The New Noir

The publisher and the University of California Press Foundation gratefully acknowledge the generous support of the George Gund Foundation Imprint in African American Studies.

The New Noir

RACE, IDENTITY, AND DIASPORA IN
BLACK SUBURBIA

By Orly Clergé

UNIVERSITY OF CALIFORNIA PRESS

University of California Press, one of the most distinguished university presses in the United States, enriches lives around the world by advancing scholarship in the humanities, social sciences, and natural sciences. Its activities are supported by the UC Press Foundation and by philanthropic contributions from individuals and institutions. For more information, visit www.ucpress.edu.

University of California Press
Oakland, California

© 2019 by Orly Clergé

Library of Congress Cataloging-in-Publication Data

Names: Clerge, Orly, author.
Title: The new noir : race, identity, and diaspora in black suburbia / by Orly Clerge.
Description: Oakland, California : University of California Press, [2020] | Includes bibliographical references and index. |
Identifiers: LCCN 2019014745 (print) | LCCN 2019018669 (ebook) | ISBN 9780520296763 (cloth : alk. paper) | ISBN 9780520296787 (pbk. : alk. paper) | ISBN 9780520969131 (ebook)
Subjects: LCSH: Middle class African Americans—New York (State)—New York—Social conditions. | Middle class African Americans—New York (State)—Long Island—Social conditions. | African diaspora—Social conditions. | Queens (New York, N.Y.)—Race relations. | Long Island (N.Y.)—Race relations. | Immigrants—New York (State)—New York. | Immigrants—New York (State)—Long Island.
Classification: LCC E185.86 (ebook) | LCC E185.86 .c564 2020 (print) | DDC 305.5/50896073074721—dc23
LC record available at https://lccn.loc.gov/2019014745

28 27 26 25 24 23 22 21 20
10 9 8 7 6 5 4 3 2

To my mama and parents, Marie Deesse and Antoine Sherer, whose ordinary decisions made the extraordinary possible. And to zansèt nou (our ancestors), who made a way under impossible circumstances.

Table of Contents

Illustrations

Acknowledgments

Men anpil, chay pa lou ("many hands, the load is lighter")

Haitian proverb

The book completion process is enriched by the community writers have around them. My first expression of gratitude is to God for providing me with the strength and endurance to complete this ten year plus project. I am thankful to the many families, individuals, and organizations who allowed me to come into the interior spaces of their lives. Their extraordinary stories are imprinted in my mind and spirit, and I hope that through this book, their narratives become a part of the Black diaspora's rich archives. Archival research for this project was made possible by the Schomburg Center for Research in Black Culture, the Queens Public Library, and Hofstra University's Center for Suburban Studies and Special Collections. Fieldwork was supported by the National Science Foundation Research Grant, the Society for the Study of Social Problems Minority Fellowship, and Brown University's Population Studies and Training Center, The Center for the Study of Race and Ethnicity in America.

I owe a sincere thank-you to Jose Itzigsohn for his support. Generations of scholars have benefitted from his mentorship, and I feel lucky to have been his student and advisee. I am also grateful to Hilary Silver, whose commitment to urban justice served as an important model for how one should use research to change cities and suburbs for the better. This book has benefitted immensely from the thoughtful feedback and moral support of Kara Cebulko, Cedric De Leon, Zophia Edwards, and Trina Vithayathil. I have been lucky to have them as intellectual interlocutors and friends. I reserve a special thank-you to Grey Osterud who gave the manuscript careful attention; this is a stronger book because of her insights. I am also grateful to my UC Press editor, Naomi Schneider, for her insight, and managing editor, Benjamin (Benjy) Malings, for his attention to detail. I am especially appreciative of Jody Agius Vallejo and anonymous reviewers for their feedback. Thank you to the wonderfully talented artist and friend who created the amazing cover art for this book, Nathalie Jolivert. I am very appreciative of the incredible creative insight of Nikki Terry, whose support helped me assemble this book in its final stages and get it out into the digital world.

I feel a deep sense of gratitude toward my undergraduate mentor, advisor, and friend, Michelle Harris. Her generosity was a turning point for me as a college freshman, and she and Harvey Charles have been a continued source of love and support throughout my career. I am also grateful to our collaborators, Sherrill Sellers and Frederick Gooding, with whom I met frequently to complete our coedited book as I wrote this book. Working with them was a reminder that transformative and liberatory sociology is possible. Thank you to Megan Reid and Amanda Reid, who both provided great academic and publishing advice. I am also grateful to several scholars for their guidance, mentorship, and support from the conception of this book to its completion: Karyn Lacy, Juan Battle, Alford A. Young, Marcus Hunter, Andrew Deener, Joyce Bell, Phil Kasinitz, Ranita Ray, Koritha Mitchell, Joyce Bell, Sherie Randolph, Shawn Christian, Kijan Bloomfied, Rachel Heiman, and Sylvia Dominguez. Thank you to my amazing academic teammate, Nalo Hamilton, with whom I met weekly while writing this book. Nalo shared very helpful insights throughout the ebbs and flows of work and life's circumstances that helped me tremendously.

I am also deeply grateful to my Brown University/Providence community. Graduate school is a rigorous process; however, some of my most cherished memories and friendships formed during this period. Thank you to Paget Henry, Barrymore Bogues, Michael Kennedy, Nancy Luke, Susan Shorts, Ebony Bridwell Mitchell, Nitsan Chorev, Greg Elliot, Michael

White, Marion Orr, Gianpaolo Baiocchi, Ann Dill, Dennis Hogan, and Evelyn Hu Dehart for faculty support. To the friends I gained: Monique Brown, Jessica Chery, Kathy, Bernard Onyango, Jing Song, Sukriti Issar, Roland Pongou, Gabriella Sanchez-Soto, Holly Reed, Kasahun Admasson, Besenia Rodriguez, Erica J. Mullen, Kathy Cooper, Blessing Mberu, Maya Mesola, Salome Wawire, Rachel Goldberg, Julia Drew, Jennifer Darrah, Karida Brown, Marcelo Bohrt, Tina Park, Yara Jarallah, Thandi Hlabana, and Michael Rodriguez, thank you. I owe a special thank-you to Noelle Hutchins Kelso, with whom I started and finished graduate school and who has been a source of boundless sisterhood on this academic journey. I am also grateful to Gayatri Singh, Bernadette Ludwig, and Irvin Hunt who read early articles that informed the book. They showed me the importance of writing in a supportive community, and I am very appreciative of our writing meetings in New York coffeeshops.

Thank you to the organizations where I conducted my earliest scholarly and pedagogical work: the Leadership Alliance and the Institute for Recruitment of Teachers: Medeva Ghee, Barbara Khan, Sharon Gamble, Luisa N. Borrell, Chera Reid, Reginald A. Wilburn, and Alexandra Cornelius. I am also thankful to the scholars whom I met in graduate school and have supported my career development: Tiffany Joseph, Saida Grundy, L'Heureux Lewis-McCoy, Maria Johnson, Keith Robinson and, Abigail A. Sewell. They each taught me the strength of graduate student support networks when I did not quite know my way around the academic world. I had the good fortune of working at the Russell Sage Foundation, and benefitted from working with various visiting scholars. I am especially thankful to Pyong Gap Min for his mentorship and Galo Falchetorre for taking me on as his student.

I've written this book in many cities and institutions. The early drafts of this book were written during my postdoctoral position at Yale University. I've benefitted greatly from working with Elijah Anderson. Anderson's Urban Ethnography Workshop was a critical intellectual space for me to present my work and be exposed to exciting ethnographic research in addition to his intellectual generosity. A special thank you to Fred Wherry, who after I shared the findings of my research helped me brainstorm an early chapter outline for this book—which marked the moment that my dissertation became a book project.

The bulk of this book was written at Tufts University. I am grateful to Tisch Library for providing the space and the resources needed to complete this book. I am thankful for the support of my colleagues and staff from across the university: Pawan Dhingra, Helen Marrow, Freeden Oeur, Ryan Centner, Paula Aymer, Sarah Sobieraj, John Libassi, and Victoria Dorward. The Center for Humanities at Tufts was an excellent intellectual space, and along with the Race, Colonialism and Diaspora Consortium and the Center for the Study of Race and Democracy, the Africana Studies Program, and the Africana Center, I was exposed to new literatures, ways of thinking, and scholars who helped me transform this project for the better. Thank you to Lisa Lowe, Adriana Zevala, Adlai Murdoch, Pearl Robinson, Modhumita Roy, Monica Ndounou, Khary Jones, Kris Manjapra, Kerri Greenridge, Sabina Vaught, Areej Sabbagh-Khoury, Julian Agyeman, and Katrina Moore. Thank you to Yolanda King for providing me with the unique opportunity to be a scholar in residence and share my research and activism with the broader Tufts community. I am especially appreciative of Natalie Masuoka, who has been a wonderful mentor and friend.

A writing residency at Tufts in Talloires, France, gave me a memorable space to think about transnational problems of colonialism, exile, and diaspora. I owe a special thank you to Kendra Field, with whom I started at Tufts as a colleague and, at my departure, felt I was leaving a dear friend. To the vibrant community of intellectuals in the Boston area who became friends, thank you to Sarah Jackson, Saher Selod, Sylvia Dominguez, Derron Wallace, Regine Jean Charles, Ohene Asare, Fox Harrell, Vincent Brown, Ajantha Subramanian, Vivek Bald, Sneha Veeragoudar, Patrick Sylvain, Francis Sullivan, Elizabeth Hinton, Ashley Farmer, and Rashauna Johnson. A sincere thank you to Patrick Sylvain, who provided important insights on English-Haitian Kreyol excerpts in the text. I completed this book at the University of California–Davis. I am grateful for the interest and engagement of scholars in the Department of Sociology, Department of Education and African American and African Studies. Thank you to Maisha Winn and Lawrence Winn of the Transformative Justice in Education Center who have been especially helpful. I am also grateful for a University of California–Davis publishing grant that supported the completion of the book.

I am also thankful to Wheaton College professors and administrators, particularly Hyun Kim, Javier Trevino. Thank you to Marta Elena, Leroy

Foster, Debbie Bial, Rico Blancaflor, Laura Brief, and the POSSE Foundation for the opportunity of a lifetime. I am indebted to Luis Baez, with whom I learned how to do activist sociology as an undergraduate student, and has been a dear friend since. Thank you to Sierra Freeman Jerez, a loving friend and writing confidant who read many drafts of chapters in progress and reminded me how important it was to maintain the book's New York authenticity. A heartfelt thank-you to my friends whose phone calls, prayers, and meet-ups sustained me: Vernick Smith, Alana Smith, Julie Kapur, Marsha Muschette, Jewel McGowan Watson, Jason Watson, Geraldine Aine, and Zarius Durant. A special thank-you to my dear friend Shantini Alleyne for reading early chapter drafts, visiting me during challenging periods, and providing valuable marketing advice.

I don't think there is a truth more universal than that we strive to make our parents, biological or adopted, proud. During the moments when I did not know if I was going to be able to complete this book, I channeled my parents unconditional love and bottomless support. Our conversations enriched this project, their care helped me complete it. My parents have been my fiercest advocates, reminding me to take care of myself when the workload was heavy. We experienced life-altering and heartbreaking setbacks as I wrote this book; however, they always graciously prepared food for my soul, extended hugs, and welcomed me home when I needed to replenish. They have given me a great push, but have also reminded me of our family's extraordinary migration journey through their beautiful storytelling. Along with my siblings, they have kept me grounded and I can never thank them enough for all that they have done for me. This book is my gift to my parents, whose sacrifices were numerous, yet often went underappreciated. To my siblings, Jens Arthaud Charles, Claudia Warrington, Samarah Ghunney, Naama Charles Allonce, and Cadiz Clergé, my early skills as a sociologist were learned by watching your every move, fascinated as I followed in your shadows, and piecing together the stories you shared and sometimes hid from my girl-child mind. My brother's swag and singing voice taught me the importance of cultural expression. My sisters' confidence, beauty, and intellect taught me how to stand on my own in the face of life's challenges. Thank you for your love, protection, and encouragement despite it all. Thank you especially to Naama, who read my writing, provided incisive feedback, and helped me brainstorm new ideas.

To my nieces and nephew, Felicia, Naaji, Imma, Max, Jenskito, Jennah, Jensey, and Jenny, my hope is that I can inspire you to amplify your gifts as much as you have inspired me to do so. I love you dearly. To Uncle William, and my uncles, aunts, and cousins, you are the diaspora of my heart. To my grandparents, Ada France, Marcel France, Felicia Tanis, and Andre Tanis, and the ancestors, I hope you will gather for a book club to read the translated version of this book in heaven. I miss you. Special gratitude is reserved for Darnel Degand, who expressed excitement about the possibilities of this book in its early stages, read elements of the work, and provided important insights along the way. I disappeared to my office, local cafés, and libraries at odd times, and for long durations. Coming home was a source of joy and reprieve from what at times seemed to be an endless road. For your partnership, I am grateful.

Preface

APERITIF

The rules of Black Society could not be any more complex than
they are in New York.

Otis Graham, *Our Kind of People*

My fascination with neighborhoods and identity likely began when I was
around eight years old. I was born and raised in Flatbush, Brooklyn.
Occasionally, my family visited friends from the old country who lived in
Queens, the Jean Baptistes. One evening we dressed up to attend a first
communion party for their daughter, Fabiola. Fabiola's mom, Guerline,
and my mom grew up attending community picnics and walking through
shared *lakous* (backyards) together in the south of Haiti. Like mother-
daughter pairs sometimes do, Fabiola and I became best friends. As my
family and I left our three-bedroom apartment that evening and exited
the lobby, we saw red and blue lights of NYPD cars flashing and heard
ambulance sirens wailing. My mom's Chevrolet Celebrity was parked in
the center of the commotion, and a crowd was forming on the sidewalk
behind her car. We crossed the street, and next to our car lay the deceased
body of a young man, half-covered by a white sheet.

I watched the scene as my father pulled off and swerved between the
police cars. He drove to the Belt Parkway. Queens was our destination, a
place where the murders, drug dealing, and theft that surrounded us in
Brooklyn did not seem to happen. In our neighborhoods, my father was
held up at knife- and gunpoint several times going to and from work at the

mechanic shop; my mom's car was broken into frequently, making her late for work at a nursing home. Haitian families in Queens did not seem to encounter these problems. They were *well off* in my girl-child eyes. Fabiola's party was filled with the stereotypical joys of a suburban childhood. When she opened greeting cards, money fell out. A lavish amount of food was laid out in the dining room with international dishes I had never seen before. Fabiola and her brother each had their own room. They could play in their green backyard. She had the newest sneakers, her brother a Nintendo gaming system. Her parents' cars did not stall at red lights. They were living in what seemed to be a demi-paradise. In contrast, my family of eight was living across borders; my parents and I were in Brooklyn and my siblings were in Port au Prince. My parents worked to make ends meet and to create a pathway to bring my siblings to New York. And there began my consciousness of class, migration and place and my fascination with how *the other half* of the Haitian diaspora *lived*.

My childhood impressions of Queens were of course limited and naive. Queens was a class-diverse place. Yet moving between the world of Brooklyn's tenement buildings and the one-family homes of Queens was meaningful for the formation of my class consciousness. Queens taught me the spatial politics of class, but fault lines in Flatbush illustrated intersectionality—the overlapping systems of racial, status, spatial, gender, and ethnic oppression that reflected hidden elements of the "Empire State" of mind, so to speak. A walk two blocks west of our apartment building was Ocean Avenue, a physical color line that imprecisely separated Blacks and Whites. I crossed the color line into Ditmas Park regularly. Hand in hand, my parents and I often walked to Newkirk Plaza to catch the D train into the city (Manhattan). We passed grand Victorian houses with wrap-around porches. When it was time for my first communion, my parents had a celebration for me in our three-bedroom apartment, and the Soca Boys' song "One Cent, Five Cent, Ten Cent Dollar" was the event's soundtrack. Between the ceremony and the party, my father walked me over to the houses on Ocean Avenue. He snapped staged photos of me in my poofy dress, a veil coiffed over my sweated-out hair press, and awkwardly smiling in front of the manicured lawns and large homes of the monied White ethnic families who had not left with the exodus of Jewish, Italian, and Irish renters in the 1970s and 1980s. These experiences in Ditmas Park and at the Jean Baptistes' in Queens were my earliest exposures to suburban-style places within city limits. I became acquainted with Long Island when the Jean Baptistes moved there after selling their home in Queens. These were the points of departure for my childhood understanding that New York was an unequal city and that my Black working-class immigrant family had a complicated relationship to it—raising questions that have been central to my sociological imagination.

Flatbush is bounded by Prospect Park and Brooklyn College. My side of Flatbush had all the indicators of what sociologists describe as impoverished, disadvantaged neighborhoods: high crime rates, low household incomes, densely populated housing, poor social services, and heavy policing. My dad often shared stories of his first impressions of racial disparity in this section of New York. When he arrived in Flatbush in 1981, Italian, Irish, and Jewish residents would hang out for hours on folding chairs in front of their apartment buildings. As Blacks moved in, it seemed as if these White ethnics disappeared in the middle of the night. Businesses and city services departed with them. None of these characteristics, however, told us much about the soul of the neighborhood, the people and their strivings.

Additionally, Flatbush represented the cultural, religious, ethnic, political, and social diversity of Black people in the U.S. My parents were politically engaged, and I grew up overhearing at home debates about the Rodney King uprising, the trial of O. J. Simpson, and the Jewish-Black tensions in Crown Heights. The political rallies organized by the Haitian community to usher in Haiti's first democratic election, won by Jean Bertrand Aristide in 1990, were household events. My mother let me tag along with her when her Filipina and Jamaican coworkers were protesting for better wages and benefits in front of city hall with the 1199 Service Employees International Union. Growing up in a Black diasporic city, you were pan-African, transnational, global, and a labor activist by osmosis.

My downstairs neighbors were Puerto Rican. Those on our left were from North Carolina, and those on the right were from Spanishtown, Jamaica. Our landlord was a Hasidic Jew, and the building super was Dominican. My classmates' families were from every Caribbean country from Cuba to Venezuela, and my teachers were the descendants of Puerto Ricans and Italian, Irish, and Indo-Trinidadian immigrants. We purchased our vegetables in Chinatown and our bagels in Italian Sheepshead Bay. The sounds of salsa woke us up in the morning, reggae marked the end of the school day, and hip-hop/soul put us to bed at night. Botánicas and apartments where voodoo ceremonies took place lived across the street from storefront Pentecostal churches. We took for granted that English, Patwa, Spanish, and Kreyol were the neighborhood's official languages and that goat, collards, pork, fried plantains, and sweet potato pie were Thanksgiving staples.

I have fond memories of growing up on Ditmas Avenue. My parents were strict, but when I could, I would stay out a little late, attempt to learn Double Dutch (which I never mastered), go to the Puerto Rican store to buy sour power, or meet up with friends in the lobbies of their apartment buildings to talk about the latest songs from Bad Boy Entertainment or listen to one of our friends tell us that they were the flyest on East 21st Street. This was all hype, of course. We were wearing Catholic school uniforms and had varying levels of parental supervision, but none of us were running, let alone controlling, the streets. We just thought it was cool to have a tough mentality, to break open fire hydrants for water fights in the summer and in the winter to get into fights on street corners over whose shearling coats or Timberland boots were knock-offs. I didn't have much to contribute to these conversations. I was just an observer. My family could not afford the latest styles from Karl Kani, FUBU, or Tommy Hilfiger. My family was split across borders, and the money my parents earned was to keep us afloat in Brooklyn and support my siblings in Port au Prince who were facing the volatile politics of the Aristide era and U.S. imposed embargoes.

Brooklyn was my home for sixteen years until my family purchased a home in Queens. My parents were among many families who had benefitted from a growing national economy and had house-buying fever during the 1990s. They wanted to use it as a source of shelter for the family. When someone lost a job, they could come home. If a romantic relationship failed, the door was open. As a teenager, I no longer thought that Queens was particularly remarkable. Instead, it represented a landscape of boredom and isolation. In order to continue attending my high school in Sheepshead Bay, I found an afterschool job in Brooklyn, even though it meant a two-hour commute home. Sometimes I stayed with my sister and brother-in-law, who had an apartment in Canarsie. I kept this up for over a year until I went away to college. I felt I was a Brooklynite visiting Queens, never truly belonging in the new neighborhood. I was reluctant to trade Flatbush Avenue for Jamaica Avenue, or Prospect Park for Flushing Meadows Park.

As I look back, our move from Flatbush to Queens seemed to be an overnight event. I have no memory of the moving trucks or my last days on Ditmas Avenue. I remember our many journeys from Flatbush to Queens to visit family friends, but now it was my family's turn to *have a place of their own*.[1] As a teenager, I was immersed in my life and friends in Brooklyn, which the move threatened to rupture. It represented something quite different for some of my peers. Although Queens is a large and diverse borough, with pockets of poverty and affluence, many Black Brooklynites imagined it as a faraway promised land where the well-off went. I learned later that some of my peers who believed my family was on welfare because we were Haitian were stunned when I told them my family had bought a home in Queens.

When I was in college, I had no plans to return to Queens permanently after graduation. My sights were on graduate school. Second-generation Black immigrant millennials like me were a growing demographic group, and our incorporation had important implications for American politics and culture. A series of news reports drew my attention back to Queens, planting the intellectual seeds of this book. In 2004, the *New York Daily News* covered an incident at a public elementary school. Two Haitian students had been involved in an encounter, and as punishment a White administrator ordered them and other Haitian students to sit on the floor of the cafeteria and eat their lunch of chicken and rice with their hands while their peers watched. "In Haiti, they treat you like animals, and I will treat you the same way here," the school administrator told them. I worried that the anti-Haitian sentiment that my siblings and I confronted in Brooklyn schools was à la mode again. I knew intimately the brand of anti-Black racism that these young students experienced. I had recently sat in the office of a Jewish college administrator who praised my academic achievements. Then, knowing little about my family, he joked that my parents could not have predicted the success of their daughter when they were off the shores of Miami, on a boat with sharks nearby. The arduous journeys of many Haitian refugees to Florida's shores became the target of his casual racism, and my family and I the subjects of his insults.

Anti-Haitian discrimination was not new to me. However, what I found surprising was that the incident occurred at a school in Queens. My experiences with the Jean Baptiste family had left me with the impression that

Black families seemed to prosper there, and I assumed that children of the well-to-do were welcomed in neighborhood institutions. It struck me as odd that Black Haitian families would have to wrestle with the same strand of racism in middle-class spaces that those in lower-income urban areas encountered.

A couple of years later, when I was working as a research assistant at the Russell Sage Foundation, Queens was back in the news. A *New York Times* article circulated that stated that Blacks in Queens earned higher household incomes than Whites. Racial inequality in the United States is such that Blacks seem to be permanently sorted by White institutional actors into lower-income occupations and positions. Queens represented a sort of anomaly, a hidden and unique site of Black achievement. The juxtaposition of Queens's Black affluence and its nativist racism gave me pause as a budding sociologist. I wondered: How could a place where some of the most affluent Blacks in New York and the country live have schools that treat their children with ethnoracial animus? Didn't money and suburbanization act as buffers between them and racial injustice?

As a graduate student, I searched for studies that might explain what was happening in Queens. But the vast body of scholarship on immigration and migration emphasized the experiences of urban, low-income immigrants. The stories of Black middle-class suburbanites and immigrant integration into those communities were hidden. Recent research on the Black middle class elucidated that Black middle-class outmigration did not lead to a promised land, but introduced new, underappreciated forms of racial segregation and inequality compared to the White middle class. However, this body of literature did not provide insight into the migratory experiences of Black middle-class people from different regions and nationalities. Growing up in working-class Brooklyn and traversing other New York neighborhoods, the Northeast, Africa, and the Caribbean, I became a student of the geographical and cultural complexity of Black life. It was at this nexus of personal and sociological inquiry that I began to identify neighborhoods to study the relationships between migration, mobility, and suburbanization among New York's Black diaspora. From these events, *The New Noir* emerged.

1 Village Market

ENCOUNTERS IN BLACK DIASPORIC SUBURBS

Food has not just been fodder for our journeys, but embodies the journeys themselves.

Michael Twitty, in *The Cooking Gene*, p. 72.

There are two kinds of people in the world, those who leave home and those who don't.

Roy, in Tayari Jones's *American Marriage*

Located on a main boulevard in Cascades, the Village Market, the community's largest local retailer, is the pulsing heart and soul of the neighborhood.[1] The name of the market recalls the countries and regions from which Cascades's residents come. Although Queens is a part of New York City proper, its eastern sections are considered "suburbs in the city" due to their tree-lined streets, Tudor-style homes, manicured lawns, and wider open spaces compared to Harlem and Bedford-Stuyvesant. At the Village Market, middle-class residents find the meats, produce, and spices they need for home-cooked meals. A casual visitor immediately notices that the market is neither an ordinary Pathmark or Shop Rite nor a higher-end Whole Foods or Zabar's. Nor is Cascades your typical New York City area: not only are its residents predominantly Black, but they are also palpably multinational. Their range of accents, skin tones, and styles of dress demonstrate that this is a central meeting place for various diasporic groups. The marketplace is a diverse, multilingual space, and many of its clientele own suburban-style homes with well-tended gardens and entertain weekend guests with dishes that bring New Orleans, Cap-Haïtien, and Spanish Town, Jamaica, into their suburban kitchens. On an evening stroll through the neighborhood, the aromas of oxtail, rice and beans, spiced cabbage, jerk chicken, salted pork and grits, fried fish, and baked mac and cheese waft through the air. While to White observers these might seem like exotic cuisines, they represent the culture of places I call Black diasporic suburbs.

When you cross the main boulevard to get to Village Market, you move between MTA buses and wave away a dollar van driver with his locs held together in a beanie hat of black, red, and green stripes. The bass of a Beres Hammond lovers rock song vibrates the street, and the van's reggae air horn sounds to announce the beginning of a dancehall music set. When you come into the parking lot, men of various colors and ages ask, "Taxi, taxi?" To the left, there's a man selling Nollywood movies. The crowd of customers at the entrance to Village Market indicates its popularity. An older Black woman holds her young granddaughter close to her tiered skirt of blue cotton while she picks out yellow plantains. Next to the plantains are mangoes, strawberries, blueberries, cantaloupes, fuyu persimmons, and grapes. The side display of fruits and vegetables announces the variety of foodstuffs found in the market, the range of places where those who live nearby come from, and the local culinary influences of New York's many diasporas. I grab a squeaky cart and walk toward the entrance. The Asian manager, likely in his fifties, and I make eye contact, and he gives me the usual nod and informal soldier's salute. I enter a brightly lit and busy produce section with a dizzying assortment of foods from all over the world.

The Korean and Brazilian yams are popular. Cassavas, maniocs, and batatas (sweet potatoes) are clustered behind the fruits section. A caramel-complexioned woman in her forties ties a knot around one bag of green beans and another of okra to weigh them. She is wearing a skirt suit, and her collar has a gold-plated name tag that says "Usher." She belongs to the after-church crowd. To the left are spice buns, sorrel leaves, and bags of brown sugar stacked one on top of the other. Further down the aisle, Black customers of all ages, shapes, and tones reach for small plastic bags to hold their grapefruit, cucumbers, ears of corn, and eggplants. Others feel papayas, peaches, and avocados to ensure that they are at just the right degree of ripeness, read the ingredients in the coconut water, or look for fresh garlic, thyme, and ginger root. Along a side wall are scallions for seasoning callaloo; collard greens and kale for side dishes; and spinach for stews, salads, and smoothies.

A young couple debates an item in front of metal containers filled with salted pork tails in brine. Behind them, a worker stocks the bacalao (salted codfish). In the meat section, three young siblings giggle near the bin of frozen goat meat. Their mother asks the butcher to slice her pork shoulder into medium-sized cubes. Untrimmed oxtail is on sale, but the smoked turkey neck is in short supply. The fish section has a long line of customers. Bachata plays in the background as shoppers take the plastic trays used to weigh whiting, conch, tilapia, blue snapper, and shrimp.

In the spices and rice section, flags from Caribbean, Latin American, African, and Asian countries are on display alongside the American flag. Basmati rice and Goya products are located directly across from the extensive collection of flours and seasonings. Jamaican jerk seasoning, Guyanese mango sour (chutney), Ghanaian fufu flour, Haitian Rebo coffee, Sylvia's Southern Spices, curry powder, butter beans, Maggi bouillon cubes, and canned mackerel are taken off the shelves and placed into shopping carts in a hurry. Near the cashier are cocoa balls imported from Jamaica and an assortment of peanut and caramel sweets. The lines for the ten cashier booths staffed by Bangladeshi women are long, often extending into the aisles.

Village Market offers a preview of the myriad of consumption practices at the center of the everyday life of this Black middle-class community. A trip to the local grocery stores in the neighborhoods of study is an opportunity to see the multiplicity of regional and national cultures that animate suburbia and the global food industry that supports it. "We have the market down der, and everyone in the neighborhood goes. I'm in der all de time," Damian told me. When Damian, a forty-eight-year-old realtor, arrived in New York from Jamaica in the 1990s, he initially came to take care of an ill parent. After their recovery, he decided to stay. He aspired to be a chef. Although he wanted to work in New York's elite restaurants, after graduating at the top of his class in culinary school he was never called back after interviews. "Everybody below me has corporate jobs right now, yuh undastan'?" Damian passionately exclaimed. He excelled in culinary school, but, because New York's restaurant scene was a racially- and gender-unequal industry, Damian's White, less-qualified classmates landed jobs in high-end kitchens as chefs. Once employers saw that he was a Black man and heard his Jamaican accent, Damian never received job offers after interviews.

Although eager to stay in the United States to be close to family, Damian also remained connected to Jamaica. He visited every year and contemplated returning permanently. But he lamented that, despite the racial barriers he has encountered from White New Yorkers, returning permanently to the island is impossible. He explained, "Jamaica had a brain drain in the late 80s and 90s. 'Cause people like us, we left. We left, and everybody left. So, we left the young kids that we should be the role models for. We left that vacuum there for them. 'Cause when I was growing up, I had somebody, a big brother I should say. When I was growing up, it used to be a village which raised the child. Now, the village left." The village Damian is referring to is the people who were the pillars of his hometown community in Kingston. The seamstresses, construction workers, factory workers, merchants, teachers, and policemen who he felt had held his town together boarded planes at Norman Manley airport, some never returning to their natal home. They were a part of the mass out-migration of Black people from the Caribbean and the US South in the twentieth century. They were leaving repressive political and economic regimes behind, as well as loved ones, longtime friends, and lands their ancestors had known for generations. They protested with their feet against the declining colonial and postcolonial conditions of life in their islands and regions.

Although their bodies were displaced, their psychic and spiritual connections to the people and places left behind remained.[2] Their minds and hearts were also impacted by the shock of their displacement, by feelings of alienation, as they encountered a foreign culture that was often unwelcoming because of White disdain towards their race and origin. Thus, for comfort and support they turned to the loved ones they had left behind. Damian spent hours at a time on the phone talking to his younger brother in Jamaica, to whom he regularly sent prepaid calling cards. Like the hundreds of thousands of other Jamaicans who have left the island since the 1960s, Damian was negotiating life as what Peggy Levitt (2001) calls a "transnational villager." People like Damian, who were once a part of villages all around the Black Atlantic, have created new villages in cities and suburbia. Their nostalgia for the places they left behind and desires to plant roots in their new homes energize their neighborhoods and local institutions like Village Market. Residents exchange a portion of their middle-class earnings to make meals that psychically transport them to their places of origin. But they also cook up new ways of knowing, being, and acting in the mélange of their encounters with one another.

This book ventures into the cultural worlds of multiethnic Black middle-class suburbs and illustrates how Damian's experiences are not unique. His negotiation of racial exclusion, social mobility, and trans-spatial ties mirrors the lives of large segments of Black diasporic people in gateway cities like New York. Many villagers have left the American South and Global South and have set up new suburban villages. I ethnographically explore two such New York suburbs, Cascades and Great Park, to address the following questions: How do middle-class Jamaicans, Haitians, and Black Americans articulate cultural identity in multiethnic and multiracial places? How do these overlapping diasporas define cultural belonging in light of their social mobility and racial exclusion in New York? Fifty years after watershed racial, immigration, and colonial policy shifts in the United States and the Caribbean, what legacies do these groups carry with them on their journeys to middle-class suburbs, and how do these histories manifest in their social identities, interactions, and micro-practices in everyday life?

Participants in this ethnographic study offered up statements such as "Jamaicans like curry, but Haitians use a creole sauce" or "Black Americans make the collards different than Trinidadians" as expressions of cultural differences within the Black middle class. These were not trivial remarks about cuisine preparation; rather, they were important insights into how the participants made sense of their shared and divergent histories. Their Black epistemologies—or how those who fit under the Black racial umbrella come to know, understand, and interact with themselves and each other in suburbia—were expressed through cultural norms, and nothing signals a group's shared beliefs and practices more than food, a necessity of everyday life. Therefore, although the book is not about food per se, food provides an entrée into the quotidian identities and politics of Black middle-class diasporas.

Ethnographically, food is a site of memory, consciousness, and community across borders. Many of my understandings of the cultures of the people whose lives fill the pages of this book arose around food: I interviewed people as they prepared dinner, met with them over homemade appetizers, and listened to their life stories while they tended herb gardens in their backyards. I spent many hours in local restaurants watching cross-ethnic encounters within them. I sat at kitchen tables and listened to the life experiences of families gathered in fellowship. Food was cooking or cooling in the background as my interviewees granted me entrance to the interior of their lives. They discussed issues of family, hardship, success, the desires of their hearts, the problems on their minds, the joys of their spirits, and the contradictions in their politics. The foodways of the Black diaspora[3] were portals into private domains and public problems of the families I spoke with. As a result, I use foods of the African diaspora as metaphors for the quotidian articulations of their identities in this text.

MIXED GREENS: THE AFRICANA CLASS MOYENNE

The Black middle class has received increased attention since the turn of the twenty-first century. Books such as *Living with Racism* (Feagin and Sikes 1996), *Black Picket Fences* (Pattillo-McCoy 1999), *Red Lines, Black Spaces* (Haynes 2008), and *Blue-Chip Black* (Lacy 2007) have elucidated the complex role of race and class for Black people who have "moved on up" out of poverty and segregated urban areas and have attained middle-class incomes and suburban lifestyles. The Black middle class negotiates a unique and peculiar position in racial capitalism. Racism and nationalism are key factors in the economic system of exchange and production. Therefore, the term *racial capitalism* provides a lens to analyze how the global economy is built on the assignment of value and power to workers based on the racial category they are put into by affluent White society. Although Marxists posit that our economic system is based on class conflict, a Black Marxist perspective argues that class and racial conflict order the global economy and, therefore, our class stratification system (Du Bois 1935, Marable 1983, Robinson 2000). For example, the Black middle class has expanded due to political mandates for Black access to desegregated schools, neighborhoods, and workplaces. However, their class ascendance is characterized by continued patterns of racial exclusion designed by White society. This book builds upon these works by deconstructing "Black" or "African American" as a racial category and demonstrates that the Black middle class consists of heterogeneous cultural, nationality, regional, and ethnic groups that differ in their relationships to the racialized economy and to multiple and overlapping Black social worlds.

The socioeconomic positions and cultural experiences of these different nationality groups vary in important ways. Since the passage of the 1965 Immigration Act, the in flow of hundreds of thousands of Black immigrants from the Caribbean and Africa have transformed Black mobility and cultural geography. Between 1980 and 2016, the Black foreign-born population in the United States increased from 816,000 to 4.2 million.[4] As Black immigrants have moved from a "presence to a community" (Kasinitz 1992), *Black* has emerged as an umbrella term, a category that now includes a myriad of nationality groups—the descendants of racial slavery in the United States, people of African descent from the Caribbean and Latin America, and African immigrants. As Black immigrants either obtained well-paid jobs soon after they arrived as highly skilled workers or professionals or worked their way up from low-paid occupations into the middle class, they have joined middle-class Black Americans in educational, work, and residential spaces. Together, Black immigrants and Black Americans have toiled in the face of White racism, economic insecurity, migration, and the problems of restrictive immigration policies and unkept promises of civil rights legislation to attain middle-class jobs, buy homes, and build lives in New York's suburban enclaves. This book is about their communities and overlooked diasporic narratives.

Large-scale Black migration from the Caribbean and Africa has raised questions in the United States about how migrants and their children will fare in a postindustrial, bifurcated, and racially segmented economy. Segmented assimilation theory, the prevailing perspective on the trajectory of Black immigrants, predicts that their children will experience downward economic mobility if they become culturally similar to poor, urban Black Americans (Portes and Zhou 1997). A variant on assimilation theory argues that low numbers of children of Black immigrants are finding their way into the so-called mainstream—constructed as White—occupations and schools (Alba and Nee 2003, Alba et al. 2011).

Models of immigrant outcomes commonly used in sociology advance assimilation discourses that are based on public and intellectual continuities of colonial racism. Old and neo-assimilationist perspectives privilege the movement of ethno-racial groups into a constructed White mainstream but downplay and undertheorize Whites' active resistance to resource sharing with racialized groups and their repackaging of biological racism as cultural, class, and ethnic difference. Assimilation discourses also overlook racial projects that divide Black people by nationality and class in order to undermine their unified political opposition to White hegemony (Bonilla-Silva 2003, Omi and Winant 1994, Pierre 2004; Winant 2001). This book is in conversation with the work of race theorists and historians of the African diaspora invested in building knowledge of Black people by bringing them from the margins into the center of cultural analysis (Bald 2006, Gilroy 1993, Guridy 2010, Hall 1990, Lewis 1995). I focus on the dynamic politics of belonging that trans-geographical Black people engage in together in suburbia and how their identities dialogue with both their histories and contemporary experiences with racial oppression and their class consciousness. Joining the effort to interrupt the reign of assimilation theory (Treitler 2015) and decolonizing knowledge production (Go 2013, Harris et al. 2013), the book focuses on Black culture not as a deficit but as a set of diverse social relations of identity making, creativity, resistance, accommodation, and collective survival across Black diasporas.[5] I argue that the Black middle class consists of overlapping diasporas (Bald 2006) whose identities and mobilities are constantly being negotiated through their encounters with different national and regional groups in suburbia.

The diasporic framework of Black middle-class life in New York organizes this book. *Diaspora* does not simply describe a people on the move, dispersed outside of their homeland. *Diaspora* is a verb.[6] It encompasses the ongoing dialogue between Africans in the Americas with the places they consider their homelands and with other Black peoples across the world. The diasporic framework provides the tools needed to unpack the cultural identities of Black Americans, Haitians, and Jamaicans as a outcomes of their racialized migrations from the American and Global Souths and b) their entrance into suburbs with complex racial and class histories that shape their experiences within them. These migrants are part of a post–civil rights movement and post-colonial generation with heterogeneous positions in the global political economy. Their identities emerge from the interactions across racial, class, gender and nationality boundaries. The myriad of ethnic groups within the Black middle class are like the ingredients in Aunties' plate of mixed greens. They share similar roots, create distinction between one another, yet work together, at times harmony through their differences across color, tastes, and preparation.

The diasporic diversity of the Black population is nothing new to New York City or the United States. At the turn of the twentieth century, thousands of Black immigrants lived in the United States, most having moved from the Caribbean and Latin America to Florida, Harlem, and Boston to escape labor exploitation in declining post-slavery agricultural economies (Putnam 2013, Watkins-Owens 1996). Together with Black Americans, they co-created jazz and hip-hop, danced to soca and reggae, shared jambalaya and patty recipes, named streets after the Tuskegee Airmen, and built pan-African coalitions to resist Jim Crow in their city. Outside of Harlem, Black southerners and Black immigrants encountered one another in New York's suburbs as early as the 1930s (Haynes 2001).

By 2012, the non-Hispanic Black foreign-born community in the United States comprised over 10 percent of the Black population (see table 1). One-third of Black people in New York are foreign born. Like the Black American population, Black immigrants are stratified by class and often live together in the same residential environments, propelled there by racial residential segregation and drawn there by personal choice. In this book, I explore the lives of people who make up the Black American and Black immigrant middle and upper-middle class.

This book explores the articulations of Black identity in suburbs where Black Americans, and Caribbean and African immigrants influence its cultural geography. New York has been for a long time a North Star for Black southerners, a gateway city for Caribbean immigrants, and a newer destination for African immigrants (Kent 2007). I focus specifically on the largest Black nationality groups in the United States and New York: the Black American, Haitian, and Jamaican diasporas. I distinguish Black middle-class people by their national origins for several reasons. First, Black Americans are a distinct group with unique cultural lexicons and migration histories.[7] Regionality is an important boundary in Black

Table 1   Socioeconomic Characteristics among Blacks by Nativity (2012)

	Black American	Black Immigrant
Total Population	25,554,024 (89.7%)	2,908,991 (10.3%)
Median Family Income	$36,000	$45,000
Median Household Income	$41,000	$52,000
Lower-Middle Class (%) ($30–$49,999)	19.8	17.2
Middle-Middle Class (%) ($50–$99,999)	28.0	30.7
Upper-Middle Class (%) ($100,000+)	14.0	21.0
Some College (%)	30.5	26.7
College (%)	16.8	28.2

SOURCE: Current Population Survey (2012). Class categories adopted from the definitions used in Lacy's (2007) *Blue-Chip Black: Race, Class and Status in the New Black Middle Class* for lower-, middle-, and upper-middle-class Blacks.

American identity formation (Robinson 2014). Cultural differences between those who identify with their Southern or Northern heritages, or a mixture of both, yield different subjectivities and practices. For example, as they encounter Black immigrant groups in diasporic suburbs, Black Americans with roots in the South erect boundaries against them because they equate Blackness with being from the South. Others maintain that they are not "African" American because, unlike recent Nigerian and Ghanaian immigrants, their ties to Africa were ruptured long ago when their ancestors were kidnapped from Africa during the transatlantic slave trade. These beliefs are a preview of the complicated identity work occurring in Black diasporic suburbs. Their inclusion of these perspectives into sociological paradigms of race, class, migration, and urban sociology improves our social theories by reflecting Black lived experiences that are hiding in plain sight.

In addition to exploring the differences between Black American and Black immigrants, this book also disaggregates the homogenizing category "West Indian" by exploring the distinct experiences of Jamaicans and Haitians Both groups bring their languages, cultures, citizenships, and patterns of mobility with them on their journeys to middle-class suburbs. The term *West Indian* was created by European empires to categorize their Caribbean colonies. Today, West Indian identity does resonate with many immigrants who feel a sense of pan-Caribbean unity and political consciousness across colonial divisions based on language and history. However, the term obscures diversity as much as it excludes. For example, Jamaicans are usually treated as the test case for the West Indian immigrant experience in research studies. Haitians, on the other hand, are often marginalized or regarded as outsiders because of their colonial and linguistic differences from English-speaking Caribbean immigrants. This marginalization is also shaped by their country's history of geopolitical power struggles with European and US imperialism. When members of their unique diasporas meet locally, however, their encounters become a recipe for comparatively understanding Black identity making in the twenty-first century, dynamics elucidated in this book.

The diasporic Black middle class is characterized by socioeconomic differences that shape their identity work. The increasing ethnic heterogeneity of racialized groups in the US labor market translates into meaningful inter- and intra-ethnic group differences, a process that José Itzigsohn (2009) calls *stratified ethnoracial incorporation*. For example, later chapters discuss that English-speaking Jamaicans' mode of entry into the United States often as skilled laborers facilitates their middle-class grounding in suburbia, while French- and Kreyol-speaking Haitians, who are more likely to enter through family reunification or political asylum (Kent 2007), have a more arduous road to the middle class. The brain drain of nurses and teachers from Jamaica translates into consistently higher incomes for them in US schools and hospitals compared to Black Americans and Haitian immigrants. Black Americans' middle-class occupations are largely in the public and financial sector. Haitian immigrants, too, have attained middle-class status through unionized health care occupations, but in contrast to Jamaicans, they largely have done this from the bottom up.

Yet my ethnographic observations demonstrate that, despite these socioeconomic differences, Black American, Haitian, and Jamaican households' cultural economies have followed similar logics of collective support. Multigenerational and single-parent households are part of the mosaic of their middle-class lifestyles. These households supply domestic and international remittances, sending money and goods to relatives across households and back home. This practice enhances their identities as monied middle-class people because they have adequate resources to share with family members elsewhere. How members of the diasporic Black middle class make, spend, and save money transgeographically illuminates the interaction between their socioeconomic situation and their cultural identities.

SUBURBAN SOIL: SAME ROOTS, DIFFERENT ROUTES

Most Black people in the United States now reside in the suburbs. The number of Black families living within New York City is decreasing; however, the suburbs saw a 30 percent increase in Black families between 1990 and 2010.[8] The historically distinct pathways followed by Black Americans, Haitians, and Jamaicans to the suburbs demonstrate the ongoing relationships within the Black diaspora outside of Africa. The African diaspora was created by racial slavery. For four centuries, European empires trafficked African peoples of different geographical and cultural origins and dispersed them throughout the Americas. After emancipation, but in response to varying conditions of racial inequality, labor exploitation, and political suppression, Black migrations from across the Atlantic to the industrial cities of the United States generated nearly unprecedented contacts among free Black people with different languages, nationalities, and colonial histories. The social structure of New York's suburbs allows us to widen the conversation about contemporary relations within the African diaspora in important ways.

The adults I interviewed are a part of the post-Break Black middle class. I use *the Break*, a term coined by Howard Winant (2001), to describe the time period when White supremacy was challenged by international antiracist and anticolonial resistance between 1945 and 1970. This epoch of wide-scale global transformation led to an unprecedented number of Black migrations from the American South and Global South to Northern metropoles. The adults I interviewed largely came of age after this Break period. The Black American middle class that emerged after the 1960s has been referred to as the post-King generation or the post-integration generation (Lacy 2007, Pattillo-McCoy 1999). These descriptions make sense when the Black middle class is understood as consisting of the children and grandchildren of the civil rights movement, the descendants of slavery in the United States. These generational markers also distinguish the new Black middle class from newly educated and monied Black people in the 1950s, whom Franklin Frazier (1957) called the Black bourgeoisie.

In order to understand the localized identities and practices of the Black middle class in the twenty-first century, however, we must move beyond the nation and use a more *global and comparative perspective* that encompasses international racial histories, migrations, and political situations. New York's Black middle class cannot be comprehended without engaging with the complicated social hierarchies of the US and Global Souths from which its members have come. The racial caste system of Charleston, the uneven industrialization of Kingston, and the dictatorship politics of Port au Prince are interrelated global processes and have shaped Black migrant experiences and perspectives. The multinational composition of the Black middle class in New York requires that we look at their lives and consciousnesses through the ways in which the nation-states to which they belong(ed) structured and articulated global White supremacy. Black people across the Atlantic have engaged in collective political action and cultural work to chip away at American and European socioeconomic domination from enslavement through rebellion, revolution, emancipation, colonialism, and independence. They are currently living in a neoliberal, colorblind era, which requires sociological attention and theorization that respects the ties that bind them and the differences that set them apart.

Separated by land and sea, Black Americans, Haitians and Jamaicans in this study all had unique and overlapping migratory histories. In the mid-twentieth century, inspired by the perennial desire to free themselves of the living legacies of racial and color caste, they left the places of their oppression. Their collective biographies are a part of global revolts against racial formations—that is, racial projects in their respective countries and regions that bolstered White domination by activating old and new technologies of racial categorical inequality. In the United States, Black people's active resistance was expressed in the movement of millions from the Jim Crow South to the North and West. Black Americans' exodus was the most important population redistribution in American history: the Great Migration, which Isabel Wilkerson (2011) aptly calls the "first step America's servant class took without asking," and also referred to as the "Great Escape" (Brown, 2018). Many of my respondents were born and raised in the South, while others had parents and grandparents who came from the eastern seaboard states of North Carolina, South Carolina, and Virginia between World War I and the 1960s.

During this same period, Black people in Jamaica and Haiti also set their sights on the North Star. However, they did so under different political conditions. As Blacks in the U.S. were demanding liberation from the terror of segregation and lynching, Black Jamaicans were fighting for their freedom from the British Empire's crippling hold on the island's affairs. England had colonized Jamaica in 1655 and created a colonial state apparatus that continued to extract the island's resources and labor but left many Black Jamaicans in rural and urban poverty. A participant in the international anticolonial movement in the Caribbean and Africa, Jamaica became independent in 1962. The transition from a colonial to a neocolonial state hampered development. Economic stagnation; the ensuing violence; and competition between the country's main political parties, the People's National Party and the Jamaica Labor Party, propelled the outmigration of Jamaican professionals and workers in search of material freedom in the land of the "almighty dolla." Largely locked out of migration to Britain, many Jamaicans came to New York—only to find backbreaking work, an ongoing desegregation crisis, and Black people from other regions and nations with the same goals and difficulties. Just as Haiti is separated from Jamaica by hundreds of miles of Caribbean Sea, the Haitian experience was strikingly different from that of Jamaicans during their era of decolonization or of Black Americans amid desegregation struggles.

During the Break period, Haiti was embroiled in a political dictatorship whose violence and repression from the late 1950s to the 1980s sent people from every class into exile in New York and Miami. The fall of the Duvalier dictatorship in 1986 led to free democratic elections, and Haitians chose Jean Bertrand Aristide, an avid advocate of the country's rural and urban poor. But within a year he was forcibly removed from office and sent into exile, later reinstated with only formal authority, and ultimately overthrown by the right wing, all with the direct aid of the US government. Amid US imperialist control and continued popular resistance, political instability crippled the economy. Haitians fled the political terror of their hometowns but actively tried to maintain connections with those they had left behind on the island.

This book reveals the global and comparative character of Black middle class identities. First, my interviewees were people whose lives, migrations, and unlikely encounters in global cities like New York emerge from interconnected national and cross-national political events. These Black New Yorkers and their families participated in mass migrations, provoked by the downfall of an empire, a brutal dictatorship, and the encumbrance of Jim Crow. However, these migrations were undertaken through the individual and household decisions of everyday people seeking a better way of life. Second, the post-Break paradigm helps us to recognize that the suburbs where Black diasporic groups meet and mix have experienced significant socioeconomic, cultural, and political changes over time that affect their power and belonging in that space. As my respondents arrived in these suburbs, they confronted the spatial legacies of colonialism, enslavement, segregation, and Black resistance embedded in the suburban soil of Long Island they inherited. The history of their suburban places, too, leave an indelible imprint on my interviewees' understanding of their citizenship as New Yorkers and as Black people in the United States.

Culturally, the term *post-Break* helps us see the Black middle class with new sociological frameworks. Cascades and Great Park are suburban villages created by global migrations and Black social movements that demanded the dismantling of racial segregation. Here diasporic people of African descent from the US South, various Caribbean islands, and immigrant Africans renegotiate their identities and belonging in and through their interactions with one another. How these Americans and immigrants negotiate their diasporic histories and define identities and belonging from the "inside out" (Lewis 1995) as they make sense of suburban life illuminates the new places in which race, class, and nation are constructed, contested, and reconstructed. In a strange journey from enslavement, colonialism, and Jim Crow to the middle class in the wake of the civil rights and decolonization movements, my interviewees, who have experienced economic mobility, have to bear the burden of making a way for themselves and their families in a White-dominated society that continuously tries to subordinate them. This reality intensifies desires for their return to their respective Souths. Many said that they are rooted in suburbia for now and resort to forging transregional and transnational ties and identities as coping strategies.

I approach this project with the recognition that the diasporic Black middle class in New York is not an entity unto itself, but rather a node in a transatlantic Black cultural world that is the product of the African, European, and Indigenous encounter referred to as the Black Atlantic (Gilroy 1993). The self-conceptions of residents of diasporic suburbs and what groups they feel welcome in are shaped by their position in a larger Black world that is simultaneously local, transregional, and transnational. Studies of Latinx immigrants in the United States have demonstrated that their ideas of social exclusion, power, and mobility are shaped by inequality in the United States and their home countries. Peggy Levitt's *Transnational Villagers* (2001), for example, illuminates the complex network of identities and practices that organize Boston's Dominican community and their hometowns in the Dominican Republic through circular flows of families, ideas, and goods. Building on these works, I analyze middle-class Black Americans', Haitians', and Jamaicans' negotiations of racial identity and social mobility as they reflect the stratification systems of New York, the US South, Haiti, and Jamaica. Their nationalities and regionalities are the prism through which they navigate their dialectical relationships to categories of race and class, often reshaping them in new and sometimes dramatic ways. Migration and media, for example, are powerful tools that have brought social practices from below (Thomas 2007) into Black middle-class suburbia.

Black middle-class immigrants are expected to mirror the identity and practices of the Black American middle class. Challenging the thesis of segmented assimilation, which contends that Black immigrants who identify with Black Americans' views on race and racism adopt adversarial views, and descend into poverty, Kathryn Neckerman, Prudence Carter, and Jennifer Lee (1999) have offered a necessary theoretical intervention. They argue that middle-class Black Americans have a "culture of mobility," a unique set of racial and class identities that help them navigate social problems in their interclass and interracial encounters with Whites and lower-income Blacks. As Black immigrants become middle class, leave economic communities, and interact with the White world in school, at work, and in their neighborhoods, they are expected to mirror what they call an African American culture of mobility.

The thesis of an African American culture of mobility created an empirical imperative to find Black middle-class communities where Black American and Black immigrants are in close proximity to one another. Physical proximity allows for cultural interaction and diffusion, and Cascades and Great Park served as key spaces for this theoretical exploration. They were Black, middle class, and multiethnic suburbs. However, upon entering the field, it became clear that I was asking questions around cultural exchange between groups without exploring the extraordinary heterogeneity of each group. Instead of asking how are middle-class Black immigrants becoming similar to middle-class Black Americans, understanding the lives of my interviewees required that my inquiries focus on how each diasporic group defined the politics of identity and belonging in its own right and how it is shaped by their social interactions with each other.

I submit that Black immigrants are not simply adopting a blanket African American culture of mobility but that, instead, Black Americans are a diasporic group with their own set of norms and practices that are specific to their experiences as native born, often Southern-origin peoples in the global city of New York. Middle-class Black diasporic groups are negotiating cultural identities in their social interactions with one another in New York's uniquely multiracial, multiethnic, and hyper-mobile milieu, making their experiences and encounters on the margins of the city fundamentally different from that of groups in Chicago; Washington, D.C.; L.A.; or Atlanta. In relation to racial identity, I find that the post-Break Black middle class is challenging and remaking the category of Black that is imposed upon them. Their trans-spatial political ties and interactions with one another are fundamental to how they articulate the contents of their racial self-conceptions. Instead of asking my respondents how they negotiate racism, for example, I asked them to describe what Blackness meant to them and how their practices reflected or contradicted these meanings. I call what emerged from their answers to these questions a *racial consciousness spectrum*. Black Americans, Haitians, and Jamaicans articulated and displayed cultural identities around Blackness that differed both *within* and *between* groups. My interviewees developed these positions through cultural pathways that are shaped by local and global understandings of race, region, and nation. In the chapters that follow, I discuss how this spectrum is related to social class and ethnic solidarities and their implications for the cultural and political geography of suburbs.

These findings may resonate with the experiences of other middle-class groups of color. Ethnoburbs, or ethnic suburbs, for example, have multiplied since the 1960s as middle-class Asian and Latinx immigrants have expanded in number and moved to the outskirts of cities. The combination of highly skilled immigrants from China, Korea, and India and the upward mobility of later-generation immigrants from Latin America and Asia has resulted in the formation of a monied Asian and Latinx middle class who express their status through the purchase of homes in old and newly developed suburbs. Ethnic suburbs such as Silicon Valley and San Gabriel Valley (Lung-Amam 2016; Li 2009; Wen, Lauderdale, and Kandula 2009) are sites for transnational social and economic activities that connect these immigrants and their children to their home countries. Found across gateway cities and new destinations from Toronto to New York, ethnoburbs express the bicultural racial and class repertoires and desires of immigrants to become rooted in the United States on their own social and economic terms. As the Black-White color line is morphing into a tri-racial system in which some Latinx and Asian people may fall into an honorary White status (Bonilla-Silva 2004), how these monied groups define racial solidarity, understand their mobility to middle-class suburbs, and make sense of their relationship to Blacks and Whites has the potential to reshape cultural and political dynamics. Future studies that compare their experiences are critical to the sociology of race, racism, and suburbs.

BLACK DIASPORIC SUBURBS IN THE WHITE EMPIRE CITY

The lived experiences of my interviewees were wedded to the residential context of Cascades and Great Park, their spatial histories, and their relationship to Greater New York. The contemporary situation of the post-Break Black middle class is the latest chapter in a long history of Africans in New York and the New World. Fifty years after the passage of the Fair Housing Act, a large and growing segment of Black people in metropolitan New York now live in the suburbs. However, the presence of Black communities on Long Island began long before the 1960s. From the docking of the first Dutch slave ship on Long Island in the 1600s to the desegregation crisis that, ironically, gave Black New Yorkers access to these postwar suburbs as Whites and White ethnic households fled to protest racial integration with Blacks and Puerto Ricans in the 1970s, Long Island has a four-hundred-year history of settler colonialism, racial slavery, and Jim Crow politics.

Colonial Long Island's history began with the erasure of Indigenous people and the displacement and enslavement of Africans and their children. This process was met with Black resistance, subversion, and radicalism. Long Island estates in Cold Spring Harbor and the African Burial Ground and Underground Railroad stations in Brooklyn and Manhattan attest to the significance of slavery in New York's economy and the bold and courageous efforts of enslaved and free Black people to envision and struggle for democratic ideals owed to them. Although the outskirts of New York City are usually imagined as White and White-ethnic spaces of potato and dairy farms, Black people established free communities on Long Island as long ago as the 1600s. Slavery on Long Island was replaced by Black codes and racial residential segregation that inscribed White control over the development of contemporary suburbs.

The spatial histories that the post-Break Black middle class inherited as they established homes in suburbia bled into their contemporary socioeconomic problems. The metropolitan, national, and global situation at the time I conducted the research for this book were spatialized continuations of racial and economic injustice Blacks have encountered for generations. In 2008, the global economy had reached its lowest point since the Great Depression, and experts dubbed the long downturn that followed the "Great Recession." The Great Recession was part of a global economic collapse caused by neoliberal deregulation and the rise of the sub-prime lending practices of predatory banks that infiltrated Black and brown communities throughout the United States. Many of the people I interviewed hesitated to identify themselves as middle class when jobs were insecure, mortgages were underwater, and income inequality was on the rise across the country. It took exceptionally high incomes to keep up with the rising cost of living. Gladys, a Black American office manager in her forties who lived in Cascades, said, "To be middle class in New York, you have to bring in at least $150,000 to $200,000 a year, and that is not living within your means and that is with debt." If a family in Queens earned $200,000, their earnings would be approximately three times higher than New York's median household income. However, the cost of basic necessities in New York, such as food, transportation, and utilities, is significantly higher than the national average. Aware of these financial realities, middle-class Black diasporas construct space- and time-specific standards for being a part of the middle class.

The Great Recession threatened and gutted the Black middle class that had emerged since the civil rights triumphs of the 1960s. The foreclosure crisis hit Queens and Long Island residents especially hard. Queens's Black neighborhoods experienced exceptionally high levels of predatory lending and in 2008–2010 had one of the highest foreclosure rates in the country.[9] Residents' family members and friends, and sometimes they themselves, were losing jobs, receiving foreclosure notices, and consoling others who were suddenly plummeting from new middle-class lifestyles into poverty. Their homes were the main source of wealth for the Black middle class, and the foreclosure crisis and widespread layoffs set back decades of advances in income and homeownership that civil rights activists had fought for. Their affluence did not shield the middle class from the exploitative lending practices and job insecurity that hit Black communities hard, and Latinx groups the hardest (Lacy 2012, Niedt and Martin 2013). The persistence of racial inequality in wealth meant they had significantly less assets than Whites to protect themselves from episodes of economic shock. This foreclosure crisis was the contemporary outcome of generations of White domination over Black economic freedom.

In the depths of economic despair that led many Black people from comfortable positions to claim that there was no longer a middle class in America, a wave of political hope was unleashed by the election of Barack Hussein Obama in 2008. Black people from a wide range of backgrounds were stunned and elated when the son of a Kenyan immigrant man and White American woman and the husband of a Black American woman became the nation's first Black president. Many perceived the Obamas as exemplars of what they wanted their children to aspire to. The Obama Presidency represented a new freedom to move around the world. The presence of a Black family in the White House suggested to many that a dream of the civil rights generation had been realized—but only this far. The political roadblocks Obama faced with Republicans in Congress and the concerted effort to discredit him and stymie his attempts to change public policy, coupled with the Great Recession and the early rise of the Black Lives Matter movement, were living contradictions that affected middle-class Black suburbanites in both material, cultural, and psychological ways.

Middle-class Black suburbanites' uncertainty about the future at this moment of national economic crisis was intensified by recent changes in New York's political economy. The neoliberal policies that had undercut middle-class jobs in the city and the rise of a bifurcated class structure since the 1970s undermined the Black middle class, as the anti-black employment practices in New York's workplaces and the recency of their upward mobility made them particularly vulnerable and insecure. Although New York has been a global city for some time, since the 1990s the circulation of capital into and through the city generated a speculative boom in real estate, encouraged the privatization of public goods, and removed the fetters from those who regard profits as more important than people. The political structure of the city, historically dominated by a combination of Manhattan's White Anglo elite and Irish, Italian, and Polish political machines in the boroughs and suburbs, has systematically kept Black New Yorkers out of positions of meaningful political power, even though wealthy Black people reside there and have also represented urban districts in Congress. Despite the prominent positions attained by Shirley Chisholm, Yvette Clark, Jesse Jackson, Al Sharpton, and David Dinkins, the ruling elite remains White, and the interests of the city's working class and poor residents of color marginal. In a metropolitan area in which people of color are a majority, White Anglos and White ethnics have continued to dominate the political infrastructure and cater to the interests of real estate developers and multinational corporations.

My respondents' middle-class, suburban identities were framed around living in or in close relationship with Mayor Michael Bloomberg's New York. In what Bloomberg's successor Mayor Bill de Blasio called a "Tale of Two Cities," the rich prospered, the poor suffered, and the middle class was disappearing. Many of my respondents remarked that, although Bloomberg's policies were seen as progressive, they were anti-Black in scope and implementation. Simeon, age fifty-one, a Jamaican Great Park resident and construction worker declared: "The only thing Black about Bloomberg is his wallet." After billionaire Michael Bloomberg, who made his fortune in finance, media, and information technology, was elected in 2002, his initiatives to attract wealthy investors and high-tech corporations to New York led to a rise in the proportion of high-income residents in the city, the intensification of gentrification in historically Black neighborhoods such as Harlem, Bed-Stuy and Crown Heights, and a sharp decrease in quality affordable housing. Following a creative-class logic, Bloomberg repurposed a former industrial city into one that attracted young, mostly White, well-educated, and monied people. With this in-migration came the dispossession of the city's poor, working-class, and middle-class Black and brown families. Many moved to areas in and around Cascades and Great Park, as part of a trend now called the suburbanization of poverty. Others abandoned New York altogether and moved down South. Bloomberg's pro-growth administration left an indelible print on Black people's sense of belonging and possibility in a city where the middle class who are at its heart were forgotten.

Bloomberg's law enforcement policies troubled middle-class parents of Black boys and girls. Raising their children in New York required them to strike a delicate balance between protecting them from harm from private citizens and law enforcement. "Too many White cops in our Black neighborhood," Simeon also remarked. "They give our kids citations for riding a bike on the sidewalk, in their own community!" Residents wanted to raise their children in safe neighborhoods; however, Bloomberg's stop-and-frisk policy heightened the awareness of Black middle-class families in Queens of their outsider status. Stop-and-frisk gave police the authority to search young Black and Latinx people without cause. Although they accounted for just 4.7 percent of the city's population, between 2003 and 2013, youth of color were 41 percent of those stopped by the police.[10] In addition to being directed against youth in lower income neighborhoods, the policy also impacted youth who resided in segregated Black middle-class areas on the margins of the city and was modeled in suburban multiracial towns on Long Island.

For the Black immigrant middle class, the underbelly of this New Jim Crow criminal injustice system was deportation for noncitizen Black New Yorkers. The 1996 Illegal Immigration Reform and Immigrant Responsibility Act (IRRIRA), the expansion of ICE, and the widespread removal of noncitizens led to family separations for a subset of the families I met. In this environment, middle-class Haitians were also strategizing how they could shelter and aid new migrants seeking temporary protected status after the devastation of the 2010 earthquake in Port au Prince. The post-Break Black middle class negotiated an array of seismic local and global events that impacted their sense of racial and class belonging in New York's global political economy in real time. They were living and making history.

PUTTING QUEENS AND LONG ISLAND ON THE BLACK MAP

Cascades and Great Park are two of the four hundred middle-class suburbs where multinational Black communities have formed in the United States (Wen et al. 2009). To understand cultural identity and belonging in diasporic suburbs at a tumultuous time in New York and US history, I spent two and half years living in Cascades, Queens, and Great Park, carrying out participant observation and conducting interviews there. Over the course of ten years, I returned to these neighborhoods to remain in contact with their residents and give attention to the transformations occurring there. In order to immerse myself in these neighborhoods' local culture, I volunteered with community organizations; frequented restaurants and retail stores; attended various church services; and went to meetings of parent-teacher associations, civic and block associations, and community boards. I was invited to social events and private parties ranging from family-friendly first communions to adult gatherings. "Thick descriptions" of social practices in these spaces were complemented by sixty in-depth interviews with Black middle-class adults (see table 2). One-third of them were born in the United States and had no recent foreign-born ancestry; one-third were born in Jamaica or had Jamaican parents; and another third were born in Haiti. Twenty-five interviews

Table 2   Characteristics of Interviewees in Cascades (C) and Great Park (GP)

	Black American		Haitian		Jamaican	
	C | GP		C | GP		C | GP	
N	10 | 10		10 | 10		10 | 10	
Average Age	53 | 53		47 | 49		55 | 58	
Sex (F:M)	8:2 | 8:2		6:4 | 5:5		8:2 | 6:4	
Born Abroad/South	5 | 3		10 | 10		10 | 6	
Adult Children of Migrant/ Immigrant	5 | 7		0		0 | 4	

with business and community leaders provided important insights into the political economy of Cascades and Great Park.

I first explored Cascades, a majority Black middle-class suburban area in the racially, ethnically, and linguistically diverse county of Queens. In 2008, when I started this project, the population of Cascades was 77 percent Black, 40 percent foreign born, and 27 percent college educated. Professionals constituted 29 percent of residents, and the median household income was $70,174, which was higher than that of Whites in Queens and nationally ($50,303).[11] Great Park, in contrast, is a multiethnic, multiracial suburban community nestled in predominately White Nassau County, a unique space in New York's racially segregated suburbs. In 2008, the population of Great Park was 29 percent Black, 32 percent White, and 32 percent Latinx; 31 percent of residents were foreign born. The median household income was $81,315; residents with professional occupations comprised 36 percent of the population, and 37 percent had at least a college degree. In each of these areas, Haitians and Jamaicans constituted the largest foreign-born Black groups (see table 3).

Cascades: Suburb in the City

The average income of Black residents in Cascades, Queens surpasses that of Whites, a rare occurrence in most American cities. Cascades location within the boundaries of New York City does not make it any less of a

Table 3 Socioeconomic Characteristics of Cascades, Queens County, Great Park, Nassau County, and New York City

	Cascades	Queens County	Great Park	Nassau County	NYC
Median Household Income	$70,174	$56,780	$82,315	$97,049	$51,746
Black Household Income	$71,148	$58,527	$91,872	$81,215	$41,589
Asian Household Income	$73,493	$55,207	$105,481	$ 116,673	$55,090
Latino Household Income	$69,112	$50,710	$58,701	$70,525	$36,022
White Household Income	$54,848	$ 62,491	$89,526	$ 102,404	$71,851
College Educated (%)	27.0	29.9	31.6	41.4	34.0
Management/ Professional (%)	29.3	31.3	35.5	43.2	38.1
Owner-Occupied Housing (%)	66.2	44.5	74.1	81.3	35.3
Poverty Rate (% with incomes below the national average)	7.3	11.6	7.3	4.0	16.9

SOURCE: American Community Survey, 2008–2012.

suburb in the imagination of its Black residents. The generations of Black families who moved from tenements or high-rise buildings in the Bronx to single-family homes felt that they had significantly improved their situation, although moving required substantial financial resources. Cascades' residents work throughout the metropolitan area on various combinations of day, afternoon, and night shifts in diverse occupations and industries. My respondents included nurses, engineers, transportation workers, postal workers, small business owners, accountants, service workers, and teachers. Over a quarter of Cascades' population is college educated, with many holding associate's degrees. Nursing is a popular occupation for women. Registered nurses earn salaries upward of $60,000, and many work overtime to boost their earnings. Not only is the average income of

Black households higher than those of Latinos and Whites, but the poverty rate is well below the city's average.

Cascades is a hyper-segregated space. While Queens County is 17.7 percent Black, more than three-quarters of the Black population is clustered in Southeast Queens.[12] As a result of racial processes of White flight and Black in-migration, Cascades is three-quarters Black. Immigrants comprise two-fifths of the population, a slightly lower proportion than in Queens County, but much higher than in New York City as a whole. Whites are a very small and rapidly decreasing proportion of the population. Many of the remaining Whites are elderly, longtime residents who did not leave the neighborhood during the desegregation of local schools and White flight in the 1960s and 1970s. Daisy, a White widow who had lived in her single-family home since the 1940s, received social support from her neighbors to meet the demands of everyday life. A Black Panamanian neighbor took charge of her care. In exchange, Daisy gifted her the rights to her property, which her parents had purchased and passed down to her.

Cascades has a concentrated Black population in one of the most ethnically and racially diverse counties in the country. Over half of Queens County residents speak a language other than English at home; they hail from over one hundred different countries and ethnic groups. The census undercounts in Black communities like Cascades, making their reports on ancestry difficult to rely on. More accurate reports from the Department of City Planning, New York City Community Board, and the Drum Major Institute indicate that Caribbean immigrants constitute the most significant pan-ethnic group in Jamaica, Queens.[13] In 2000, three-quarters (75.7%) of the population was Black. Black Americans constituted half (51.3%) of its Black residents, and Caribbean immigrants almost one fourth (23.3%).[14] The diverse experiences of immigrants from different islands shape Black middle-class life in this city within a city (Du Bois, 1899).

Since Queens is located on the eastern edge of New York City, it lies on the urban-suburban boundary that separates the urban municipality from the suburban towns. This boundary defines who has access to the resources that the city provides and pays its lower property tax rates. At the same time, these contiguous locations have affordable, integrated transportation systems and interconnected commercial areas. Despite its middle-class characteristics, residents feel the daily realities of racial segregation. Across the railroad tracks or major thouroughfares are predominantly White and Asian neighborhoods, which Black neighborhood residents believe receive more city services. Monica, forty-three, a paralegal of Jamaican ancestry, observed a delay in the city's snow removal after the blizzard of 2010: "Manhattan gets cleaned up quickly! The city cares more about them. In Queens, forget it. Down here, we have to fight for everything. We just had a big storm, now where are our snowplows? Buses are stuck on the street in front of my cousin's house. Bayside gets more than us."

Great Park: Out on the Island

Brooklyn, Queens, Nassau, and Suffolk counties are all on Long Island. When New York City annexed Brooklyn and Queens in the late 1800s, Queens and Hempstead were divided and the political boundary between New York City and Nassau and Suffolk was created. The Cross Island Parkway symbolizes the color and class line separating the city from its suburbs. The city, with a population that is diverse in class, racial, and ethnic terms and has a political system that is more representative of diverse population interests, is adjacent to one of the wealthiest, racially segregated, and politically conservative counties in the nation. Over the past twenty years, however, as poor, low-income, middle-class and affluent families of color have been pushed or chosen to move to the suburbs, Nassau County has experienced unprecedented racial and class heterogeneity and segmentation (Lichter, Parisi, and Taquino 2012).

In 2012, the median household income of Great Park was $82,315, higher than that of Queens but lower than Nassau County. Compared to the national median household income, however, Great Park residents are affluent.[15] Great Park is considered a bedroom suburb; residents commute to work elsewhere in the county or in New York City. On a given workday morning, Volvo Crossovers, Mercedes SUVs and Honda minivans fly down the main street onto the highways heading west and east. Residents are employed in health care, public service, business, construction, and professional and managerial occupations. More than one-third of Great Park residents hold managerial or professional positions. Black residents work in a range of fields: as technology specialists, nurses, doctors, engineers, and small business owners. One-third of the adults have a college degree. Like their counterparts in Cascades, Great Park's Black residents have earned associate's and bachelor's degrees at the city and state's public universities, which have enabled them to move up into the middle class.

Great Park's ranking in the hierarchy of Black diasporic suburbs translates into high prestige yet high costs for those who live there. For Black Americans and Black immigrants, owning a home in Great Park is the culmination of years of learning, earning, and saving. Parents work constantly to meet mortgage and tuition payments, while some are still paying off substantial debts for their own college education. What most clearly separates Great Park from Cascades is the exorbitant amounts residents must pay in property taxes, which may exceed $20,000 per year. The combination of high taxes and high mortgages prohibits many families from living here and stretches its residents financially. What sets Great Park's Black families apart from their White neighbors, however, is that they must pay what is colloquially called a "Black tax": they have to earn more to live in a suburb where Whites earn less than they do, and many pay more to live in overpriced homes that they purchased as housing prices were rising prior to the housing market crash.

White, Latinx, and Black diasporic families encounter one another as neighbors more often in Great Park than Cascades. Great Park's racial makeup is currently undergoing substantial change, as its Black and Latinx populations are rapidly increasing (American Community Survey, 2008–2012).[16] Between 2000 and 2010, the White population fell from 46 to 35 percent, while the Black population rose from 26 to 29 percent. The proportion of Hispanics (who may be of any race), primarily Dominicans, Salvadorans, and Colombians, experienced a similar increase, from 24 to 29 percent. Black residents are skeptical of the idea that the community is stably integrated, however. Mrs. Hughes, a Black American librarian, observed: "One year, it's like the White students just started leaving the school system. They still live in the area, but their parents pulled them right out. This was especially for the seventh grade and up." The Great Recession and the resulting inability of White families to sell their homes for a profit limited White flight. These residential realities make Great Park a key site for unpacking the qualitative experience of diasporic Black middle-class residents in a multiracial, stratified suburb and comparing it to Cascades, a suburb in the city more advanced in its transformation from White to Black-brown.

AFRO-DIASPORIC DISHES, CHAPTER BY CHAPTER

The next two chapters of this book are historiographies of migration and place. They explore the forced and voluntary movement of Black peoples and their suburban place making. Beginning from the dawn of the colonial era in the 1400s to the end of the Break period in 1970 (Winant 2001), chapter 2, "Children of the Yam," elucidates the cross-national racial formations and migrations that have shaped the long, trans-geographical journeys of Black Americans, Haitians, and Jamaicans from slavery to middle class. Chapter 3, "Blood Pudding," explores the role of racism, class, and segregation in the rural to suburban development of Queens and Long Island and how Black (im)migrants have created these places in their visions.

The following chapters unpack the structure and culture of class in Black diasporic suburbs. Chapter 4, "Callaloo," turns to the contemporary cultural economies of the post-Break Black middle class. It argues that although they are separate and unequal from Whites, there are important inter- and intragroup differences in the Black middle class migrations and socioeconomic experiences that shape how they earn and circulate money in between their households. Chapter 5, "Fish Soup," introduces the reader to the diverse class origins of the diasporic Black middle class. A significant proportion of Black middle-class people in the United States are first-generation middle class. How class origins become contentious sites of status boundary work individually and collectively elucidate their lived experiences of downward, lateral, and upward mobility. The clash between class origins and distinction work creates the parameters of belonging in a local and trans-spatial Black stratification system articulated by my interviewees.

The final chapters are in conversation with the complex meanings of race, nationality, and regionality for the post-break Black middle class. Chapter 6, "Vanilla Black," explores how the Black diasporic middle class defines, negotiates, and contests racial identity. Rather than analyzing the degree to which a person identifies as Black or of ethnic origin, it explores individuals' cultural pathways to Blackness. I examine the meaning making that respondents engage in to assert their relationship to constructions of Blackness in the US South, Haiti, and Jamaica. Through an analysis of how respondents interpret the "Black" racial identity, the chapter outlines what I term the racial consciousness spectrum, a framework for categorizing interethnic and intraethnic racial identities and practices. Despite the conventional sociological wisdom that middle-class Black immigrants distance themselves from Black identities, this chapter uncovers the diversity of definitions and performances of Blackness among middle class Black immigrants and Black Americans.

Chapter 7, "Green Juice Fast," probes the centrality of nationality and regionality in the lived experiences of the post-Break Black middle class. Ethnic stigmas characterize the social encounters between Black Americans, Haitians, and Jamaicans in their neighborhoods, workplaces, and private spaces. The overlapping encounters of these Black diasporic groups in suburbs gives traction to stereotyping, which leads to the formation of a local diasporic hierarchy. This local stratification system is informed by cross-regional and cross-national racial, class, and color politics. The negotiation of ethnic boundaries in middle-class spaces demonstrates the persistence of nationality in light of upward class mobility, its social utility in diverse contexts, and its embeddedness in racialized respectability politics. The final chapter, "Mustard Seeds," summarizes the book's main contributions to urban studies, immigration, and race and suggests future research directions on the next generation, suburban Black millennials.

2 Children of the Yam

FROM ENSLAVED AFRICAN TO THE BLACK MIDDLE
CLASS IN THE UNITED STATES, HAITI, AND JAMAICA

> Our cultural identities reflect the common historical expe-
> riences and shared cultural codes which provide us, as "one
> people," with stable, unchanging and continuous frames of
> reference and meaning, beneath the shifting divisions and
> vicissitudes of our actual history. This oneness, underlying
> all the other, more superficial differences, is the truth, the
> essence of "Caribbeaness," of the Black experience.

Stuart Hall (1990)

Walter and I sat in a local delicatessen at lunch time. As the overhead
radio played Robin Thicke's "Lost without You" and a compilation of
Diana Ross's hit songs from the 1970s on WBLS and customers came in
to buy hero sandwiches, Walter shared his first impressions of New York
City when he arrived from Louisiana:

> We came to New York—I remember it like it was yesterday. We crossed the
> George Washington Bridge ... before sunrise and every light in the city
> looked like it was on. And I was like, "oh man!" At nine o'clock down there
> in Louisiana, you can't see a light on at that time. And I was looking at this
> city, it just amazes. And then I got acclimated. You hear young men cursing.
> Adults speaking to a child and the child being rude. How I grew up and
> where I came from everybody went to church. And all of a sudden in the
> Lower East Side, I was in school with a very diverse crowd.

Walter was not only a participant in the Great Migration during the 1960s,
but also the child of immigrants from the Caribbean who had moved to
the US South in the 1950s. His story, along with many others I heard,

exploded any neat, linear assumptions about the origins, migrations and identities of the Black middle class.

Walter, sixty-three, a prominent educator, had lived in Great Park for most of his adult life by the time of our interview. He was born and raised in rural Louisiana by Jamaican and Cuban immigrant parents. His mother did domestic work; his father labored on a farm in the hot Louisiana sun. They refused to teach him and his siblings either Jamaican patois or Spanish. His father did not want his children to be targets of anti-Black and anti-immigrant sentiment in Jim Crow Louisiana. Walter's fondest memories of growing up in Louisiana revolved around eating his mother's dinners by candlelight. Only later did he realize that these special and spontaneous events happened when his parents' earnings were not enough to both keep the electricity on and feed the family.

Walter's parents arrived in rural Louisiana after the Second World War. They were leaving behind volatile political economies in Jamaica and Cuba. What they found in the South were irregular jobs, segregated schools for their children, and abuses from Jewish shopkeepers who ran after the children with broomsticks when they wanted to buy pop soda. Exhausted by the racial caste system of rural Louisiana, Walter's parents sent him to live with his older sibling in New York to "get a good education." Walter's parents' migration from the Caribbean to the South and his subsequent move to New York exemplifies the overlapping, intergenerational nature of Black migration, bold moves that call into question sharp distinctions between native and foreign-born Blacks.

As members of overlapping diasporas, the post-Break Black middle-class's understandings of cultural belonging are shaped by their migration histories, which are a "culmination of a set of movements" (Bald 2006) between multiple social classes and places. Their political and economic struggles and resulting migrations summon back memories of their racial situations in their nations and regions. The mass migration of Blacks like Walter's family across the Atlantic in the postwar period is the product of interconnected racial and labor struggles from below that resulted in the global shift from White colonial domination during the twentieth century to our current era of colorblind racial hegemony (Winant 2001). As a result, the racialized political economies of the United States, Haiti, and

Jamaica are inseparable from the migrations to and cultural repertoires of Black suburbs.

In its contemporary form, the post-Break Black middle class has brought with them the items they need to re-root themselves on suburban soils. The African yam is one of these items, a staple crop of the gastronomy of the diaspora. As the children of the African Yam, they come from lands abundant with yam fields. This tuber was brought to the West from West Africa during the transatlantic slave trade. From the dishes of colonial Virginia to the Caribbean and Africa, the yam was a part of the plantation diet. Today, customers find it in Village Market and commercial places like it. It is boiled in soups, fried in palm oil, or candied for the holidays; and it connects Black middle-class suburbanites to their ancestral pasts.[1] A symbol of wealth and seen as the king crop in Nigeria, slave traders stocked their ships with yams to feed kidnapped Africans during long, arduous, and often fatal trips across the Atlantic and into bondage. Yams were later planted as crops in the United States and Caribbean islands and became a food that enslaved Africans cooked for White masters and, when possible, themselves. It is a go-to root found in the kitchens of diasporic suburbs today, harkening back to the resistance and creativity of the diaspora's ancestors amid a history of exploitation, hardship, and mass migrations across the Atlantic.

This chapter turns to the historical racial formations and resulting migrations that have sent people of African descent from the US South and Global South to New York and its suburbs. In order to understand the cultural identities of the Black middle class, I examine the long period between the beginning of the transatlantic slave trade in the 1400s and what Howard Winant calls the "Break" in the cultural, social, and political acceptability of global White racism (1945–1970) to provide an integrated history of racial slavery, colonialism, Black revolution, emancipation and decolonization, and nation-building movements across Haiti, Jamaica, and the United States. These global shifts in racial stratification were fundamentally tied to the mass migration of Black postcolonial subjects to metropoles of empires, eventually leading to the reconfiguration of both local and global Black class stratification systems. As we will discuss in subsequent chapters, my interviewees' cultural identities were deeply intertwined with how they retold stories of these pasts in relation to their present (Hall 1990).

As children of the yam, the post-Break Black middle class negotiated the racial formations of their nation-states in tandem with their global connections to the larger African diaspora. Despite the shared racial histories of children of the West African yam, their different styles of preparing and consuming yams in the United States, Haiti, and Jamaica demonstrate the heterogeneity of each groups' nation, race, and class formations. All these diasporic groups have bought these particular histories to the suburbs where they reside. This chapter's analysis of middle-class Haitians, Jamaicans, and Black Americans serves as a backdrop for their diasporic epistemologies: their ways of knowing, seeing, and discussing their lives. The negotiations between what Stuart Hall (1990) calls *presence Africaine*—the representation of the Black diasporas' repression as the progeny of Africa by European colonization—and their self-determined national and regional identities are at the core of the cultural histories that they bring to diasporic suburbs.

THE EARLY BLACK PETIT BOURGEOISIE (1400s–1700s)

Class and status divisions among Blacks in the Atlantic world are long-standing. Their forms, symbols, and expressions, however, have changed over time (Frazier 1957). The first twenty Africans brought to British colonial North America arrived in Jamestown, Virginia, in 1619, shortly after the colony's creation. In 1675 an insurrection of landless and poor Europeans and Africans against wealthy White landowners, known as Bacon's Rebellion, prompted the British colonial government and the planter class to solidify racial slavery and provide basic guarantees of freedom to White men.[2] The tripartite Black-White-Indian racial classification system divided people into rigid status groups and locked Blacks into perpetual servitude to Whites. Indigenous people who survived the genocidal warfare of settler colonialism were forced to abandon their homelands and flee beyond the edge of European settlement or to surrender their cultures and histories in a process of forced assimilation that denied them equality and expressions of their humanity.

The early Black middle class during slavery in British colonial North America was defined by their skin color. In the plantation regime, mixed-race slaves were more likely to be free or were often afforded a higher status compared to enslaved Blacks. Their privileges included training in skilled occupations, and they were assigned as messengers between plantations. However, they, too, were subjected to coercion and violence from White masters. White landowners also tried to use mulattos or slaves who worked in the house to control Black field hands, creating divisions between these groups in an attempt to undermine their collective resistance.[3] Although mixed race people were the children of enslaved Black women who were raped by White masters (Feimster 2009, J. Jones 2009), they occupied the same political and social condition as Blacks whose ancestry was entirely African—and did so regardless of whether they remained enslaved, had bought their freedom, or had been emancipated. This one-drop of African blood ideology is unique to the United States; it ordered the social relations of slavery, Reconstruction, and Jim Crow, and was even inscribed into laws in the early twentieth century (Sharfstein 2006). Mulattos held an intermediary position between Blacks and Whites. Their lighter skin color, European facial features, and hair texture gave them a higher status than dark-skinned Blacks, irrespective of their education or wealth. Sometimes they used this position to challenge slavery. More often, they sought to retain their power by collaborating with Whites to reinforce control over the Black African population.

Mulattos' expressions of loyalty to Whites and hostility toward Blacks both within their societies and their families arose from the fact that, legally and culturally, they could not attain a White identity or the power that it conferred. Instead, some of those whose African ancestry was hidden engaged in racial "passing" in order to gain the economic and social power controlled by Whites. Others created an insular social class that used strategies such as etiquette, exclusive social organizations, and intermarriage only with other mulattos in order to reinforce boundaries between themselves and Blacks.

Status distinctions in colonial Jamaica and Haiti developed differently than in the United States. By the time enslaved Africans were brought to Virginia, Haiti had been subject to more than a century of Spanish and French colonial rule. Slavery was forged on Hispaniola (the island divided between Haiti and the Dominican Republic) with the arrival of Christopher Columbus in 1492. By 1540, thirty thousand Africans were enslaved in

Table 4   Colonial Racial Stratification in British-Controlled North America, British-
           Controlled Jamaica, and French-Controlled Haiti

British-Controlled North America	*British-Controlled Jamaica*	*French-Controlled Haiti*
White	White	White (*grand, couche moyenne, petit*)
Mulatto	Brown middle class	Mulatto/Free People of Color (*gens de couleur/affranchis*)
	Chinese, South Asian, Mulatto (sambo, quadroon, mustee, musteefino)	
Black	Black	Black, enslaved and free (*noir*)
Indigenous	Indigenous	Indigenous (*Indigene*)

SOURCES: (Dubois 2005, Dunn 2012, Dupuy 2004, Zephir 1996)

Haiti. Within a century, Haiti was the number one exporter of sugar in the world and the wealthiest country in the Western hemisphere. The Spanish ceded control of the western part of the island to the French in 1697. Renamed Saint Domingue, it became one of the richest Caribbean colonies and the envy of the British and Portuguese Empires. By the time of the French Revolution (1789–1799), the island's enslaved Black and mulatto population (five hundred thousand) vastly outnumbered the French and St. Domingue–born White population (forty thousand) (Dupuy 2004). Whites were divided into the *grand blancs*, who were landowning planters, and the *petit blancs*, who were landless. Initially the *petit blancs* were indentured servants and perceived as inferior to land-owning Whites. After repaying the cost of their journey to Saint Domingue through their labor, *petit blancs* were hired by *grand blancs* and occupied middle- and lower-class positions in the island's social hierarchy. They worked as shopkeepers, teachers, and merchants. They were anti-Black, pro-slavery, and saw the mulatto population as competitors who threatened their socioeconomic status (Zephir 1996).

Of the half a million Blacks and mulattos in Saint Domingue at the onset of the Haitian Revolution in 1791, twenty-eight thousand were free, most of them mulattos. The mulatto class in particular saw itself as a distinct status group, separate from free and enslaved Black people. In the United States, the system of racial ascription and repression excluded free and enslaved mulattos, along with Blacks, from access to such tools for upward mobility as education or land ownership. In Haiti, however, the mulatto class enjoyed social and economic privileges conferred on them by their White fathers. They came to represent an important status group, outnumbering landless Whites and, eventually, landowning Whites. Their power was used to reinforce Black repression. It was also seen as a threat to *petit blancs*, who had less access to land because, unlike mulattos, they did not inherit it. *Petit blancs* believed themselves to be socially superior to mulattos, even when they were financially poorer. The *affranchise* (free) mulatto class was socially and politically oppressed by landowning and landless Whites on the island, but at the same time distinctly oppressive to free and enslaved Blacks.

A small, free Black *petit bourgeoisie* emerged from property ownership in Haiti. In *Black Marxism*, Cedric Robinson remarked: "Some Blacks, but certainly with less frequency than occurred with what the French colonialists termed the *petit blancs*, had translated particular skills, traditional positions and knowledge into property (including slaves during the slave era)" (Robinson 1983, 179). Some Blacks were born into slavery but later freed. Members of this *noir* middle class sometimes owned land and even slave plantations before and after the Haitian Revolution. Others were sent to France to be educated and returned to Haiti to assume leadership positions. The most prominent figure in Haitian history, Toussaint L'Ouverture, once a slave, was educated on the island and later became the principal leader of the Haitian Revolution. L'Ouverture used the philosophy of Black freedom and the French revolutionary ideals of *fraternité, égalité, liberté* as models for ending the enslavement of African peoples in Saint Domingue. Other educated Black revolutionaries joined the quest for racial liberation from below. The Black middle class in colonial Haiti emerged separately but alongside the mulatto *affranchise* class. This coexistence was sometimes cooperative, as Blacks and mulattos became allies in the fight against the French. Yet the small number of landowning Blacks in positions of political leadership paled in comparison to the perpetual lower caste position of free and enslaved Blacks on the island.

Jamaica's racial stratification structure is distinct from those in the United States and in Haiti. The conditions of slavery and indentured servitude were defined by a racial classification system of White landowners at the top, enslaved Blacks at the bottom, and a multiracial brown middle class in between them. In Jamaica, the mulatto class emulated the cruelty of Whites toward enslaved Blacks that characterized racial relations in the United States. Unlike the United States, but like Haiti, Jamaica had a complicated Black-brown-White racial landscape. Unlike Haiti, however, in Jamaica the mulatto class was absorbed into a privileged "brown" middle class that also included Chinese and East Indian indentured servants, rather than forming a group unto themselves. The brown middle class preserved its social and economic power by making it impossible for Blacks on the island to acquire land or accumulate wealth.

Large-scale slavery was introduced in Jamaica in 1655 by the British. Located three hundred miles from Haiti, the island colony absorbed a whopping total of eight hundred fifty thousand Africans whom labored in the expanding and highly profitable sugar industry during the eighteenth century. In both Haiti and Jamaica, the survival rate of enslaved Africans was low, and few enslaved Africans had children. As a result, the native-born Black population was disproportionately small compared to the number of enslaved Africans brought to the islands. The racial stratification system was a three-tier hierarchy of "domestics, skilled workers and field hands" (Brown 1979). Mulattos were the preferred domestic workers, while most skilled workers and all field hands were Black. As in Haiti and the British North American colonies, the mulatto class served as an intermediary group that facilitated the perpetuation of slavery.

While the mulatto class was the early Black middle class in the United States and an entirely separate ethnoracial caste group in Haiti, during the later plantation period Jamaica's mulattos were subsumed into a brown middle class. In response to the abolition of the international slave trade, the British introduced indentured servants from China and East India, since the profitability of plantations depended on the ample supply of free and cheap labor. The abolition of slavery by the Haitian Revolution at a time when the British were still unwilling to emancipate the slaves in their Caribbean colonies accelerated this shift in the source of plantation labor. In order to avoid slave rebellion and the formation of a Black empire in Jamaica and Trinidad, the British selected Chinese and Indian laborers, whom they believed would undercut Black mobilization and serve as models of the civilized, well-disciplined labor they wanted Black Africans to emulate (Jung 2006). Their assumption was the Chinese and Indian workers would become intermediary enforcers of colonial rule because they granted them privileges denied to the Black population. This created a complex stratified racial and class structure unique to Jamaica that continues to shape encounters and experiences on the island and the diaspora today.

THE BLACK MIDDLE CLASSES AMID REVOLUTION AND EMANCIPATION (1800s)

The combination of racial oppression, demographic predominance of Blacks over Whites, and the radical politics that arose in the island colony during the French Revolution created the conditions that made the Haitian Revolution possible (Geggus, 2001). Ruling Whites used increasingly punitive measures to control enslaved Africans in Haiti. Frustrated by the hardening of the line between Whites and non-Whites drawn by the *grand* and *petit blancs*, the *affranchise* mulatto class formed opportunistic alliances with free and enslaved Blacks to end slavery. The ambivalent and fluctuating relationship between the mulatto and Black populations on the island are among many examples of the skin color continuum that has defined mulatto-Black relations and created the apartheid-like conditions that exist in Haiti today. Led by Toussaint L'Ouverture, Andre Rigaud, and Jean Jacques Dessalines, Blacks and mulattos finally defeated Napoleon Bonaparte's army in 1804 and erected the first free Black republic in the modern world, Haiti.

The Haitian revolution was the first critical rupture of global White supremacy and reordered the Black class system. The Haitian Revolution inverted the modern global order that posited that Europeans were racially and economically superior to all other contrived racial groups. The victory of skilled enslaved Africans over Napoleon's army proclaimed the humanity of Blacks who had been subjugated to centuries of bondage. Black societies in Saint Domingue, New Orleans, New York, Trinidad, Jamaica, and beyond could imagine the possibility of collective racial liberation and independent Black republics. Haiti became a beacon of resistance, dignity, achievement, and aspiration across the Black Atlantic. After the revolution, most of the White population of Saint Domingue had either been killed or fled the island and returned to France. Those without sufficient means to leave remained but lived in racially hostile conditions. Mulattos inherited the land that their French fathers left behind or seized abandoned land as the spoils of war. In the nineteenth century, they capitalized on their acquisition of property and became the dominant economic class. The Black masses acquired land, but most remained in the peasants class.

The revolution's promises of a prosperous independent Haiti were hindered by ongoing internal conflicts between Blacks and mulattos for power and position and external interventions by the governments of France and the United States. The mulatto class revered French cultural repertoires and identities, maintained economic relations with France, and controlled business and political relations on the island, becoming an urban elite that socioeconomically dominated the Black population. Blacks were largely relegated to rural poverty in a declining plantation economy. Their primary vehicle of upward mobility was attaining government positions. A Black elite emerged from those with high-ranking positions in the military. These racial, color, and class dynamics led to continuous competition over the racial control of Haiti's nation-state, inhibiting the rise of a substantial Black middle class in a predominately Black nation.

At the turn of the nineteenth century, the plummeting price of sugar in global markets posed a threat to the plantation economy throughout the Caribbean. The decline in the profitability of sugar production led to increasingly cruel and debilitating labor and living conditions for enslaved Blacks. While Haiti was in the throes of revolution, Jamaica's mulatto and Black population was held under the thumb of British rule. Africans in Jamaica rebelled constantly against their bondage. Escaped slaves known as Maroons (see Campbell 1988) built free towns in the mountainous regions and waged war against British planters in the 1730s and the 1790s. Haiti's concurrent political upheaval was an omen to White planters across the Atlantic. This signal Black victory reverberated in Jamaica, causing the British to move from signing treaties and granting Maroons local sovereignty to deporting rebellious slaves to Nova Scotia and Sierra Leone to thwart a Haitian-style revolution within their borders.

British officials' decision to abolish slavery gradually, starting with a shift from perpetual bondage to time-limited apprenticeship in 1834, met with unexpected resistance among Blacks, who demanded their complete freedom. The British then instituted a formal emancipation in 1838. White planters, however, sought to keep Black freedmen and freedwomen under their control through violence and economic repression in order to maximize the exploitation of their labor. They also resorted to replenishing their labor force with indentured servants. The British government, meanwhile, continued promoting the importation of bound, "coolie" labor from its colonies in South Asia and China. Thus, race became further imbricated in class stratification, as mulattos, Indians, and the Chinese became the socioeconomic middlemen between the newly freed Blacks and the White British upper class. Indentured Asian laborers received inferior treatment compared to Whites, but when their time was up, they were given credits and loans to start business ventures and plant roots on the island. They also enforced measures of surveillance and violence that kept Blacks in positions of peasantry and servitude. Although occupying a lower position than White Britons, Indians and Chinese laborers were made to understand their position in the racial hierarchy as superior to that of Blacks and given opportunities to enter a professional middle class. These practices created ongoing racial, ethnic, and class distinctions that continue to animate contemporary social stratification on the island.

In Haiti, the sociopolitical and economic changes in slavery and colonialism after the Revolution created significant uncertainty in plantation societies in the United States and the Caribbean. Migration became a primary tool for elite and non-elite Black communities across colonies and in nation-states to find security and upward economic and social mobility in a time of major upheaval. The new Black republic of Haiti also desperately needed labor, so the government invited Black Americans to immigrate to the island, promising them land and financial support to get started. Only a few took up this offer. The emigration of Black Americans to Haiti and West Africa was made possible by the American Colonization Society (ACS) in the 1820s, a White organization invested in deporting enslaved Blacks as an alternative to emancipation. Emigration was later promoted by more Black grassroots efforts to find liberation for the enslaved in territories outside the United States in the mid-nineteenth century (Horton and Horton 1998). At the same time, migrants from Haiti and Jamaica were either coercively or voluntarily moving to or through the port cities of New York, Cuba, and Venezuela in a process of circum-Caribbean migration that laid the groundwork for radical pan-African political identities and allegiances (Putnam 2013). These crosscurrents of migration between spaces of Black enslavement and freedom, as well as colonization and independence, facilitated the formation of Black identities and the emergence of a *noir* middle class on the move across the Black Atlantic.

This increased social and spatial mobility of Blacks, however, it did not prevent the re-entrenchment of White colonial and imperial domination. After the Haitian Revolution, mulattos and Blacks, as well as slaveholding Whites, fled the French Caribbean. Many boarded ships to New Orleans, which was then a French colony. By 1810, Haitian immigrants accounted for one-third of New Orleans's slave population. In *Slavery's Metropolis*, Rashauna Johnson (2016) emphasizes that this migration led to captivity instead of mobility and freedom for Haitian mulattos and Blacks. "The auction block was among the first places that these migrants entered, and through naked force it transformed them from free persons to Louisiana slaves" (39). Others fled to New York, seeking safety from the ongoing battles between Blacks and mulattos over land and power in Haiti. The color conflicts on the island were brutal, and many mulattos went into exile, abandoning the land their French fathers gifted them. Members of this class of mulatto migrants integrated into New York's Black urban elite. In *Negroland*, Margo Jefferson (2016) remarks that the families with French last names in New York's Black bourgeoisie circles originated in Haiti: "Some arrived from Haiti alongside Whites fleeing Toussaint L'Ouverture's Black revolution: their ranks included free mulattos and slaves, who, after some pretense of loyalty, found it easy to desert their former masters and go into the business of upward mobility. From New Orleans to New York, men and women of mixed blood insistently established their primacy" (p. 11).

A key entrée into the circular migrations around the Black Atlantic between the Haitian Revolution and Emancipation in the United States is through the family histories of preeminent leaders of Black liberation. In the autobiography of W. E. B. Du Bois, the prominent sociologist, philosopher and historian had to piece together the story of his own family's diasporic history. Du Bois's paternal grandfather was from Haiti, settled in

Connecticut in 1830, and returned to Haiti just before the Civil War. He conjectured that his paternal grandfather joined the collective of Black American émigrés who sought land and freedom in post-Revolution Haiti and may have owned a plantation and had trade connections with the United States (Du Bois 2014).[4] Du Bois surmised that his grandfather may have left Haiti because of the impending war with France. These geopolitical events effectively undermined Du Bois's grandfather's socioeconomic status and led him to move back to the United States with Du Bois's Haitian-born father. His grandfather's return to the island just before the Civil War, while his father remained in his adopted country, signifies the continuing ties that joined Black people in the two countries.

As Haitian mulattos settled in New York and Black Americans sought liberation in Haiti, they entered stratified societies that were being reshaped by national crises. In the U.S. fugitive slaves and freed people arrived in Northern cities in search of safer havens from Southern racial repression. In places like Philadelphia and New York, they found poor housing conditions, low-wage work, and White American and European immigrant institutions and mobs that abhorred their presence and attacked their neighborhoods. Together, free and enslaved Black migrants from Northern, Southern, and Caribbean societies of various classes formed what Du Bois (1899) called a city within a city. In this segregated space, a respectable elite, many of whom were mulattos, emerged alongside a larger number of working-class and poor Black people.

After the passage of New York State's gradual emancipation law in 1827, class distinctions within the Black community were reshaped. A stratification system that had been based on color and free or enslaved status became increasingly based on color, social status, and family name. A small group of entrepreneurs and artisans was composed of people who were literate and churchgoing, most connected to the Anglican religious tradition. As tensions over the expansion of slavery gripped the nation, New York was seen as a destination and a gateway to Black freedom. For example, a myriad of Black churches and schools in Manhattan and Brooklyn were Underground Railroad stops. This demonstrates New York's geographical and social importance in the long, often thwarted journey from slavery to freedom. The respectability elite were invested in the fight for Black liberation and formed churches and schools to serve the wider Black community. At the same time, they also strategically built boundaries between themselves and the Black masses. The city's Black poor were confined to demeaning, low-wage work and overcrowded housing in Manhattan and Brooklyn, while the Black elite became entrepreneurs in ghettoized areas. Because Black-owned businesses could not serve White clientele, they relied on the patronage of the larger Black population for their economic success. Yet they actively erected class and color distinctions between themselves and the Black communities where they lived and worked.

Reconstruction after the Civil War and Emancipation was the beginning of a long, grueling struggle for Black freedom. Four million Black people who had been legally defined as property were to be incorporated into the United States as citizens. Freed people's struggle with White landlords over the control of their labor turned into sharecropping and tenancy arrangements that resembled slavery. During the Reconstruction period, unprecedented numbers of Black people pursued the promises of citizenship: they sought and won political office, opened businesses, and migrated north to escape endless toil in the declining agricultural economy and to seek opportunities in the expanding industrial economy. The White-controlled southern states responded to these efforts by establishing Black codes that severely restricted freed Black people and their freeborn children. These laws were enforced by a combination of state-sanctioned police and prison authorities and civilian racial terrorism. Black Americans were denied freedom of movement and assembly. Some were determined to work in family groups to avoid working under the supervision of Whites, but the majority of Blacks had little control over the terms of their labor. In addition, White tyranny ensured that they were denied the rights to vote, bear arms, and hold public office. A system of arbitrary incarceration and convict leasing kept Blacks as captive labor (Cox and Cox 1973), one of the many strategies used by White Southerners to suppress Black progress during this critical period in American history.

YAM JOURNEYS: THE GREAT MIGRATION AND CARIBBEAN IMMIGRATION (1900–1945)

The massive political and economic transformations of the early twentieth century continued to reshape the African diaspora in the United

States and the Caribbean. While plantation economies were declining and European and American imperial interests were being challenged, the industrial economy was reconstituting the Black working classes and middle classes in the United States, Haiti, and Jamaica. Industrial technologies ushered in a revolution in the pace of capitalist mass production and the distribution of consumer goods that propelled the United States into a position of global economic leadership (Zunz 2000). Expanding industries attracted Black Americans and Black immigrants to rapidly growing cities in the North, Upper Midwest, and West. Black migrants and immigrants arrived at the same time as Southern and Eastern Europeans, and these groups came into competition and conflict over access to jobs and housing. Between the Black and Asian diasporas, in contrast, there was more blending. In the nineteenth century, early Chinese immigrants in New York lived side by side with Blacks before the rise of Chinatown (Tchen 2001). Bengali immigrants settled in Harlem in the early twentieth century and formed alliances with their Black neighbors (Bald 2013). Black Southerners and Caribbean immigrants became an even more important source of labor when the demand for workers soared during World War I and the supply of European immigrants was curtailed, first by war and then by restrictive immigration policies in the 1920s. In New York, Black southern migrants and Caribbean immigrants encountered one another in greater numbers than ever before. Together, they created the uniquely dynamic Black diasporic culture of early twentieth-century Harlem (Kasinitz 1992; Watkins-Owens 1996).

In *The Warmth of Other Suns* (2011), Isabel Wilkerson calls the Great Migration "an unrecognized immigration within the country" (542). The family migration histories of US–born respondents show that they participated in both the first phase (1910s–1945) and the second phase (1945–1970) of the Great Migration. At its core, this "movement with their feet" was a deeply political process. Black migrants fled the racial oppression that dominated their daily lives in the rural and urban South. Internal colonial practices of White tyranny took the form not only of Jim Crow segregation, disfranchisement, exclusion from employment, and barriers to property ownership but also of beatings, lynching, rape, incarceration, and convict leasing. Whites violently repressed any sign of Black mobility

Figure 1. Men, women, and families waiting for the train giong up north at the Union Railroad Depot in Jacksonville, Florida, in 1921. Many could not afford the price of a train ticket for all their family members, so pioneers traveled alone and sent their wages or train tickets back to their family members so they could join them.
Source: State Archives of Florida. http://www.inmotionaame .org/gallery/detail.cfm?migration=8&topic=99&id=465409&page =4&type=image.

and resistance. Millions of Blacks responded by leaving their homes, if not psychically, at least physically.

During the early twentieth century, Black Southerners got a foothold in northern and western cities and founded an array of cultural, economic, and religious institutions. During the second phase, which was precipitated by wartime employment opportunities, five million Black people—almost twice as many as had left the South during the first phase—made their way to established Black communities in the North and West or created new ones. Their number one destination was New York, followed by Chicago and Detroit. The image of northern cities as a promised land where Black Southerners could find opportunities that did not exist in their native region was a significant draw. Black newspapers that circulated nationally ran job

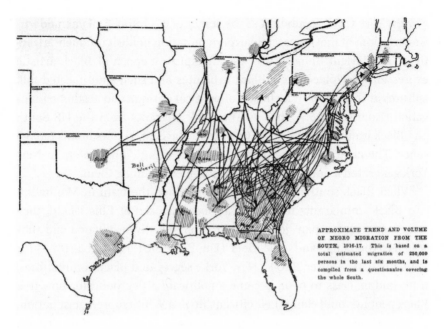

Figure 2. Migration map from W. E. B. Du Bois's report on the Great Migration for *The Crisis*, May 31, 1917. Courtesy of the Schomburg Center for Research in Black Culture, New York Public Library.

advertisements. Employers in need of labor publicized their willingness to hire Black workers and, sometimes, to pay their train fare.

Newspapers like the *Chicago Defender* and personal letters written by loved ones portrayed sites outside the South as cosmopolitan, liberating places where Black Americans could escape the economic and cultural limits of racism and poverty (Watkins-Owens 1996). In a 1917 issue of *The Crisis*, the magazine of the National Association for the Advancement of Colored People (NAACP), W. E. B. Du Bois analyzed the push and pull factors that animated the Great Migration: Black people's rejection of the White mob violence and determination to escape the chronic and economic problems in the South, coupled with the prospects of better-paid employment and greater safety in the North and West. In particular, parents sought to protect their daughters from the rampant sexual exploitation of Black girls and women by White Southern boys and men and offer them better educational and occupational prospects (Chatelain 2015).

New York City's reputation as the center of cosmopolitanism, modernism, freedom of movement, and experimentation made it uniquely attractive. The Harlem Renaissance was an explosive epoch of Black artistic expression that placed new Black urbanites and their multifaceted folk cultures at the center of its fusion of political critique and aesthetic innovation (Adams 2005, Ogbar 2010). Black migrants from the US South and Black immigrants from the Caribbean played vital roles in this renaissance. The creative energy sparked by these groups' encounters in New York generated a new wave of social movements among them.

When Black southern migrants disembarked the train in Manhattan and Black immigrants from the Caribbean docked at Ellis Island, they were met with rampant job discrimination, racially segregated and substandard housing, and race riots (Du Bois 1901 Haynes 1913, 1918; Lemann 2011; Trotter, 2004). New York's segregated Black communities, from middle class to poor, became a political battleground for how free Black people would claim their citizenship in a White supremacist nation.

As the tide of Southern migrants grew, the city's established Black elites were ambivalent about the newcomers. Some organized benevolent associations to ease the difficult transition for southerners; others believed that the masses of uneducated Black migrants were culturally and morally inferior and could not readily be uplifted. Regardless of how the city's longtime Black resident felt, however, the southernization of New York's Black population was inevitable and would leave an indelible print on the city's culture and politics. Doctors, students, domestics, and laborers; uncles and aunts; siblings and cousins made bold decisions to leave the places where their families had lived for generations. Few returned, but many of their family and friends soon joined them. Southern migrants first settled in lower and midtown Manhattan in the Tenderloin district, and later were pushed northward by the building of Penn Station and frequent race riots (Wilkerson 2011). By the 1910s, Harlem was the emerging Black cultural capital of the world (Jackson 2001).

The changing demographics of the Black community brought significant shifts in the politics of color, ethnicity, and class. Increased occupational diversity, the newfound wealth generated by a growing industrial economy, and greater access to higher education transformed the pattern of class stratification. The mulatto elite continued to have a strong hold on

Figure 3. Black patients in Ellis Island Library, circa 1920. Soon after arriving at Ellis Island, immigrants underwent mandatory medical evaluations. Those deemed ill were treated onsite for diseases; others were returned to their home countries. Courtesy of the National Archives (90-G-125-48).

middle-class identity and culture, but a growing stream of educated, skilled, and well-paid darker-skinned migrants formed a more varied Black middle class (Frazier 1957).

Equally important, the politics of class and race were also reshaped by the Caribbeanization of Harlem in the early twentieth century. In *Caribbean New York* (1992), Philip Kasinitz demarcates three major periods of West Indian migration: 1900–1930, 1930–1965, and post-1965. Before 1930, unprecedented numbers of immigrants from Jamaica, Barbados, and Panama arrived in New York. Their arrival coincided with a flood of Southern and Eastern European immigrants who were fleeing economic and demographic crises as well as pogroms. Italians, Irish, Jewish, and Polish immigrants encountered anti-immigrant sentiments from native-born residents who regarded them as undesirable foreigners; some were initially referred to with the derogatory n-word by White Anglo-Saxon Protestants (WASPs).

Between 1900 and 1940, forty thousand immigrants from the British West Indies arrived in New York (Watkins-Owens 1996). In sharp contrast to the experiences of most Southern and Eastern Europeans, the entrance of Caribbean immigrants into New York was shaped by profound racism. While Southern and Eastern Europeans were often excluded from WASP organizations, they were still afforded social privileges that were denied to Black migrants and immigrants. Blacks experienced racial exclusion and discrimination in the job and housing markets and were the targets of mob violence from White ethnic New Yorkers. In racial contestations over space, White immigrants and their children pushed Black residents out of lower and midtown Manhattan and outward into Harlem or Brooklyn. In this social environment, newly arrived Black migrants and immigrants relied on social networks to find housing and work. Although Black Harlem was driven by tensions of class and nationality, Caribbean immigrants became an integral part of the political, cultural, and economic life of this Black Mecca.

Global changes in the power of empires shaped the local patterns of class and ethnic stratification in Harlem. Jamaican immigrants were leaving behind an island entrenched in British colonial domination and embroiled in economic turmoil. The deterioration of the sugar plantation economy led to entrenched poverty, inhumane working and living conditions, and stagnant mobility—conditions much like those of Black Americans in the South. Jamaica's emerging banana export industry kept its economy afloat. While cities like Kingston were expanding and the mulatto elite and White colonizers managed to maintain and compound their wealth, large numbers of the rural peasant class and the urban poor lived in squalor. Many Jamaican immigrants arrived in the United States with a formal education. Others had occupational skills that were valuable in their place of origin, but their human capital or skill level did not matter in New York; they were segregated into low-wage work. Some were career migrants, and New York was their second or third settlement site after migrating around the Caribbean. Jamaicans became "ghetto entrepreneurs" or worked as domestics and laborers alongside Black American and Irish women.

W. E. B. Du Bois and Marcus Garvey are towering figures in the Black class struggle, the rise of Pan-African internationalism, and the movements for decolonization and civil rights that reshaped the Black Atlantic's middle class in the early to mid-twentieth century. Harlem became an incubator where their political agendas were debated and disseminated. Both Pan-Africanists with transnational heritages, Du Bois and Garvey engaged in intense debates over strategies for Black liberation and mobility. These conflicts were shaped not simply by differences over strategy, but also by differing relationships to nation and class.

Class inequality between Black, mulatto, and White colonizers in Jamaica influenced the rise of the Pan-African Movement. Marcus Garvey, who founded the influential Universal Negro Improvement Association (UNIA) and the Back to Africa Movement, appealed to the Black peasant class in Jamaica and abroad. His message of 'Black pride,' liberation from White supremacy through Black-led enterprise, and repatriation to Mother Africa through the Black Star steamship line was supported by hundreds of UNIA chapters in places ranging from Central America to Oklahoma (Brown 1979, Field 2018, Buffonge 2001, Zips 1999). The child of parents locked into Jamaica's peasant class, Garvey became a champion of the Black laboring class in Jamaica, the Caribbean, and Latin America.

Garvey's political ascendency occurred as Jamaica's Black class structure was being altered. In the early twentieth century the British expanded colonial schools in Jamaica, giving Black rural and urban youth access to education. This project was designed to cultivate a native class of colonial subjects who would manage governmental and business affairs on the island. The schools instilled the idea that Jamaicans were British subjects and formed the first cohorts of an educated Black middle class. Emerging organizers of the rural and urban working class, such as the light-skinned, British-educated Norman Manley and Alexander Bustamante, operated within the confines of the White colonial apparatus. Garvey, a dark-skinned Black man who embodied the plight of the excluded Black masses, demanded the end of White economic domination over Blacks on the island and internationally. Disenchanted with the colonial incorporation and racial accommodation framework, he criticized the "depth of self-hatred that was manifested as color prejudice in the Jamaican social conglomerate" (Brown 1979, 124). Garvey campaigned throughout the Caribbean, witnessed the economic stagnation of the Black proletariat across locales, and later moved to New York to find a more suitable platform for his campaign for Black economic progress.

Figure 4 and Figure 5. Right: Marcus Garvey, founder of the Universal Negro Improvement Association (UNIA) and Back to Africa Movement. Below: Universal Negro Improvement Association convention parade through Harlem, New York, 1920. Garvey's message resonated with Black southern and Caribbean migrants in New York, and Black women's contributions was central to the movement. Photo Courtesy of Schomburg Center for Research in Black Culture, New York Public Library.

W. E. B. Du Bois was a preeminent scholar and activist for Black freedom. In contrast to Garvey, he was a Massachusetts-born, light-skinned, third-generation Black American of Haitian descent and had an elite education in the United States and Europe. Du Bois recognized that Garvey was a charismatic leader with a Pan-Africanist agenda of racial pride and autonomy that appealed at the grassroots level. Moreover, he was himself a Pan-Africanist, tracing the roots of Black culture in Africa and allying with anticolonial movements on the continent. However, Du Bois regarded Garvey as an opportunist and used *The Crisis* as a platform for criticizing the Back to Africa movement. He believed that Garvey did not have the business experience and organizational skills that his enterprises required, and he contended that his vision of Black entrepreneurship amounted to little more than Booker T. Washington's ideology of self-help.

Garvey had a significantly larger following than Du Bois and the NAACP. The UNIA had a broad-based appeal. The organization had chapters from the Midwest to South America. Garvey's rallies drew thousands of working-class and poor Blacks, including substantial numbers of women. Garvey used his newspaper, *Negro World*, to oppose Du Bois, often in direct response to criticisms Du Bois expressed in *The Crisis*. Seeing his rival in terms of the tensions between Jamaica's Black and Brown classes, Garvey contended that Du Bois wanted to establish a mulatto aristocracy, was an intellectual elitist, and was out of touch with the soul and struggles of the Black working class.

Neither leader was as elitist or directionless as his opponent charged, but the two men came to represent the status, nationality, and gendered tensions among Black New Yorkers as well as their alternative visions of political liberation.[5] Du Bois and Garvey epitomize the racial, class, and color problems faced by the Black Atlantic only a couple of generations removed from slavery. It mattered that these debates on Pan-Africanism happened on the stages of Harlem streets, making New York a central site for continued transnational Black political dialogue and class struggles (Rogers 1955; Rudwick 1959).

Jamaican immigrants who arrived in New York when the UNIA was flourishing were involved in all sectors of the Black economy and cultural institutions. According to Irma Watkins-Owens (1996, 3), "A small but visible educated elite—a Caribbean 'Talented Tenth'—were among the immigrants. Other middle-class immigrants possessed a sound grammar school education and often a skilled trade. Thirty-one percent reported occupations in industry and 10 percent in commerce. About 40 percent of those arriving reported occupations as laborers and servants."They worked as business owners and domestics and served as church leaders and political activists. Unaccustomed to the stark color line that permeated everything from their place of residence to their relations with employers, many joined movements for Black liberation. After initially expressing their ethnic distinctiveness, Jamaicans eventually became absorbed into the Black community of Harlem and then moved out to different areas of New York City, its suburbs and beyond (Bald 2013, Haynes 2008).

Jamaican and Haitian immigrants who arrived in New York during the early twentieth century came from societies with different legacies of racial slavery and class formations. Britain maintained its colonial control over Jamaica, while the United States focused its imperial interests in the Caribbean on Haiti (as well as on Puerto Rico and Cuba). These distinct experiences with empires led to the islands' divergent relationships with the United States, differing migration pathways, and varying contexts of their reception on arrival. For half a century after enslaved and free Africans declared Haiti independent of French colonialism and immediately emancipated all its citizens, the United States refused to recognize the autonomy and sovereignty of the Black republic: "Haiti was not immediately recognized nor was she welcomed into the family of nations" (Wesley 1917, 370). The United States was the last global power to recognize Haiti, formally doing so only in 1862. Throughout the nineteenth century, the United States made repeated attempts to undermine the country's economy and limit its participation in international trade, while also refusing to engage its political leaders on a basis of equality (Dupuy 2004).

American efforts to dominate the global economy by seizing the colonies of European empires led to chaotic internal battles within island nations, inflamed anticolonial revolts, and furthered US military control in the Caribbean. The United States cemented its power over the Caribbean and Latin America through the Spanish-American War (1896–

1900), taking possession of Spain's colonies in the Caribbean and the Pacific, asserting its sovereignty over Puerto Rico, and occupying Cuba (Vargas 2000). The American attempts to establish an empire that would usurp those of Spain and France paralleled the nation's initial interests in capital accumulation through the seizure of land and resources from Indigenous peoples during the settler colonial period and the exploitation of Black and Asian labor in the South and West.

The US occupation of Haiti from 1915 to 1934 undermined foreign competitors from the island's economy and established American control of its politics. The multiple changes in political leadership and financial indebtedness as a result of the intervention were used to legitimize the United States' domination of Haiti's markets and governmental affairs. The "Haitian problem" was managed by the imposition of policies ostensibly aimed at stabilizing its government and economy and building an American-style middle class (Trouillot 1990). In reality, this set of practices only served the United States' interests in extending its domination over the region. Black Americans deeply disapproved of the US invasion of Haiti, which they viewed as the center of the Pan-African struggle for human rights and Black dignity. Du Bois argued that the invasion of Haiti had done little to bring democracy to the country or to alleviate poverty. Instead, he contended, the "United States was at war with Haiti" (Coupeau 2008, 72).

The US invasion introduced an educational system that shifted the class and occupational structure of the Haitian populace. Until then, despite the nominal existence of a national public educational system, those who could afford to pay tuition sent their children to private or Catholic schools. After the US authorities created vocational and agricultural schools, agronomy and medicine became leading occupational aspirations for young Haitian men in rural and urban areas. Women were largely relegated to domestic service work or agricultural labor which undermined their prospects for economic mobility. Moreover, following the British model of using the educational system to create colonial subjects in Jamaica, education was designed to create a local elite that would work as public servants in the US-controlled economy. Simultaneously, the United States undermined political stability by continuously backing mulatto political leadership at the expense of Black political participation.

While these schools did expand the Black middle class in Haiti, they also helped to create an educated class of Blacks who would eventually challenge White American economic intervention and mulatto hegemony on the island (Brutus 1948, Cook 1948).

The twentieth century marked new forms of Black resistance to global White oppression, which was often articulated by radical members of the diasporic Black middle class. The rise and expansion of Jim Crow and the US invasion and occupation of countries inhabited by the "darker races" took place simultaneously on the local and international stage. Harlem's New Negro Movement of the 1920s challenged the cultural and philosophical landscape of the Black community. Demands for Black political progress were echoed in the Black Atlantic, and culture, literature, music, and dance that featured the African heritage of Black people took center stage as political resistance projects. Groundbreaking artists such as Langston Hughes, Zora Neale Hurston, Alain Locke, and Claude McKay used literature to forge new forms of Black cultural life. Many Harlem Renaissance writers adopted Black diasporic subjectivities, bringing together the Black American and Caribbean experiences through imagined and lived migrations to demonstrate the interconnectivity between Black struggle in the United States and abroad. Zora Neale Hurston's *Tell My Horse* (1990) and Claude McKay's *Home to Harlem* (1928) are emblematic of the transnational Black literary approach that evoked ties between Black America, Haiti, and Jamaica.

While Jamaicans were bringing the Caribbean to New York through the 1940s, Haitians were Haitianizing the Dominican Republic and Cuba, and then New York. During the first half of the twentieth century, over two hundred thousand Haitian immigrants traveled to Cuba and the Dominican Republic to work in the sugar industry. These migrations were the result of the destabilization of agricultural industries by the US occupation and the denial of educational opportunities to the children of Black peasants, as well as the demand for labor on Cuban plantations. The Cubans subjected the migrants to anti-Black xenophobia and projected stigmas that Haitians carried contagious diseases. They criminalized the practice of vodou, an African form of spiritual worship and healing that was mixed with Catholic beliefs and practices. Anti-Haitian sentiment in Cuba was a product of the colonial tradition of degrading African people and their faith traditions, which were deemed inferior to Spanish culture and Christianity. Cuba's heritage of colonial Christianity meant that Haitian migrants encountered Spanish imperial agendas during their journeys. But many made intra-Caribbean migration to the Dominican Republic and Cuba a strategy to recoup economic losses suffered at home. It also helped Haitians to forge hybrid, modern identities as migrants who worked seasonally in Cuba and returned to Haiti with savings to invest in entrepreneurial pursuits or to purchase land. Others returned home impoverished, and many remained in Cuba (Coupeau 2008).

In Haitian cities, as in the cosmopolitan Black political and cultural epicenter of Harlem, Black society was experiencing its own renaissance. Through the organization of the country's educated elite, artists and the intelligentsia forged new agendas to counter racial and colonial projects of the United States and European powers in the 1920s and 1930s. In the aftermath of the US occupation, the radical Black political movement known as *noirisme* reshaped the country's political ideology. Articulated by the educated class on the island, noirisme called for the total control of the Haitian nation-state by Black people. The movement sought to overturn White and mulatto domination of the country's political economy and called for centering the African heritage of the nation. Africa was central to the image of the island nation in the eyes of *noiristes*, and, like the New Negro Movement and Pan Africanism, they sought to remake Black citizens and challenge their unequal relationships to the American and European empires.

From the end of World War I through the aftermath of World War II, large-scale opposition to European imperialism and internal colonialism spread throughout Haiti. The Black middle class, led by popular novelists, writers, and intellectuals, advocated recognition of vodou, not Christianity, as the religion of the people and demanded that Haitian Kreyol, rather than French, become the country's official language. They partnered this racial ideology with the mounting cry for economic equality through adapting Marxist ideology as a remedy for their colonial situation. Like the labor movements led by Garvey, Bustamante, and Manley in Jamaica, Haitian intelligentsia was at the forefront of this movement. They were a part of a global shift occurring in the Caribbean, Africa, and the United States that mobilized laborers against the economic, cultural, and political domination of elites within their countries and in Europe. Black people sought economic liberation, but the racial capitalism of the West promised to keep them oppressed. Much of this culminated in a Pan-African movement toward socialism and increased political ties between the Black Atlantic and the Soviet Union in the early to mid-twentieth century (on Black Bolsheviks, see Putnam 2013).

The cultural importance and political centrality of Blackness in the African Atlantic made the New Negro, noirisme, and Négritude movements distinct but parallel political visions with the same goal: Black liberation. Négritude was the brainchild of a growing number of Black students in French universities in the 1930s. Led by Martiniquan and Senegalese intellectuals including Aimé Césaire, Léon-Gontran Damas, Léopold Sédar Senghor, and Cheikh Anta Diop, Black youth sought to break down nationalistic boundaries and build a common racial consciousness vis-à-vis French colonialism. They challenged French imperialism through the empowerment of Black internationalism. Négritude transformed global Black identity in France, the French Caribbean, and French Africa. Like the New Negro movement, revolutions in Black arts and culture helped to generate bold political statements asserting Black humanity and power. Together with the increasing domestic and international migrations around the Black Atlantic and the calls of Marcus Garvey for "Africa for Africans," these movements advocated the total transformation of global racial power relations. They were crafted by transnational Black allegiances forged and solidified by radical post-emancipation Black migrations across the Atlantic (Rabaka, 2015).

In the United States, by contrast, the end of World War I and the restriction on international immigration slowed the entrance of Blacks from the Caribbean. Jamaicans set their sights on prospects in Britain. After World War II, Britain sought the labor of Jamaicans, Trinidadians, and Barbadians to aid in rebuilding its war-torn infrastructure. Many Jamaicans, including well-educated teachers and civil servants, were promised British nationality through the Immigration Act of 1948 and traveled across the Atlantic on board the *Empire Windrush*. These pioneers became known as the "Windrush Generation." Despite their contributions to the rebuilding of England, they have been treated as outsiders-within in British society. Recently, after seven decades of regarding themselves as British, those who had arrived in Britain and obtained residency permits but had not been formally naturalized were threatened with deportation by the British government.

LIFE AT THE BREAK: GLOBAL POLITICAL RUPTURES, BLACK MIGRATIONS AND THE *CLASS MOYENNE* (1945–1970)

The end of World War II marked the beginning of a new era for the Black Atlantic. White societies that had exploited Black labor were recovering from the financial and moral devastation of the war. The Holocaust prompted those whose empires were built on White supremacy and scientific racism to reflect on their own society's racist foundational values. In the United States, Black veterans demanded equal access to the promises of citizenship after having fought against facism abroad. Black parents demanded the end of laws and practices that relegated their children to segregated schools that were inherently unequal. Black communities called for an end to White racist terror in the form of lynching, violent attacks on Black communities, and intimidation at the polls. In the Caribbean, the Black masses demanded their liberation from European empires and an end to their exploitation on White- and foreign-owned plantations. Egypt, Ghana, Kenya, and India were at the forefront of this anticolonial chorus. By the turn of the twenty-first century, mass migrations from both the US and Global South, widespread boycotts, protests, and political pressure from below forced empires to relinquish their formal authority over colonies and forced White Americans to strike down the racial barriers to education, housing, work, and migration that subordinated the colonized groups within the nation. The Break era ushered in a new *noir* middle class that was multiethnic, multiregional and increasingly suburban. The contemporary Black middle class are children of the yam whose ancestors had been enslaved, freedmen, and second-class citizens. They're now middle-class suburbanites, living their ancestors wildest dreams. However, does this socioeconomic stratification among people of African descent represent progress? What a conundrum!

The post-Break Black middle class in the United States emerged from two important transformations: first, the mass migration of Black people from the southern states, and secondly, the end of colonialism in the

Caribbean and the achievements of the civil rights movement in the 1960s. During the early 1940s, the wartime labor shortage created a demand for workers in factories, railroad companies, foundries, and automobile plants, opening opportunities for Black migrants from the American South in New York. However, access to employment was coupled with racial and gendered segregation and wage inequality. The repressive conditions in northern cities were challenged by community organizations led by the Black bourgeoisie and the working class. Entrenched racial segregation, racially exclusionary trade unions, substandard housing conditions, and voter suppression led to organized local and national urban Black political movements. These organizations were the seeds that grew into the mid-twentieth century civil rights movement.

The Black middle classes in the United States, Haiti, and Jamaica were at the forefront of Black liberation struggles during the postwar period. In Haiti, the political leadership of a rising Black middle class inspired by noirisme eventually led to the end of US occupation. Yet this pro-Black ideology was adopted as the political platform of the repressive Duvalier dictatorship (1957–1986), which led to the mass migration of middle-class and poor Haitians to the United States. In Jamaica, the large-scale decolonization movement of the peasant and middle class led to independence in 1962. The rise of Rastafarianism and Black Power in Jamaica was the legacy of Marcus Garvey. Each of these movements in the Caribbean was occurring at the same time that marches, boycotts, and uprisings organized by Black churches, student groups, political leaders, and community organizations were sweeping across the United States. These civil rights demonstrations and their violent repression by White authorities exposed the racism that belied the United States' democratic ideals of freedom and democracy. Acting on a global stage, Black Americans showed that they would no longer tolerate Whites' imposition of second-class citizenship upon them. By the mid-twentieth century, these radical Black movements among the poor, working class, and middle class had mobilized Black and mixed-race people to reshape global systems of White imperial domination around the globe. Through the cracks of a shaken racist apparatus, the families in this book emerged: a generation of trans-geographical Black middle-class people and their children who negotiate Pan-Africanism, class, and nationality through their encounters with one another.

During the 1940s and the postwar period, Black New Yorkers made important progress in finding employment in the manufacturing and retail sectors. The limited supply of labor in wartime and collective racial protest meant that Blacks gained access to decent jobs. Black migrants encountered new spaces, technologies, and race relations, which required them to reconcile or negotiate the identities and cultural repertoires of their southern origins and the emerging cultures of New York. The migrants in the second phase of the Great Migration were more educated than migrants in the first phase. Upon arrival in New York, however, few were able to translate their education into well-paid, dignified jobs.

Southern migrants encountered a range of status groups among Black New Yorkers. The preexisting and deeply rooted class of light-skinned Blacks of bourgeois families in parts of Harlem and Brooklyn was at the top of the Black stratification structure. Some were porters, domestic workers, or caterers. Others were business owners, doctors, and lawyers who built their own insular societies to display and reproduce their class status (Graham 2000). Yet the pervasive perception that southern schools were inferior created a clear boundary between New York's small Black elite and these newcomers, blocking the upward mobility of many migrants who were educated in segregated southern high schools and historically Black colleges and universities. Many found themselves working in factories or as domestics for White families in the city and suburbs (Wiese 2005). From the 1950s on, the departure of the manufacturing industry and the rise of the service and information economy undercut blue-collar occupations. The bifurcation of the class system in the 1970s meant that Black New Yorkers either became affluent or were stuck in low-wage work. A working class emerged in the service sector, while the middle class was found in the expanding public, health care, education, and self-employment sectors.

CARIBBEAN EXODUS: DECOLONIZATION AND DICTATORSHIP

As migration from the US South tapered off in the 1970s, a new wave of Black folks came to New York from the Global South. Instead of speaking with a southern accent, they had patois, British, French, or Spanish accents. This unprecedented influx of immigrants from the Caribbean was triggered by the combination of anticolonial movements and the passage of the 1965 Hart Cellar Act, which broadened country-specific quotas, encouraged the immigration of skilled labor, and promoted family reunification. Haitians and Jamaicans constitute the largest Black immigrant groups who came to New York City during this period. They met a burgeoning Puerto Rican migrant population upon arrival. The Jones Act of 1917 extended US citizenship to Puerto Ricans, and mass migrations ushered in large numbers of Afro–Puerto Ricans to New York in the 1950s–1960s. Each diaspora left behind a collection of political, economic, and environmental problems. They wanted to find steady work, join family members, have a political say, send their children to good schools, and remit money to family. Some immigrants believed they needed US citizenship to achieve these goals, while others opted for other incorporation strategies (Rogers 2006).

Large-scale political shifts in the British Caribbean and Haiti created the impetus for this Caribbean exodus. The increase in working-class uprisings, solidification of global Black consciousness, and the calls for decolonization in the United States, Caribbean, and Africa were challenging centuries of Western domination. After a forty-year lull in mass immigration to the United States, the blocked borders of the United Kingdom, the loosening of US immigration restrictions, and the decolonization of the British Caribbean created the conditions that encouraged mass migration from Jamaica.

Haitians, too, were allotted a larger number of immigrant visas. But Haiti was unique among Caribbean nations. Although the free Black republic had been independent for 150 years, Haiti had been subjected to continuing foreign political and economic intervention. From 1957 on, however, Haitians were also battling the Duvalier regime, which initially enjoyed the support of the Black lower classes but soon became a repressive dictatorship. In addition, Haiti struggled to establish and defend its sovereignty from United States military intervention and imperial economic exploitation, as well as from European powers' damaging trade policies. In the 1970s and 1980s, underdevelopment, chronic unemployment, and deepening poverty coupled with violent political repression created a new generation of migrants from Haiti. Between 1961 and 1992, 248,000 Haitians entered the United States (Zephir 2001). Between 1964 and 1980, over three quarters of a million (781,213) immigrants arrived from the West Indies and Haiti and entered the United States (Kasinitz 1992). By 1975, migration from the Caribbean had exceeded that of the previous seventy years. Roughly half of these migrants settled in New York City.

The class composition of these migrant families is central to understanding their journeys to New York and its suburbs. The first wave of Jamaican immigrants to the United States after 1965 came from the educated and professional Black and brown middle class (Vickerman 1999). The brain drain of Jamaica's professionals was prompted by their targeted recruitment by agencies in New York, as well as the instability of the postcolonial economy. The early twentieth-century working-class movements forged by Marcus Garvey had morphed into 1970s Black power movements that mandated the meaningful inclusion of Black people in political and economic affairs. Although Jamaica became a sovereign nation in 1962, it remained part of the British Commonwealth. Its major political parties (the People's National Party and the Jamaican Labour Party) were engaged in cyclical conflicts over power and position. Election campaigns were fraught with violence, which party leaders used to suppress opposition (Thomas 2004). Constrained class mobility, political uncertainty, and urban violence encouraged an increasingly heterogeneous assortment of urban and rural poor and working-class people to pursue emigration to the United States (Brown-Glaude 2011). Many worked as teachers and nurses after arrival, often employed in under-resourced schools and hospitals in New York. Others held jobs in retail, clerical, or personal service occupations (Kasinitz and Vickerman 2001, Vickerman 1999).

Today's Jamaican middle class has been shaped by the politics of status and color on the island. Although the class composition of the Jamaican diaspora in New York became more heterogeneous in the 1980s and 1990s, it continues to have high numbers of educated and skilled immigrants, many of whom either bring with them divisive politics of race, color, and class from the island nation or work to challenge it. The status markers spawned by slavery and colonialism continue to define relations within and outside the community. One Jamaican respondent in Cascades, Betty, age fifty-two and a teacher, displayed portraits of her Scottish ancestors on her living room wall, insisted that she was not "Black," and was disturbed by the rigid racial classification system in the United States, which lumped her into the same group as everyone else. Her husband, Donald, was fair skinned, and she boasted about her daughters having "long hair down to their back." Like many other Jamaicans who came from the Brown middle class or married into it, she emphasized their allegiance to the British government, argued that they spoke the Queen's English, and exuded identities that distinguished them as superior to Americans in general and Black Americans in particular. Another respondent exclaimed, "Everyone thinks 'cause I'm Jamaican, I smoke weed or am a criminal." Others from urban working-class origins expressed disdain toward the British government, deplored neocolonialism, and promoted Black political consciousness. In subsequent chapters, we will explore these complex racial identity negotiations in greater detail.

Early cohorts of Haitian immigrants came from the country's French-speaking, light-skinned, upper class and were encouraged to escape the rampant human rights violations orchestrated by Francois Duvalier. President John F. Kennedy granted many elite Haitians refugee status before 1965. Duvalier's militiamen, the Tonton Macoute, gripped the country politically and repressed opposition through intimidation, violence, and murder. They rose to power with a noiriste agenda, a Black radical political platform that was a response to the mulatto aristocracy that had been in direct competition with Black political leadership since the Haitian Revolution. As a result, affluent Haitians were entering the United States under markedly different circumstances than Jamaicans did when immigration quotas expanded. They were followed by the Black middle class in the late 1960s, and the proletariat class thereafter, many beginning their lives as immigrants in Brooklyn, New York.

The Black middle class in diasporic suburbs are the children of the yam. Like the African yam which was brought to the Americas on slave ships, the Black middle class in New York's suburbs are the agents and products of multiple forced, prompted, and voluntary migrations. The migration narratives of Black Americans, Haitians, and Jamaicans illustrate that they and their families have circulated throughout the Atlantic for generations. In this chapter, I've outlined the histories of these migrations and their relationship to racial and class formations in the US South and Global South. My Black American respondents were Great Migrants or their children who had traveled to New York from the South. The Haitians and Jamaicans I interviewed were mostly first generation immigrants who had flown into Kennedy airport. A few had both Black American and Caribbean ancestry or were the children of Caribbean immigrants who settled in the US South before migrating to New York.

First forcibly taken from Africa to North America, and then making bold decisions to leave societies that constrained them by enslavement, racial caste, labor exploitation, colonial rule, imperial domination, and violent dictatorship, my respondents and their ancestors were active participants in epic local and global transformations. The movements for decolonization and civil rights that propelled their migrations were the culmination of four centuries of Black resistance to racist political economies that persisted in various forms until that global order of White supremacy was ruptured in the mid-twentieth century. Amid the global transformation in power relations between White Europeans and Americans and peoples of African descent and the rise of the Black middle class, migrants have brought the political and cultural legacies of stratification by race and color with them from the South, Haiti, and Jamaica like the foods and medicines that they packed in their luggage for the journey. The next chapter explores the legacy of racial segregation on Long Island that the post-Break Black middle-class newcomers inherited when they moved to the suburbs. Long Island's long history of Black settlement and the clash of state sanctioned racial segregation, White tyranny, and Black agency led to the creation of their contemporary diasporic spaces in Queens and Nassau counties.

3 Blood Pudding

FORBIDDEN NEIGHBORS ON JIM CROW LONG ISLAND

African communities in the Diaspora are living, breathing,
dynamic entities, made such by the very environment in
which they are forced to exist and by their very struggle to
survive. Because of their unique characteristics—skin color,
history and others—the establishment of a Black community anywhere in the world outside of Africa has usually
been a gigantic task and a constant signal to Whites to
oppose its formation.

Ronald W. Walters (1997)

Blood pudding is considered a delicacy in European and African diasporic
gastronmies. Pig blood is the main ingredient, and the dish is less a pudding and more a sausage. Blood pudding was brought to the Americas by
British colonizers and prepared by enslaved African cooks, who added to
it their own herbs and spices. From Bahia, Brazil, to Jamestown, Virginia,
its rich flavors make it popular, but its blood content leaves many suspicious of its spiritual and culinary character. In Jamaica, it's known as
black pudding. In Mexico, it's called *morcilla*. In Guadeloupe, you'll find
it on menus as *boudin noir*. In Trinidad, blood pudding is popular with
hops bread and is served up as a Christmas delicacy.

During one holiday season likely catered with blood pudding and sorrel
drink and animated by Christmas songs and church services, the joyful celebrations came to a devastating end for an immigrant family in Queens. On
New Years Eve in 1974, Ormistan and Glenda Spencer were awoken in the
middle of the night by a loud noise. A firebomb had been thrown through

Figure 6. Glenda and Ormistan Spencer (front, center) in prayer with their congregation in Queens after the bombing of their home by white supremacists. Image courtesy of Bill Moyers, "Rosedale: The Way It Is" and WNET, New York Public Media.

the front window into their living room. The perpetrators were a group of White men from their Queens neighborhood. A written message accompanying the weapon read, "Viva Boston, KKK." The neighborhood terrorists were celebrating the violent refusal of White parents to accept the busing of Black students to schools in South Boston, the latest anti-integration protest in two decades of widespread White resistance to mandated school desegregation since the US Supreme Court case *Brown v. Board of Education* (1954). In addition, the Fair Housing Act of 1968 made the discriminatory practices that Whites historically used to create lily-White neighborhoods illegal. The Spencers had purchased their seven-room, Tudor-style home in Queens just as White rage began to mount against these policy shifts across segregated cities and inner-ring suburbs. Before the Spencer family moved in, their house had been set ablaze. The Spencers' sole transgression was that they wanted a place to call home in a postwar residential area where first- and second-generation Italian, German, Polish, Jewish and Irish immigrants had taken up residence.

In a scene from "Rosedale: The Way It Is," Bill Moyers's public television exposé of racist violence in Queens, a soul-shocked Glenda Spencer sat in her living room next to her husband and stated in a soft voice with a distinct Trinidadian accent: "The only reason this is happening is because we are Black. So, whether this is Rosedale or the neighboring communities, this can happen anywhere. This isn't happening because they are like, "hey, this is cause of your ideas." No! This is happening because we are Black. And what are we going to do about it? What are we as a people going to do about our Blackness? Hide it? Become invisible? We can't do that."

In a subsequent scene, a group of working-class White ethnic men discussed their views: "We are going to keep this neighborhood. We are going to keep Rosedale predominately White, the way it is, and we are not going to let a bad element in. This is our right, too. You know, they talk about rights for minorities. Where the hell are the rights for Whites? That's what we are all about, equal rights for Whites."

From the perspective of these self-appointed neighborhood gatekeepers, they had the right to dictate the racial composition of their neighborhood. White ethnic neighborhoods on the city's margins were also expressing the same anti-Black sentiments in the 1970s. In *Canarsie* (1985), Jonathan Rieder uncovers how the Canarsie, Brooklyn community responded to school desegregation. Italian and Jewish residents of this mixed-income suburb in the city rejected and terrorized low-income and working-class Black Americans as they moved into the neighborhood. White ethnics were internally conflicted about the impact of liberalism in the post–civil rights moment. They resented being mandated to integrate their neighborhoods and schools by Manhattan's White political and educated class, whom they referred to as "limousine liberals."[1] Both 1970s Canarsie and Rosedale demonstrate the repertoires of anti-Black racism that are fundamental to Southern and Eastern European racial identity formation (Treitler, 2013). Their attainment of Whiteness hinged upon their ability to reside in all-White spaces where "no Blacks were allowed." As the Spencer family moved into their new home, they were confronting the long history of Black spatial exclusion in New York that preceded them. They, along with Black Americans and other immigrants from the Caribbean, were the *forbidden neighbors* (Wiese, 2005) of postwar suburban New York.

The Spencers encountered the culture of White residential segregation, which used intimidation, violence, and legal tactics, to exclude Black families from what they regarded as "their" neighborhoods. The White ethnic working-class residents accused the Spencers of being blockbusters, recruits of real estate agents intended to create racial panic among White residents and encourage them to sell their homes for less than they were worth. Outside the Spencers' home, their White neighbors held frequent protests, chanting "Equal Rights for Whites" and "Spencers (n-word), Go to Hell." They organized a group called Restore Our Alienated Rights (ROAR) to ensure that Whites who were leaving the neighborhood sold their homes only to White buyers. Local newspapers reported that these suburbs were rapidly changing from White ethnic working class to Black working and middle class. Whites' response to desegregation was contested, as some supported their new Black neighbors' right to housing while many others sought to exclude them.

The Spencer family's story uncovers the silenced history of the Jim Crow North (Glenn 2011, Hunter and Robinson 2018). Institutionalized racial segregation was not confined to the South but was widespread across Northern cities and suburbs. White supremacy has been at the core of New York's housing and education structures and Black diasporic suburbs emerge from this racist legacy. In the postwar suburbs of Queens and Long Island, which housed upwardly mobile European immigrants and their descendants and ushered them into the privileges of Whiteness, Black newcomers encountered resistance, avoidance, and violence, including cross burnings and fire bombings during the Break (1945–1970) and post-Break period (1970–present) in global White supremacy. In New York, Black families targeted by White suburban violence came from across the diaspora. The Spencers were one of many Black families who moved to Queens and Long Island from Harlem, the South Bronx, and the US South and Global South in the 1970s. These Trinidadian immigrants had migrated to New York after living briefly in England. Tony was a photoengraver in Manhattan. He and Glenda sought to enjoy the promises of the American Dream and the civil rights movement: access homeownership to their own home, open space, good schools for their two sons, and privacy. Instead, they were met with acts of terror, an American nightmare.

Black families who encountered the racial trauma of desegregation found healing in Black spaces of worship and kinship. A scene in "The Way It Is" shows the Spencer family seeking refuge in their Black church in Flushing, Queens. Reverend Timothy Mitchell of the Ebenezer Baptist Church prayed over the Spencers in Sunday service: "Right now, Lamb of God, we ask that you would bless this family. Somehow be a hedge all around them. We are not praying a new prayer. Black folk have been praying for four hundred years to the God of their salvation. In our troubles, we cry out—there must be a God somewhere." In Queens and Long Island suburbs across the nation, Black families were challenging a new form of White supremacy. As explicit racial exclusions had transformed into a hegemony hidden in the cloak of racial progress in the 1970s, the desegregation crisis was the newest site where White racism reared its ugly head. New York, like the US South, had a centuries-long history of racial slavery, Black codes, Jim Crow, and civil rights struggle. Therefore, the assurance of divine protection for Black families in a metropolitan area historically entrenched in White supremacy seemed far away.

Various Black institutions in Manhattan and Queens rushed to support the Spencer family, a collective response that resembled patterns of community organizing in the civil rights struggle. For example, the Broadway cast of Lorraine Hansberry's *A Raisin in the Sun* dedicated the proceeds from their show to help the Spencers pay for the damages to their home. Robert B. Nemiroff, husband of the late Black liberation activist, playwright, and writer, Lorraine Hansberry, orchestrated the fundraiser. Nemiroff recalled that during Hansberry's childhood, her family, who moved into Washington Park, Chicago, was terrorized by White neighbors, culminating in the 1940 U.S. Supreme Court decision *Hansberry v Lee*, an experience which shaped Hansberry's artistic and activist imagination.[2]

As the Spencers' story demonstrates, New York's suburbs have complex and dynamic histories of racial segregation and White anti-integrationist action that influence the neighborhoods that Black middle-class migrants and immigrants enter. In this chapter, we explore the history of Black life in New York's hinterlands-turned-suburbs. We examine the ingredients and preparation involved in the making of the multiethnic Black middle class in Queens and Long Island spaces that have historically excluded them. Like the imaginings of blood pudding, the Spencers were misunderstood, maligned, and rejected by White residents. New York is widely regarded as a diverse and welcoming city to newcomers. However, when its silenced history of Jim Crow is uncovered, we are reminded of the strategies that Italian mothers, Polish fathers, and Irish grandparents used in an effort to prevent Blacks from the US and Global South from settling among them. The sense of distaste and rejection elicited by the iron-rich blood pudding is reminiscent of Whites' reaction to the prospect of Black neighbors. Whites have ostracized their Black blood cousins by excluding them spatially in the post-Emancipation era. While they have constructed Black people as subhuman, heathens, and impure, they have exploited, sexualized, abused, and surveilled them from the colonial period to our current colorblind era. In this chapter I take a long view of the beginnings of these racial realities in New York. The pages that follow explore the Black presence on Long Island, which began with racial slavery; the formation of a rural servant class; and the local, national, and international events that propelled Black New Yorkers from the city into the suburbs. We discuss how larger numbers of Black New Yorkers came to reside in Queens and Nassau County, Long Island during the civil rights struggle, and the racial legacies of structural racism and resistance that my interviewees inherited.

As the diasporic Black middle class set up new lives in suburbia, the histories of these places inevitably affect how they interact with their neighbors, community institutions, and trans-geographical networks. From the colonial era through the civil rights movement, Long Island has been a central site of Black community development amid racial capitalism and self determination in the face of repeated attempts to relegate them to second-class citizenship. This chapter recounts the origins of community life of the Black diasporic groups on Long Island over four periods: colonialism, racial slavery, and unequal labor, 1600s–1865; Black American and Caribbean migration and the expansion of Greater New York, 1866–1945; the postwar rise of White suburbia, 1946–1954; and Long Island as a battleground of civil rights struggle and Black middle-class suburbanization, 1955–1970s. This historical view of Queens and Long Island demonstrates that middle-class Black Americans, Haitians, and Jamaicans negotiate of New York's racialized housing market as well as legacies of Black place making and agency that shape their identities and practices in everyday life.

The narratives of Black diasporas on Long Island have largely been written out of suburban history. This omission is particularly odd because Long Island's rural hinterlands have been shaped by Black peoples from across the diaspora since colonization and racial slavery. Long Island is a large, geographically distinct landmass that is now organized into four counties: Brooklyn, Queens, Nassau, and Suffolk. Before the late 1800s, Queens and Nassau counties were considered part of New York City's hinterland. The annexation of Queens County into New York City solidified its incorporation, while Nassau became an iconic suburban county. In the imaginations of most New Yorkers, Queens and Long Island were a collection of rural towns ripe for suburban development. Although Queens is a borough of New York City, eastern sections of Queens are considered suburbs within the city limits.

THE COLONIAL HISTORY OF ENSLAVED AND FREE BLACK COMMUNITIES ON LONG ISLAND, 1600S–1865

The formation of Black diasporic communities on Long Island began with colonization and racial slavery in the 1600s. The Dutch purchased the island of Manhattan in 1626; decades later, they violently seized Long Island from the Canarsee, Meroke, Patechoag, Montauk, and Manhasset peoples. During two centuries of European settler colonialism, Long Island was one of the many centers of the genocide of Indigenous peoples and the transatlantic slave trade. When Dutch settler colonizers in the Hudson Valley were unable to enslave the Native population to work the land and build infrastructure, they turned to West Africa as a source for exploitable labor. Long Island's ports became a central nexus for the distribution of enslaved Africans across the Americas. They were used for agricultural labor in the colony as well as traded for the products of slave labor on southern plantations. Although slavery is portrayed as a Southern institution, urban and rural slavery was integral to the economy of New York. Racial slavery permeated every aspect of life, defining how land, chattel property, labor, and freedom were defined, manipulated, and contested. The exploitative nexus of capital, race, and labor that was formed in the colonial era shaped the long history of Black diasporas on Long Island.

Slavery in New York was imposed by the Dutch West India Company in 1626, the same year that they founded New Amsterdam on Manhattan. Paul d'Angola, Simon Congo, Anthony Portugese, and John Fancisco were

Figure 7. Map of New York City metropolitan area (1842). Courtesy of Queens Public Library Archives.

among eleven enslaved men who were transported there like cargo. The Dutch enslaved Africans and sold them in Brazil and the British colonies in North America. In fact, the Dutch empire was built by the labor of Black people. Enslaved Africans cleared swamps, farmed the land, and constructed buildings and roads. The Dutch trafficked a continual supply of enslaved Africans to New Amsterdam.[3] Many toiled to build such key colonial structures as Fort Amsterdam, the headquarters of Dutch and later British rule. In 1655, the Dutch extended "half freedom" to a group of Black men who asserted that they had come to the colony as indentured servants. Like propertyless Whites, they paid annual dues to the West India Company but worked on their own account. In contrast to Whites, their children remained bound.[4] Together they formed the earliest society of free Africans in the Americas (Berlin and Harris 2005).

When the British captured New Amsterdam from the Dutch in 1664, they changed its name to New York. The British rapidly superseded the Dutch in the international slave trade, and the city continued to receive newly captured Africans and "seasoned" slaves from the West Indies who were sold to the highest bidder at the docks of Lower Manhattan and Long Island. As a result, those who were enslaved in New York included some Africans who were brought directly from West Africa and others who were transported from Caribbean islands. This heterogeneous enslaved African society came from a myriad of language groups, cultures, political systems, and tribal identities. In the colonies, the slavery capitalist class homogenized them under a Black racial category that stripped them of human rights and subjugated their bodies and labor.

Enslaved and free Africans in New York had experienced multiple forced migrations and diasporic encounters. Between 1701 and 1725, for example, 2,195 enslaved Africans were brought from the Caribbean and West Africa to New York (see Wilder 2000, 16). The majority came from the British West Indies; slave owners thought that enslaved Africans who had been "seasoned" under cruel and inhumane work conditions in the Caribbean were more likely to survive than newly captured Africans had skillsets valued in the slavery economy. Under British colonial rule, slavery was more punitive than it had been under the Dutch. The British established slave codes that restricted Blacks' physical movement and limited their ability to purchase their freedom. The racial system defined anyone with African or mixed indigenous and African ancestry as Black and in bondage for life. Europeans were defined as White and free. Propertyless men served for a term as indentured servants to repay the cost of their passage to the colony. Although oppressive laws legitimized the control of enslaved Africans, they constantly strategized, periodically revolted, and frequently escaped.

Unlike the urban slavery of lower and midtown Manhattan, where enslaved Africans worked on docks, in construction, and in White households, Long Island was mostly rural, and Black slaves worked on farms and as domestic servants. Jamaica, Queens, which was named for its indigenous inhabitants, the Jameco people, grew rapidly when European colonizers from Kings County, eastern Long Island, and Connecticut seized the land. Its proximity to Jamaica Bay made it a hub of international trade, and churches, schools, and judicial institutions were established there in the eighteenth century. By 1727, there were over thirteen hundred slaves in Queens County.[5] The town of Hempstead, located east of Jamaica, was a key site of colonial government on Long Island, and enslaved Africans were trafficked there as well. By 1698, there were over a thousand slaves in Nassau County. As in Queens, Blacks performed strenuous labor amid poor working conditions on farms and in households.[6]

Resistance to European domination marked social relations in Manhattan and Long Island. Several examples of Indigenous and African resistance to the quotidian practices of White control elucidate the racial tensions that characterized colonial society. For example, "In 1709, an enslaved man and Black woman murdered their out-plantation owners when they were denied the customary Sunday freedom other Newtown slaves enjoyed; the pair was publicly executed in Jamaica, the county seat" (Sanjek 2000).

The principles of human freedom espoused by White New Yorkers during the American Revolution contradicted their commitment to the continuation of racial slavery. As the White populace celebrated their independence from the British Empire, New York's slave owners and provincial government were reluctant to emancipate enslaved Africans. Instead, racial slavery became increasingly punitive through the passage of slave laws that controlled every aspect of life for enslaved Africans and their descendants.

Figure 8 and Figure 9. Left: Advertisement for the sale of fifteen young enslaved Africans at a public auction in Hempstead, Long Island. Photo courtesy of the Schomburg Center for Research in Black Culture, Photograph and Prints Division. New York Public Library. http://digitalcollections.nypl.org/items/510d47dc-491f-a3d9-e040-e00a18064a99. Below: "$1 Reward. RAN AWAY from the subscriber, on the 30th ult. an indentured colored Boy named Tom. All persons are forbid trusting, harboring or employing said Boy. Jarvis Jackson. Newtown, Sept. 10, 1849." Advertisement for capture of a runaway slave in Newtown, Queens. Newtown is now called Corona. Courtesy of Queens Library Archives.

The Revolutionary War (1775–1783) caused significant disruption to the slave trade and posed serious challenges to the slave economy. During the chaos brought by a war in which New York City changed hands more than once, enslaved Africans fled their masters and sites of bondage. This mass escape undermined slave owners' assumption that independence from the British crown would bring them sole control over trade and labor. Thousands of Blacks were manumitted, first by the British and then by the rebels, as both sides offered them freedom in exchange for their military service.[7] Black people were on the move in search of freedom and liberation. Roughly three thousand Africans left New York when Britain evacuated the ports it had occupied. Many who remained on Long Island scattered across the territory or migrated into the city and formed an expansive free Black society in Manhattan.

The public life of Black New York was being remade during the late eighteenth and early nineteenth centuries. Its many diasporas, coming from New England, the West, the South, Long Island and the Caribbean, were active participants in the process of creating the communities, institutions, and cultures that built present-day New York. For example, in 1787 Pierre Toussaint, born into slavery in Saint Domingue (Haiti), was brought to Manhattan by his owner, Jean Bérard. Like many French and mulatto members of the planter class, Bérard was escaping the warfare in Saint Domingue that soon evolved into the Haitian Revolution (1791–1804). Pierre worked as a hairdresser, and after he was freed upon the death of his owner, he continued to work for New York's White elite. With his earnings, he purchased the freedom of his sister, Rosalie; his wife, Juliette Noel; and his niece Euphemia, whom he and Juliette adopted after her mother, Rosalie, died. The family attended daily worship services at St. Peter's Catholic Church on Barclay Street in Lower Manhattan for six decades, and Pierre and Juliette raised money for charity and housing, educated and employed the city's orphans, provided medical assistance to the ill, and founded community organizations. Pierre used his language skills to serve Haitians who migrated to New York after the slave rebellion that overthrew French imperial control. Recently he was again recognized for his contributions to New York society. He was honored with the title "Venerable" by Pope John Paul II and is currently being considered for sainthood. This is not without controversy, as many Black Catholics argue that Toussaint's freedom, wealth, and apolitical repertoire during racial slavery made him more servile than holy.[8]

New York was one of the last states in the North to end slavery. A gradual emancipation act passed in 1799 stipulated that all Black persons born to enslaved mothers after July 4 of that year would be freed after completing twenty-eight years as an "apprentice," supposedly to repay their owners for the cost of their upbringing. In 1817, a new law passed in response to antislavery agitation provided that all slaves born before 1799 would be emancipated in 1827, but some younger slaves were held for another decade. After serving out their indentures, many young adults left Long Island for Manhattan. Whites were intensely hostile toward free Blacks, but they found solidarity and created community in segregated areas such as the Tenderloin district. Although all Black people who had been born in New York were free by 1840, nonresident slave owners could still bring slaves from other states into New York. Free Black citizens in New York had to guard against White kidnappers who not only captured runaways but sold free Blacks into slavery out of state, especially after the passage of the federal Fugitive Slave Act in 1850 (Gellman 2006). Free Blacks created scattered communities on Long Island, especially in Jamaica, Glen Cove, Long Beach, Freeport, Roslyn, Hempstead, Inwood, Huntington, Wyandanch, Manhassat, Port Washington, and Rockville Center. In partnership with antislavery Quakers, free Blacks came to the aid of fugitive slaves through the Underground Railroad. Some formed the towns of Jericho and Westbury, where they assisted escaped slaves' journeys to Canada (Velsor 2013).

A distinctive feature of Long Island was the presence of Black workers in coastal industries. It's coastal towns were a major site of oystering during the colonial period, and in the early nineteenth century fishing became a lucrative industry. Many Blacks plied coastal waters as seamen and boatmen. Blacks across New York and Long Island were intent on building new lives as free people. They rented, bought, and built homes, organized African Free Schools for their children, established their own churches and secular organizations, and pursued literary and artistic endeavors. "The Negroes of Long Island," published in the *New York Times* in 1858, observed that many Blacks took advantage of the availability of cheap land. They purchased "homesteads for themselves," and Black communities expanded in Jamaica, Flatbush, Oyster Bay, and Sag Harbor.

Although Congress had outlawed American participation in the international slave trade in 1808 and no slaves were recorded in New York by 1840, New York's political economy remained deeply connected to slavery. Elderly and infirm Black people remained in bondage under the estate of their former masters, a legal provision that had been designed to prevent Whites who had grown rich on slave labor from making their impoverished ex-slaves dependent on publicly funded relief. The same *New York Times* article that announced that "Negroes abound" on Long Island demonstrates that Blacks there were still subject to racial restrictions. While White society expected elderly ex-slaves to "dry up and blow away," they denied young freedmen and freedwomen access to public education and social advancement.

Furthermore, New York's banking institutions continued to finance plantations in the South and the Caribbean well after the abolition of slavery in the state. The city's merchants traded in sugar, cotton, indigo, and tobacco products extracted from southern slave labor. These products were transported, warehoused, and exported through New York's ports, contributing to its prosperity. In a cruel irony, many free Blacks (as well as European immigrants) were employed on the waterfronts (Wilder 2000).

Throughout this period, state-sanctioned socioeconomic discrimination against New York's Black citizens, which was supported by the city's economic dependence on the products of slave labor, hindered Black community formation and progress in post-emancipation New York.

A TALE OF TWO BLACK SUBURBANIZATIONS: WORKING-CLASS AND MIDDLE-CLASS FLOWS, 1865–1945

In post–Civil War New York, the Black population of Queens and Long Island grew. Black men in eastern Long Island worked in shipping, whaling, agriculture, and fishing, as well as in artisanal crafts. Women toiled as cooks, cleaners, seamstresses, and laundresses for White households. Those who lived in Black areas of Queens and western Nassau County were more likely to be skilled and semi-skilled workers in the construction industry, such as carpenters, painters, and masons. Those in closer proximity to the industrial economy of Manhattan clustered in manufacturing.

Other men worked as barbers, coachmen, tailors, and waiters. Women served as nurses and teachers in segregated institutions of health care and education, often opening their own schools for Black children. By the late nineteenth century, several Black families in Long Island became financially successful through businesses such as catering and careers in banking, and civil service (Day 1997).

As Black communities grew on Long Island, New York City annexed Brooklyn, Staten Island, and Queens, while Nassau County emerged as a desirable suburb for the city's White elite. Queens became a quasi-suburb within city limits. With the extension of the subway system and the Long Island Railroad, areas such as Laurelton and St. Albans became the sites of country clubs, housing developments, and businesses. The city's aristocracy and burgeoning business elite established luxurious estates, which were often tended by Black gardeners and domestic workers. Suburban communities for affluent Whites formed in close proximity to established poor and working-class White and Black communities. Trolleys and ferries connected towns like Great Park to Jamaica, Hempstead, and Brooklyn. Land development in Jamaica, for example, flourished when Manhattanites en route to eastern Long Island viewed Whites' stucco homes surrounded by green lawns through the windows of Long Island Railroad trains. Houses in these "garden suburbs of New York City" were advertised for $6,999. Developers appealed to "discriminating buyers"—that is, Whites who appreciated the suburb's "careful restrictions"—who wanted to live where they could commute to Manhattan but sought physical distance from the city's increasing numbers of Black, immigrant, and poor residents. Initially developed as a rural resort town, Great Park and its adjacent areas catered to more affluent Whites in the expanding financial and cultural economy of the early twentieth century.

The development of Cascades in Queens and Great Park in Nassau County was marked by national patterns of racially discriminatory policies and practices in employment and housing. The Supreme Court decision in *Plessy v. Ferguson* (1896) upheld the constitutionality of racial segregation. Whites racially engineered residential space on Long Island. Its towns were developed as a system of racially separate and unequal housing that predated apartheid in South Africa. The increased occupational diversity of segregated Black towns in Queens and Nassau County in the

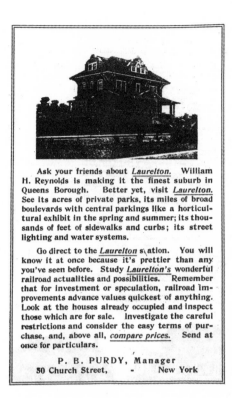

Ask your friends about *Laurelton.* William H. Reynolds is making it the finest suburb in Queens Borough. Better yet, visit *Laurelton.* See its acres of private parks, its miles of broad boulevards with central parkings like a horticultural exhibit in the spring and summer; its thousands of feet of sidewalks and curbs; its street lighting and water systems.

Go direct to the *Laurelton* s\ation. You will know it at once because it's prettier than any you've seen before. Study *Laurelton's* wonderful railroad actualities and possibilities. Remember that for investment or speculation, railroad improvements advance values quickest of anything. Look at the houses already occupied and inspect those which are for sale. Investigate the careful restrictions and consider the easy terms of purchase, and, above all, *compare prices.* Send at once for particulars.

P. B. PURDY, Manager
50 Church Street, - New York

Laurelton Long Island

THE GARDEN SUBURB IN NEW YORK CITY

Unexcelled Transit - All Public Utilities
A well developed community on the south side of Queens Borough
Wonderful shade trees and beautiful flowers
Highly restricted but moderately priced
Twenty-five minutes from Manhattan

LAURELTON SALES COMPANY, Inc.
LAURELTON BUILDING
Thirty-third Street and Seventh Avenue
Phone 1119 Greely   Office on Property

Figure 10 and Figure 11. Left: Advertisement in *Brooklyn Life*, March 5, 1910. Courtesy of the Queens Public Library. Right: A page from *The Queens Borough, New York City, 1910–1920*, a promotional book published by the Chamber of Commerce of the Borough of Queens in 1920. Courtesy of Queens Public Library Archives.

late 1800s meant that residents had heterogeneous class statuses. Like the Black neighborhoods studied by W. E. B. Du Bois in *The Philadelphia Negro* ([1899] 1996), Black households on Long Island at the turn of the twentieth century ranged from low income to affluent.

The Black towns on Long Island were largely unincorporated, which meant that they recieved few and inferior municipal public services. During the first wave of the Great Migration, many Blacks who left the South and the Caribbean joined the preexisting Black population. Working- and middle-class families wanted to live outside of the city and own their own houses but could not cross the color line. In Jamaica,

Queens, and on Long Island, Black folks encountered suburban versions of Jim Crow. Whites had created a web of real estate and land use regulations that undermined Black home ownership. They used a battery of economic, social, and political tactics to confine Black suburbanites to low-wage jobs and substandard, rental housing. White employers paid them poverty wages that undermined their ability to improve their situation. Many performed domestic services for White families; others were employed by White-owned manufacturing businesses on the other side of the railroad tracks. As a result, Great Park and Black areas like it on Long Island were poorly constructed and left to fend for themselves by local municipalities (Wiese 2005).

Black working-class suburbs were racially gendered spaces. As White middle-class families moved to Long Island, they hired Black and Irish domestic workers to relieve White women of the quotidian, gendered tasks of cooking, cleaning, and childcare. Single Black women, particularly recent migrants from the South, sought work on suburban estates because they also boarded there, which enabled them to save their cash wages. Domestic workers who did not live in their employer's household resided in nearby working-class suburbs in flats that were inferior to the White residences where they worked. These women were often the first in their families to move to the suburbs. They used their wages to support their families in the city or the South and encouraged other Black women in their social networks to move to the suburbs for similar work opportunities.

The sex ratio of the Black population in suburban towns reflected the gendered as well as racial sorting of occupations. Their demographic makeup differed, depending on the specific demand for labor in nearby White towns. Service occupations were predominantly female, and manufacturing employment predominantly male (Wiese 2005). Southern Black men were eager to obtain manufacturing jobs, which paid steady wages year-round that enabled them to live better than they had as tenant farmers or field hands. Southern Black women on Long Island no longer had to perform agricultural labor, but they continued to toil in domestic service. Even those with some formal education and occupational skills lacked the opportunity to enter other occupations. For Black New Yorkers in the pre-World War era, the sharp national inequalities of class, race, and gender were mapped onto local spaces in the suburbs.

From Harlem to the Outskirts of Town: Jazz and Elite Migration
to Queens

Although Jim Crow permeated New York's urban and suburban neighborhoods and institutions, many neighborhoods were well-known sites of
Black aspiration, achievement, pleasure, and creativity. Nowhere is this
more evident than in early twentieth-century Queens, which the Flushing
Town Hall has dubbed the "home of the Jazz."[9] Well before Queens was
incorporated into New York City, roads, horsecar lines, and the Long
Island Railroad had solidified Jamaica's position as a transportation hub.
During the Harlem Renaissance, Queens became a site of second settlement for Blacks who wanted larger living spaces than Harlem could provide. Many were jazz musicians, artists, and intellectuals; some belonged
to the old Black bourgeoisie (Gregory 1998).

In the early twentieth century, Black migrants from the South and
Caribbean immigrants turned Harlem into an unparalleled center of African
diasporic cultural and political creativity. The fusion of the Black Atlantic's
musical expressions—the blues, call and response, and improvisation—with
European band music gave rise to jazz in New Orleans and Harlem. The
subsequent migrations of hundreds of jazz musicians from Harlem to suburban Queens represented both an imagined return home to rural southern
life as well as a sign of their desires for liberated futures in the urban North.

Jazz singer Eva Taylor and her husband, Clarence Williams, a music
publisher and businessman, were the first Black jazz musicians to move to
Queens. They purchased a home and several adjacent lots in a rural area
of Jamaica in 1927. Clarence Williams was from Louisiana and preferred
the country-like atmosphere of Queens to Manhattan. Many of those who
followed him there from Harlem originally came from the American
countryside and Global South. The attraction of suburbia lay in its resem-
blance to spaces where they felt at home, recreating the psychic sense of
connection to the homelands they remembered in Alabama, Tennessee,
North Carolina, and Virginia.

The enormous popularity of jazz provided the wealth that many musicians used to purchase homes in Corona, Flushing, Jamaica, Addisleigh
Park, and Forest Hills. When the Triborough Bridge facilitated automobile travel from Harlem to Queens, hundreds of jazz musicians and many

Figure 12. Map of the Queens Jazz Trail, 1998. Art by Tony Millionaire, concept by Marc H Miller and JoAnn Jones, published by Flushing Town Hall.

more Black working- and middle-class families moved to Queens. Commuters rode the F and J trains or the Long Island Railroad alongside Irish, Italian, and Polish immigrants and their descendants. Louis Armstrong purchased his home in Corona in 1943. Billie Holiday, Dizzie Gillespie, Count Basie, Fats Waller, Ella Fitzgerald, James Brown, and Jackie Robinson purchased property in Black New York's *Gold Coast*— "named for the mansions that lined the north shore of Long Island"—or the Black suburban demi-paradises of Jamaica, Queens. These neighborhoods became known for housing some of the country's most affluent Black people.[10] They were joined by acclaimed African American author, playwright and activist Shirley Graham, who moved to a modest home in Addisleigh Park in 1947, and husband, W. E. B. Du Bois; they married

Figure 13. Louis Armstrong in front of his home in Corona with children from the neighborhood. Courtesy of Louis Armstrong House Museum.

afterward in 1951. At their wedding reception, guests at Graham's and Du Bois's home "dined on toasted sandwiches, canapés, ice cream, and sparkling punch."[11] The French-style hors d'oeuvres, drinks, and desserts signify the performance of refined consumption styles and respectability politics of the educated, traveled, and cosmopolitan Black bourgeoisie.

Upwardly mobile Black families selected Queens because of its suburban appeal and location on the outskirts of the city. In defiance of anti-Black covenants, some White homeowners sold their homes to elite Black buyers. Black media outlets such as *Essence* and *Ebony* magazines advertised local real estate opportunities to affluent residents of overcrowded areas like Harlem and portrayed moving to Queens as a sign of upward mobility and Black progress. But Queens could not rival the large estates owned by White

Figure 14. Shirley Graham Du Bois, 54, and W. E. B. Du Bois, 83, were married at their home in Addisleigh Park, Queens, on February 27, 1951. Courtesy of the Department of Special Collections and University Archives, W. E. B. Du Bois Library, University of Massachusetts Amherst.

millionaires, many of whom were entertainers and athletes and other members of the political and financial elite, less than twenty miles east on Long Island.

Behind the large backyards, colonial revival houses, tree canopies, lavish dinner parties, and easy commutes to the city and its jazz clubs was the specter of the continuing significance of race in the lifestyles, consumption patterns and freedoms of elite Black residents. In Queens and Long Island, White retaliation against monied Black neighbors mirrored national trends of suburb making. As housing development revved up in the 1920s, so did the political and social articulations of White power over them. The 1920s saw a surge in the presence of the KKK in Queens and Long Island. One in seven Long Islanders was a member of the KKK (Verga 2016). In 1927, one thousand white-robed Klansmen marched in a Memorial Day Parade along Queens Boulevard in Jamaica. When police turned them away from the civic celebration, a brawl ensued, and seven people were arrested.

The KKK's White supremacist agenda in Queens and Long Island reflected the rampant racial tensions that had characterized the social order of Greater New York since the colonial era. Its anti-Black, anti-Semitic and anti-Catholic stance reflected the power structure of the city and its suburbs. Violent antagonism toward Irish and Italian Catholics, who were gaining political power, and widespread intimidation designed to prevent Black people from moving into White neighborhoods were fundamental to its activities in the Empire City. The prewar and wartime development of New York's suburbs involved a collision between White efforts to maintain exclusion and Black working-class and middle-class placemaking. In Queens and Long Island neighborhoods, Black families just a generation or two removed from slavery encountered systematic White institutional and sociocultural retaliation against racial progress and a deliberate campaign to fortify the color line and entrench it in new suburban spaces.

The Cascades and Great Park that were inherited by the diasporic Black middle class were created in Jim Crow fashion. Cascades was designed to cater to Italian, German, Irish, and Polish immigrants and their children. These European immigrant groups' tenuous status in the racial hierarchy created a vicious anti-Black culture among them, and the greater their physical distance from the city's expanding Black population, the closer they came to Whiteness. White ethnic real estate entrepreneurs seized the opportunity to purchase farms and woodlands, converting them into neat suburban subdivisions for sale only to White buyers. Overcrowding and deteriorating housing conditions in Manhattan and Brooklyn in the 1920s, coupled with anti-Black sentiment, led to the out-migration of Germans, Italians, and Irish to new real estate on the outskirts of the city. Jews experienced exclusion in housing and occupied a racially liminal position. They often formed their own enclaves, also participating in anti-Black housing practices. These new suburbs were often ethnically segmented developments on the outskirts of the city, but racially unified in their desires to keep Black people out of their residential spaces. This trend was curbed during the Great Depression, but it accelerated in the postwar period, particularly among veterans' families. In the next section, we consider Blacks' and Whites' uneven access to the suburbs as racial segregation and inequality in housing, education, and wealth were institutionalized in Greater New York.

WHITE SUPREMACY AND POSTWAR SUBURBAN EXPANSION (1946–1954)

Postwar suburbs played a crucial role in helping Southern and Eastern European immigrants cross the boundaries around Whiteness created by White Anglo Saxon Protestants. Suburbs became tools for culturally and religiously heterogenous European immigrant groups to build White racial solidarity and identity (Bonilla-Silva, Goar, and Embrick 2006). These groups were often internally conflicted and politically divided. However, suburbs were their ethnic projects—the tools they needed to assert their Whiteness, middle-classness, and Americanness by collectively subjugating Black Americans (Treitler 2013). The postwar suburbanization of Southern and Eastern European immigrants and their journey to Whiteness and middle-class status are central to the development of Cascades and Great Park. Cascades was initially peopled by European immigrants and their children, whose claims to Whiteness were tenuous at best. When the Irish, who had migrated into New York after the potato famine in the late 1840s, had gained a foothold in unskilled and factory labor, they formed anti-Black unions and neighborhood gangs that violently attacked Blacks, whom they regarded as competitors in the labor and housing markets (Ignatiev 2009). They strategically attained membership in White America by segregating themselves from Blacks. Many shed their last names, accents, and traditions. When new waves of Irish and Italians entered New York in large numbers at the turn of the twentieth century, they were systematically excluded from White Anglo-Protestant institutions because of their darker complexions and Catholic faith.

Although military service in the world wars helped many Southern and Eastern European immigrants into Whiteness, it was a reminder to Black veterans that they were continued outsiders in their own land. Government programs enabled veterans of European descent unprecedented opportunities to obtain a college education and buy suburban homes. In sharp contrast, many Black veterans and their families remained confined to the Lower East Side, Brownsville, and South Bronx neighborhoods that White ethnics were leaving. In Queens and on Long Island, these upwardly mobile newcomers reproduced prewar racially discriminatory practices in housing, embraced White supremacist ideologies espoused by the KKK, and solidified their Whiteness through their separation from Black and Puerto Rican New Yorkers.

The Federal G. I. Bill (the Serviceman's Readjustment Act of 1944) ushered in a new phase of institutional racism in New York's complex urban and suburban housing structure. Federal programs provided Americans of European origin access to crucial tools of social mobility. In what Ira Katznelson (2005) describes as "affirmative action for Whites," the federal government supported millions of White veterans by providing them tuition for vocational and college education, low-interest loans to start small businesses, and subsidized and insured mortgages to helped them buy and build equity in their homes. These programs expanded the economy after the Great Depression and the exigencies of the war and encouraged long-term economic growth through the formation of a large, consumption-oriented White middle-class. Sam LeFrak and Fred Trump were among the major real estate developers in Brooklyn and Queens who exploited this policy, building middle-class houses and apartments exclusively for White families.[12] During the late 1940s and 1950s, these public and private investments intensified preexisting racial and spatial inequalities and facilitated the creation of segregated suburban housing and schools that Black diasporic middle-class families navigate today.

The social mobility of poor, working- and middle-class Whites occurred in tandem with the systematic racial exclusion of Blacks from higher education, homeownership, and government subsidies for entrepreneurs. The racial segregation of the armed forces was reproduced in the provision of separate and unequal benefits to Black veterans. The implementation of the federal GI Bill was left in the hands of local, city, and state officials who benefitted from and upheld White supremacy. Black veterans were systematically barred from gaining mortgages from banks and excluded from suburbs through restrictive covenants on deeds and White terrorism in the form of firebombs and burning crosses. They were hindered from enrolling in historically White public and private colleges and universities, and at the same time attended historically Black colleges and universities that were financially stretched.

Black veterans fought against fascism abroad but confronted entrenched segregation at home. As European immigrants and their children were ushered into the fold of Whiteness, the color line drawn against Blacks became more blatant. Government-sponsored suburbanization allowed them to develop a White habitus (Bonilla-Silva et al. 2006), segregated spaces where Europeans of diverse national, religious, and linguistic origins could build White racial solidarity and middle-class consciousness. People of European descent formed friendships, intermarried, and networked in spaces where they believed themselves to be the moral center of American society. Suburban Whites rarely came in contact with people from the Black, Latinx, and Asian diasporas in their communities, and prevailing images of them as abnormal, bestial, criminal, disorderly, violent, hypersexual, and lazy—as inherently defective in their moral character or as coming from a pathological culture of poverty—could go unchallenged by direct experience.

The GI Bill combined with the racially biased governmental policies to create nearly impenetrable walls of racial and class segregation nationally (Rothstein, 2017), trickling down to New York City and its suburbs. The Federal Housing Administration (FHA) began as a New Deal agency designed to revive housing construction, an industry devastated by the Depression. The FHA made it easier for buyers to obtain mortgages with little or no down payments at low interest rates. Even more important, it established a systematic appraisal system that not only assessed borrowers' assets and home values, but also evaluated the neighborhood around the home (Gregory 1998). According to internal, subjective assessments made by the FHA, houses in suburban areas were more valuable than the same houses in urban areas. Those in predominately White neighborhoods were appraised at higher values than those in Black, Latinx, or Asian neighborhoods. These policies tied housing values to the racial composition of their neighborhoods, reinforcing the Jim Crow practices that prevailed in the North and thwarting the goals of the civil rights movement to strike down separate and unequal policies and practices in housing during the 1950s.

As early as 1938, antiracist activists in Jamaica, Queens, publicized many cases of the "FHA . . . systematically refusing to underwrite mortgages for Black home buyers." "As the NAACP protest forewarned, FHA policies played a critical role in articulating the meanings of racial categories and in shaping the specific institutional and popular forms that racism would take in urban communities. If White homeowners were worried that an influx of racial minorities would provoke a decline in property values, their worries were well founded" (Gregory 1998, 62). Cascades and other prewar middle-class neighborhoods and suburbs were social laboratories where the American experiment of White supremacy was tested and reaffirmed. Countless lawsuits, protests, and uprisings by Black New Yorkers contested this discriminatory project at every turn.

The large-scale development of exclusively White suburban towns on Long Island during the postwar period set the tone for how Great Park evolved from a White rural resort town to a multiracial middle-class bedroom suburb. The iconic suburb of Levittown was built in Nassau County in 1947. Levitt and Sons created the first mass suburban housing complex of its kind in the country. Built on a twelve-hundred-acre potato farm, Levittown was comprised of more than two thousand homes. In order to encourage European immigrants and their descendants to move there, the developers offered affordable mortgages with no down payment, the GI Bill provided federally subsidized mortgage loans to White veterans' families, and mandatory, racially restrictive housing covenants ensured that the suburb would be "for Whites only." Levittown's cookie-cutter homes and manicured landscapes created an image of middle-class success.[13] Management was invested in controlling the physical appearance of these suburban properties. Although Whites in middle-class residential areas of Queens sought to deter the arrival of Black families, this was an uneven process because of New York City's more democratic structure, established civil rights organizations, and entrenched taxation system. Levittown, however, was anti-Black by design. Black veterans quickly discovered that Levittown was a Jim Crow suburb.

The policy of excluding Black residents reflected the Levitts' political and economic philosophy and moral bankruptcy. When William Levitt was criticized for institutionalizing racial discrimination against Blacks when European Jews had just been subjected to racially motivated genocide, he responded by saying that as a real estate developer he was investing in solving housing problems, not racial problems. In defense of Levittown's anti-Black covenants, he stated:

> The Negroes in America are trying to do in 400 years what the Jews in the world have not wholly accomplished in 600 years. . . . As a Jew, I have no room in my mind or heart for racial prejudice. But I have come to know that if we sell one house to a Negro family, then 90 or 95 percent of our White customers will not buy into the community. This is their attitude, not ours. As a company, our position is simply this: We can solve a housing problem, or we can try to solve a racial problem, but we cannot combine the two.[14]

He went on to create Levittowns in Pennsylvania and New Jersey with the same Jim Crow North policies. When the Myers, a Black family, moved into Levittown, Pennsylvania in the summer of 1957, the quiet, majority-White cookie-cutter suburb turned into a site of massive White resistance and violence overnight.[15] In separating moral decisions from business interests and shifting the blame for racial exclusion from his company to White homebuyers, Levitt was articulating a viewpoint that was widely shared. After all, the same policy was embedded in the FHA's appraisal system. The private housing market was based on racial capitalism, and racial categories were used to define what groups were desirable or forbidden as neighbors and schoolmates. The expansion of Long Island suburbs and the private and public apparatus that supported it served Whites whose prosperity, mobility, and self-esteem were founded on the subjugation of Black people. This is the legacy of suburban development which the diasporic Black middle class confronted.

Federal housing policies were exploited by White municipalities, residents, and developers in Long Island's suburban towns. The racial segregation and neglect of prewar Black working-class neighborhoods in unincorporated towns made them vulnerable to White real estate developers. In order to clear space for Whites living in New York City to move to suburbs in Nassau County and for real estate developers and banks to capitalize on governmental subsidies, local suburban governments and community organizations engaged in what Andrew Wiese (2005) calls "suburban racial cleansing," displacing Black residents in order to redevelop these localities as prime real estate. Working-class Black neighborhoods established in the late nineteenth and early twentieth centuries were labeled slums and treated as "problems that needed to be dealt with." In a process similar to urban renewal in cities all over the country, White residents on Long Island used federal, state, and local policies and funding to demolish many Black residential areas on Long Island, such as Rockville Center, Port Jefferson, and Huntington, and rezoned them for commercial use. "Suburban Negro removal," in tandem with redlining, racially restrictive housing covenants, and White terrorism, were the central tools used by Whites to control land use, property, and community formation in Nassau County.

STRIVING AMID THE STRUGGLE: BATTLEGROUNDS OF CIVIL RIGHTS IN HOUSING AND EDUCATION IN QUEENS AND LONG ISLAND, 1955–1970s

During the late 1950s, Queens and Long Island, like Birmingham, Alabama, and Charlotte, North Carolina, became local battlegrounds for civil rights. Black people from across the class spectrum organized to combat racial discrimination in public accommodations, education, voting, and housing. In response, White suburban residents sought to deter middle-class Black families from purchasing homes in their towns and enrolling Black children in their schools. In 1954, the same year the Supreme Court mandated the desegregation of public education, Clarence S. Wilson purchased a home for his family in elite Copiague, Long Island. Wilson was the president of a Brooklyn barbershop supply company. After receiving multiple death threats from the Klan, he fled the neighborhood to keep his family safe. Wilson was one of many middle-class Blacks who sought to purchase a home in Queens and Long Island only to realize the Thirteenth Amendment's promises of freedom, prosperity, and citizenship were denied. Instead, he was left with a decision imposed on Black pioneers of desegregation: live elsewhere or constantly combat tyranny from White neighbors.

Although Whites' "massive resistance" to desegregation in the South was in the national spotlight, similar struggles occurred in the urban and suburban North, Midwest, and West. Rev. Martin Luther King Jr. toured towns on Long Island several times during his national campaigns against racism, the war in Vietnam, and poverty. The Congress of Racial Equality (CORE) invited King to give speeches connecting the racial problems of New York's suburbs to the national Black freedom struggle. During a visit to Long Island in 1965, Dr. King called for the improvement of education for Black children at a CORE rally in the town of Malverne and toured the substandard housing conditions of local Black communities, calling for racial justice.[16]

As White supremacy was challenged by the civil rights movement, the middle-class parents of the Black men and women in this book took significant steps to make their dreams of homeownership a reality. Johnny, fifty-four, an information technologist and Great Park resident with roots in the US South, grew up in Jamaica, Queens, in the 1960s. He recalls that after his father had found "a good job" and "purchased a lot in Great Park," every Sunday after church he and his sister would ride with their father to visit the site where their house was being built. These trips to Great Park resembled their summertime visits to relatives in North Carolina. He recalled:

> My cousins and aunts live in a town with one passageway [street]. We always, when we were younger, we would visit. It was really funny. When we moved from Queens, my sister and I . . . we actually said when we were driving along the main highway that we were moving from the city to the country, not the city to a suburb. It was so flat and open. Great Park is a lot more popular now. But where [my cousins] live it's very comfortable. It has good streetlights and a general store. Everybody basically knows one another there.

Johnny's parents had met and married in North Carolina. His mother came to New York to find work, leaving him in the care of his grandmother, and then he and his father joined her. The family's ties to North Carolina remained strong, and he and his sister enjoyed endless summer days playing outdoors, eating fresh food, and exploring the countryside with their cousins. Johnny's parents continue to spend the holidays in the small town where his father grew up, and recently returned for their high school reunion.

Table 5   The Black Population of Queens and Nassau County in 1910 and 1960

Queens	1910	1960
Black	3,198 (1%)	145,855 (8%)
White	280,691 (99%)	1,654,959 (91%)
Nassau County		
Black	2,317 (3%)	39,350 (3%)
White	81,541 (97%)	1,258,039 (97%)

SOURCE: U.S. Census, 1910, 1960.

Like many Black children of his generation, Johnny's family was a part of a growing exodus of middle-class Black families to Great Park in the 1960s and 1970s. The *Long Island Daily Press* reported in 1957, "LI's Non-White Population Jumps 113% in 7 years," and in 1962, that "218,240 Negroes Live on Long Island."[17] Like the Black families who bought property in Queens during the early to mid-twentieth century, Johnny's family sought a semiru-ral landscape that offered privacy, quiet, and the natural beauty they remembered from their hometowns in the South. Yet Great Park in Nassau County was distinctly different from Jamaica, Queens. While Cascades was affordable and accessible by public transportation, Great Park had higher housing prices, property taxes, and commuting costs. Fewer Black middle-class families lived in Great Park than in Cascades.

As the drama of racial integration played out in Canarsie, Jamaica, Corona, and Mount Vernon during the 1960s and 1970s, Great Park's location an hour from midtown Manhattan made it the preferred site of third settlement for middle-class Whites leaving the city to avoid Black, Latinx, and Asian neighbors (Sanjek 2000). The Black middle-class families in Brooklyn, Harlem, and Queens who moved to Great Park at that time were escaping the ghettoization and neglect of their urban neighborhoods.

New York City underwent significant demographic change as well as economic and financial crises in the 1960s. Puerto Rico experienced its own Great Migration. The small community that had existed in New York City since the early twentieth century, when Puerto Rico became a

US possession, was joined by about six hundred thousand people from the Caribbean island (Weil 2004). Arriving at a time when employment opportunities and the supply of affordable housing were declining along with the city's public services, Puerto Ricans faced difficulties they had not expected as US citizens. Immigrants from Asia, whose entry was less restricted after passage the of the Hart-Cellar Act, arrived in unprecedented numbers after 1965. Since New York's neighborhoods remained rigidly segregated, Puerto Rican migrants and Asian immigrants were crowded into neighborhoods that were already densely populated by Black Americans. In Harlem, Bedford Stuyvesant, Jamaica, and Morrisania–Mott Haven, the music, foods, and faith traditions from the Caribbean and Latin America thrived alongside Black Americans' rural and urban southern and cultures. Black residents struggled to desegregate and assert community control over the public schools, while wealthy White and White ethnics maintained their control over the city's economy and its social policies.

Rampant discrimination in the real estate market excluded Black Americans, Puerto Rican migrants, and Asian and Caribbean immigrants from White neighborhoods, while federally funded urban renewal projects destroyed large numbers of housing units where they lived. Tens of thousands were left in search of decent housing with rents they could pay from their discriminatorily low wages. Slum clearance projects prescribed by the 1949 Federal Housing Act were implemented to demolish housing in low-income areas of Manhattan and Brooklyn. Under the direction of Mayor William O'Dwyer, New York City's Slum Clearance Committee orchestrated the public purchase of areas inhabited by disempowered groups and their sale to private investors for redevelopment. Real estate speculators obtained what they deemed potentially lucrative sites (Wilder 2000). A policy criticized as "Negro removal" systematically displaced Black and Latinx residents on a massive scale, while few low-income families were offered subsidized housing, and real estate discrimination and rising rents kept many neighborhoods out of reach for families of color. The problems of densely populated Black neighborhoods were compounded by an epidemic of arson, high and rising rates of joblessness, the infiltration of drugs, and rampant governmental neglect, which became particularly visible in places such as the South Bronx, Brownsville, Harlem, and Corona.

Overcrowding and urban renewal stimulated the outmigration of low- and middle-income Black families from Harlem, Bedford Stuyvesant, and the South Bronx to Queens and Long Island. In a stratified process, low-income families found apartments in places such as Lefrak City, Canarsie, and Jamaica, while the middle class bought homes in residential areas and suburbs like Mount Vernon, Rosedale, Hempstead, and Roosevelt. Between 1960 and 1980, the Black population in the suburbs more than doubled (see Wiese 2005, 212). Black Americans were increasingly followed or accompanied by immigrants from Jamaica, Haiti, Trinidad, and the Virgin Islands (Zephir 1996).

The overlapping migrations caused by global, national, and local political and economic shifts created the heterogeneous middle-class neighborhoods of Black New York. In addition to removing racially restrictive quotas, the 1965 immigration reform prioritized the recruitment of highly skilled immigrants and family reunification. Educated citizens in postcolonial island nations were attracted by recruiters who promised lucrative employment opportunities, especially for medical professionals and educators, causing a brain drain in their home countries (Bailey 2013). Members of Haiti's elite came to New York in unprecedented numbers to escape the rampant human rights violations of the Duvalier dictatorship (Zephir 2001). These immigrants not only had human capital but benefitted from affirmative action programs and their ties to a growing diasporic economy to pursue desired middle-class lifestyles, homes, and neighborhoods. This period ushered in a new phase of social and spatial identities and encounters of Black diasporas. As a response to these international, national, and local events, Queens and Long Island became a key site of the southernization and Caribbeanization of New York.

White residents of urban New York responded to middle-class Black immigrants as they did to Black Americans who moved to the suburbs: first fight, and then flight. School desegregation was a flashpoint for racial tensions. A decade after the Supreme Court had ruled segregated schools unconstitutional, most African American and Puerto Rican students attended schools whose student body was less than 10 percent White. So Black parents and civil rights activists staged a boycott. Led by Bayard Rustin, who had just organized the March on Washington, and Milton

Galamison, a pastor and community organizer from Bedford Stuyvesant, 460,000 students did not attend school on February 3, 1964. Leaders of the boycott reported that Black and Puerto Rican students were assigned to schools whose facilities, teachers, and curriculum were consistently inferior to those of schools attended by Whites. Black parents and civil rights protesters had grown tired of waiting for the Board of Education to fulfill its promises. Their calls for equality were met by White parents who organized community meetings, held anti-busing demonstrations at City Hall and the offices of local officials, and directed intimidation and violence toward Black students. This was White New Yorkers' form of Jim Crow tyranny, which extended from city to suburb.

Integrating the schools in Cascades and neighboring communities was a social burden imposed on Black children and their parents. As children of the civil rights movement, many of my respondents, who were among the first Black families to live in Cascades and attend local schools, endured White intimidation and violence, as the White ethnic working and middle class of Elmhurst, Corona, Canarsie, and Rosedale sought to bar them from accessing these advantages (Gregory 1998, Rieder 1985, Sanjek 2000). Petal, fifty-one, grew up in the Cascades area in the 1960s. Her parents had left her and her sister, Meg, with family in Trinidad until she was five. Once they settled in, they returned to retrieve their daughters. Petal met White people for the first time on their block; she had never interacted with Whites in Trinidad. Growing up, she saw Whites as "an ugly, ugly group of people." Petal and Meg were bused to a school north of Cascades. Their worst fear was missing the morning school bus and having to walk. Petal recalled:

> When we arrived that first time, the yellow buses arrived; all those White parents were out there calling us names and everything. And the police officers there did nothing. They were throwing stuff and everything. They escorted us. . . . In reflection now, what I saw later on in life about the South was just like what we had to go through. We entered the front door the first time. That first day. Afterwards they just dropped us off and those parents protested. The White parents protested vehemently. So that was my first introduction, realizing that this was not a very pretty place. . . . If we missed the bus, we had to walk from here to there to the school. Sometimes you had to run.

Like Black children across the South, these newly arrived Caribbean immigrants in Cascades had to run the gauntlet of angry White parents without police protection. Soon all their White neighbors fled to Long Island, New Jersey, and Pennsylvania.

By the late 1960s, countless Black and White civil rights activists in the North as well as the South had laid their lives on the line for racial justice. The passage of the Fair Housing Act in 1968 was the capstone of federal legislation ensuring equal rights in public accommodations, education, employment, and voting. The implementation of race-blind housing policies, however, was met with at least as much resistance and violence, and given the private control of the real estate market, it was much easier to evade. Black newcomers in formerly White neighborhoods were met with acts of White terror that reminded those from throughout the Black Atlantic that, although violent miscegenation had bound the blood of Europeans and Africans, that sharing residential and intimate spaces of life between the races was forbidden by White supremacy.

By 1970 the White population of Queens had plummeted, and most of the Whites who could not afford to move were adamantly opposed to integration. White ethnic working- and middle-class families refused to allow Black people in their neighborhoods or schools, and many colluded to terrify Black newcomers. Soon they sold their houses in a panic, left neighborhoods like Cascades altogether, and relocated to lily-White areas of northern Queens, Staten Island, Long Island, and New Jersey. The same families who during the 1950s and early 1960s had come from lower-income areas of the Lower East Side, Brownsville, and the South Bronx in order to solidify the social distinction between themselves and Blacks by creating a physical separation between racially distinct neighborhoods left within decades when Black families arrived. The Cascades area was largely abandoned by White ethnic families, businesses, and institutions during the 1970s to the 1990s. The children and grandchildren of early twentieth-century European immigrants moved into suburban shadows. With some exceptions, they largely relinquished identifiable ties to their ethnic heritages to gain acceptance from White Anglo-Saxon Protestants and construct and consolidate their Whiteness. When symbolic ethnicity is expressed through Jewish greetings, Irish flags, or Italian cuisines, it is no longer a socioeconomic handicap. Instead, it brings pleasure without cost to Whites, while reaffirming Black people as perpetual racial outsiders in America (Waters 1990).

During the 1970s New York City's working-class residents, who were now increasingly Black Americans and immigrants of color, suffered from a precipitous decline in manufacturing jobs, which had afforded many White immigrants ample opportunities to enter the middle class. Factories moved to the suburbs, the Sunbelt, or foreign countries. The city was facing a fiscal crisis. The massive out-migration of middle-class families led to a decrease in tax revenues and massive deficit spending. Conservative voters and business interests attacked social welfare expenditures, which they blamed on the city's increasingly impoverished Black and Latinx residents. Racial tensions were exacerbated by the economic crisis, but they were rooted in a long history of spatial segregation. The exodus of Whites from New York and the in-migration of Black Americans from the South and Puerto Ricans and immigrants from the Caribbean, Latin American, and Asia were transforming New York from a predominately White city to a city of people of color.

This chapter has traversed the geography of Long Island, where the post-Break Black middle class arrived and encountered its spatial legacies. The racial history of Queens and Nassau County reveals that White supremacy has been embedded in spatial segregation ever since colonialism slavery, and Whites defended their exclusive control over urban and suburban spaces throughout a long struggle for Black freedom and civil rights. The desegregation crisis of the 1970s resulted in the exodus of Whites and the formation of Black diasporic suburbs. Whites in the Jim Crow North have used physical distance from Blacks to ensure their social, cultural, and political power against Black Americans and immigrants of color. In order to dominate those whose shared ancestry (through violence) they persist in denying, Whites on Long Island created sinister apartheid-like conditions to distance their families from their darker skinned kin.

Although blood pudding is considered a delicacy and served on tables of the residents of Cascades and Great Park, Whites' rejection of this dish despite its European gastronomic roots is a metaphor for the paradoxical mix of dependence and repulsion Whites on Long Island have historically practiced and felt toward enslaved Africans, Negroes, Afro- or African

Americans, and Black people. White society has depended on the unpaid and low-paid labor of Black Americans to build their towns and take care of their homes and their children. They have designed legislation and informal codes to confine Blacks to substandard housing in segregated neighborhoods, only to remove and replace them by better-off Whites. Blood pudding conjures up rejection and feelings of repulsion in many who believe that eating it crosses religious, spiritual, or physical boundaries. Colonial Christianity instructs followers that it harkens back to sacrificial practices tied to African folk religions. Like recent revelations of African ancestry among people who had always seen themselves as purely White, it crosses barriers that have been historically constructed to define White racial identity as separate from and superior to Blackness, however intermixed people actually are.

In my travels in White spaces as a young Black academic, I have odd encounters with Whites who came of age during the same period as my interviewees. During small talk, I usually share that I am doing ethnographic work in Queens and Long Island neighborhoods. They sometimes reply, "I used to live there, but my family left when I was young. Then we moved to the Island." Although White flight is discussed as a spontaneous response to Black in-migration, White fight and flight were well thought-out, collective, strategic, and immoral acts against Black people condoned by the state. A similar scenario unfolds when I encounter White people who say that they, too, grew up in Flatbush when it was "a nice place to live." In their eyes, it ceased to be a good place to live when Black families like my own moved in. We were seen as racial outsiders, culturally deficient and unworthy of being in the presence of Whites who enjoyed or aspired to a superior status through racial separation. Racial panic is neither a legitimate nor financially sound reason to sell a family's home. The racial politics of the Jim Crow North shaped the development of the middle-class neighborhoods of New York, leaving Cascades and Great Park residents with spatial legacies they must continue to grapple with in local schools, commercial centers, and residential neighborhoods in yet another period when middle-class jobs are unstable and housing values are vulnerable.

In this chapter, we have uncovered the silenced but central role that the African diaspora has played in the formation of New York's urban and suburban neighborhoods. The long arc of anti-Black oppression from the colonial period to the twentieth century is propelled by Whites' determination to assert racial control over the distribution of space. These spatial articulations of racial capitalism that have shaped the experiences of diasporic Black communities in New York's middle-class suburbs are not past history, but instead living history. New York's neighborhoods continue to be marred by segregation. Black institutions and communities, however, are embedded in histories of anti-racist collective actions to ensure that Black families from across the diaspora have the right to property ownership and prosperity. The next chapter explores the contemporary socioeconomics of the post-Break Black middle class since the 1980s and the cultural economies of their own households.

4 Callaloo

CULTURAL ECONOMIES OF OUR BACKYARDS

Kalalou pa manje avèk yon sèl dwèt (Okra is not eaten with
one finger)

Haitian Proverb

"We ran out of porridge. We have callaloo and saltfish," Benjamin told me.
I was meeting Hazel, a small-business owner, at Black Star, a go-to
Jamaican restaurant in Cascades. Hazel ate a cup of cornmeal porridge as
she shared her extraordinary story of coming to New York, working as an
apprentice, and opening her own home supplies shop. Her story com-
pelled, while breakfast satisfied my appetite. "Callaloo and saltfish it is
then," I told Benjamin. It came with boiled bananas on the side, country
style.

Callaloo is a leafy green, a cousin to spinach and collard greens. Native
to the African continent, it was transported to the colonies of the West
during slavery and remixed into Black diasporic cuisines. In Jamaica, it is
often served with the national dish of ackee and saltfish. Haitians have a
slightly different take. Their kalalou is not a leafy green but is instead
okra, a staple food that is fried, mixed into soup, boiled, or sautéed. From
the kitchen table to intellectual circles, callaloo is culturally significant.
Edwidge Danticat, a famous Haitian-American writer and activist outlined the cultural power of kalalou for *Callaloo*, a flagship journal of
African Diaspora arts and letters (Mirabal and Danticat 2007). When the

journal's founder, Dr. Charles H. Rowell, was in conversation with his colleague Dr. Leila Taylor, she likened his family's gumbo to her family's Trinidadian callaloo. Founded in 1976 to showcase southern Black writers who were marginalized by the northern Black Arts Movement, *Callaloo* later expanded its scope to Black writers globally. Rowell's goal was to "create a representational space for southern Black cultures" (Jackson 2007, 15).

Like the yards where callaloo and its leafy green cousins are grown and prepared in the South, Haiti, and Jamaica, the kitchens of Black diasporic suburban homes are the places where families gather to solve socioeconomic issues, while meals simmer on the stove. These transplanted lakous and yards are where the cultural economy, or the social practices around the material conditions, of the home are displayed, season to season. In this chapter, callaloo serves as a portal into the diverse cultural economies of post-Break Black middle-class households. We explore the shared and divergent socioeconomic and related cultural characteristics of Black Americans, Haitians, and Jamaicans in the postindustrial, bifurcated, and hyperglobal economy of New York.

Important elements of culture both shape and are shaped by one's economic position and relative power. Neckerman, Carter, and Lee (1999) argue that what they define as the "African American Culture of Mobility" is shaped by distinctive problems that the Black American middle class faces in their interactions with Whites and low-income Blacks. Yet they acknowledge that "ethnic variation in problems of inter-class relations" (p. 952) exist and recognize that these interactions are shaped by a group's socioeconomic condition. Culture also emerges from organic forms of self-expression and creativity (Kelley 2001). Black people are actively segregated into second-class economic positions. Contemporary White society uses racialized ideologies of cultural deficiency locally and globally to justify subjugating Black communities. Counter to this racial apparatus, this chapter turns to the ways people in Black communities learn, earn, share, spend, and save as important elements of their agentic identities. Recognizing those variations helps us to understand how they negotiate inclusion and exclusion in a racialized economy. The three family stories that follow provide an entrée into these experiences, which are as much cultural as they are economic.

THREE STORIES: SARAI, AUTHARD, AND TAMMY

"I can say growing up on Long Island made me who I am today. People want to say your circumstances make you who you are. But I think being an underdog from my all-Black town made me a stronger person." Sarai has lived in Great Park for almost twenty years, and her home is within a couple of miles of where she spent her childhood. She values her privacy and doesn't know much about her neighbors, who are mostly White. I met Sarai at a Parent Teacher Association meeting at Great Park High School. Sarai is a working mother; she has two teenagers and serves as a manager at a financial firm. She and her husband, Jesse, an engineer, own a ranch-style home that they have lived in since the 1990s. Great Park's racial diversity and its close proximity to a direct train to Sarai's Manhattan office made it an ideal place to live for her.

Sarai's parents purchased property on Long Island during the late 1960s, when Sarai was very young. They were among the many middle-class Black families who left tenement apartments in Harlem and moved to Long Island in search of better schools, cleaner air, and quality homes. Intent on exercising the hard-won rights of free movement and property ownership at the heart of the civil rights struggle, Sarai's family was a part of a new chapter in Black American history.

When her family arrived on Long Island, Sarai was the only non-White child in her kindergarten class. By the fourth grade, however, one by one, the White girls and boys she had befriended had disappeared and been replaced by Black children whose families migrated from the boroughs or other towns on Long Island. Memories of this racist reception became fuel for her young adult ambitions. When Sarai's parents became successful in the city's growing financial sector, they saved money and purchased a single-family suburban home. She recalled that her parents wanted to buy a home on Long Island in order to "claim their piece of the pie." The neighborhood had been created to house White veterans and their families, and the first Black families to arrive watched Whites swiftly leave the neighborhood. Evoking the Norman Rockwell painting *New Kids in the Neighborhood* (1967), Sarai's White neighbors saw and treated her as if she were not just a stranger, but also an alien. Some of her Black classmates had done well; others had not. Forty years later, Sarai's lifestyle demonstrated that she had beat many of the odds stacked against Black children coming of age in segregated suburbia.

Sarai's narrative underscores that suburbs were sites of both overt and covert racial violence. The childhoods of Black boys and girls were compromised in the social experiment of integration. Strategic public and private decisions by White residents led to disinvestment in spaces where Black families congregated. Sarai experienced White hostility in a racially changing suburb, and as an adult she has observed similar patterns in Great Park. As a teenager, she was an active member in her public school and community until she attended college. After completing her degree, she landed a lucrative job at a financial firm. In the 1980s, it was still taboo for a woman, and a black woman especially, to hold a leadership position in a white male-dominated financial industry. Today Sarai is one of the top managers at her firm, and her household income is upwards of $150,000.

Sarai believes that she has attained the American dream. She and Jesse were able to pool their savings and 401(k)s to purchase their home. They could take vacations and provide security for their children, even though her husband was laid off during the Great Recession. Sarai attributes much of her endurance and success to her upbringing in a tightly knit Black suburban community. Although White suburbanites marked her childhood suburb as an undesirable place to live, Sarai believed that its rich social and cultural resources encouraged Black children growing up amid the desegregation crisis to excel. "I just feel that that background and the closeness of the community in those days helped me become the person that I am today. And also knowing that people didn't expect much of you made me even more of a fighter."

The gap between the experiences of Authard, a Haitian immigrant, and Sarai, a child of southern migrants, reflects Black diasporic groups' different journeys into the middle class. Authard and his wife, Paulette, were raising their children in a multifamily house on a tree-lined street in Cascades. He is a contractor in the public sector, and together he and his wife, a nurse, earn approximately $120,000 a year. They and their teenaged children live on the first floor of their multifamily home. Authard's brother and sister-in-law reside on the second floor. Their parents occupy the ground-level apartment when they return to New York from sojourns in Haiti. "I bought this house because my brother was getting married, and my parents were retiring. I wanted to make sure they were all OK, so here we are," he said, laughing with his hands in the air.

Authard was born in a rural town in Haiti and grew up as one of the thousands of "barrel children" in the Caribbean and Latin America. His parents, like many others of their generation, had emigrated and left their children in the care of loved ones until they established themselves. He endured long periods of separation from his parents because of a combination of legal status issues and their work schedule in the United States. His parents mitigated the emotional challenges of these circumstances by periodically shipping basic material necessities to Authard and his siblings in large cargo barrels.

Authard arrived in Brooklyn in the 1970s, almost a decade after his mother and father had come to the United States. His parents were part of the stream of middle-class Haitians escaping the repression of the Francois Duvalier regime, which often targeted the country's mixed race and business-owning class. Thousands of Haitians flocked to Miami, New York, Boston, and Montreal in search of places where they could either shelter in place until the fall of the dictatorship or establish long-term homes. Emigration of the country's poor and working class increased in the 1980s, greatly expanding the size of the Haitian diaspora. Before Authard's parents left in the 1960s, they asked his uncle to enroll him in a boarding school near Port au Prince. "I didn't understand how my parents could leave like that. I know they were making a sacrifice, but it was hard on us." When his parents "sent for him," New York was in the midst of an economic crisis. "I remember everything in Pitkin Avenue being so dirty. There was broken glass on the floor, crack vials." He learned English in public school, as well as by watching children's television programs. After acquiring a command of the English language, he excelled in school and graduated from college with a degree in engineering.

Despite his income, education, and residence in Cascades, Authard felt that he was pseudo middle class. As a young boy growing up in Haiti, he had imagined that in New York the "sidewalks would be lined with shiny pennies." He thought that in order to be middle class, you had to make at least $150,000 and "live in a neighborhood that you feel safe in." By the standards of much of the United States, Authard's family income makes them appear affluent; in New York, the median household income hovered around $55,000 when I was conducting interviews. Yet the family's expenses for housing, private school tuition for their children, their own student loans, transportation, and remittances to Haiti leave them with little money at end of the month. Transportation was a significant issue. Authard had a ninety-minute commute from southeast Queens to his job in Manhattan. His "saving grace" is the *dolla van* (which costs two dollars one way), a Caribbean immigrant men–run van line that shortens residents' travel time across the boroughs of Queens and Brooklyn. Dolla vans, which are predominately driven by Black men, are heavily surveilled by the New York Police Department for licensing and insurance infractions. "The other day, I was on a van, then we saw the police lights. And everyone had to get off and find their way," Authard shared. In spite of this, they alleviate congestion in public buses on main thoroughfares.

Authard sometimes regrets having bought a house in Cascades. "We lived in a neighborhood before this in northern Queens, and I found out that they have a better public school district than we do here. But I bought this house in a rush and didn't think about the public school district. We were too focused on private, private, private. That was a mistake." Even worse, Authard's teenage son fears going outside because of his past run ins with neighborhood boys. The family feels that their neighborhood does not give them the peace of mind that their careers and incomes are supposed to afford. Authard's family situation exemplifies a widespread struggle among Black middle-class families in New York: the high cost of living means that professional degrees and earnings do not provide comfort and security, and long commutes undermine their quality of life. This financial strain is especially pronounced for Black middle-class families, native- and foreign- born, who have less wealth and are subjected to racially constrained access to neighborhoods near their places of work.

Tammy, who lives several blocks away from Authard in Cascades, retains a close connection to her home community on the island of Jamaica. When I interviewed her, the family was preparing to travel home for summer vacation to visit relatives and relax at a beach club. I waited at the front door of their single-family home until Tammy pulled her late-model Toyota Camry into her driveway. She had picked her teenagers up from school, and on their way home they stopped at Target to purchase summer clothes for her son to wear in Montego Bay. It was Thursday, Tammy's regular day off from her job at the hospital. On a typical workday, she would be in her nurse's uniform preparing for her 3 p.m.–11 p.m. shift and dinner would already be prepared. She usually cooked a dish of rice and beans, a meat stew, a side of greens, and chicken nuggets for her daughter, who did not like traditional Jamaican food. All her husband, Jimmy, would have to do when he returned from work at 5 p.m. was warm up the food.

Tammy grew up in a middle-class family in Jamaica. While she was down to earth and tried to give off that sort of vibe, she articulated a respectability repertoire characteristic of Jamaica's brown middle class. She expressed disdain for the casualness she sees in the United States, exemplified by the culture of her workplace. "In Jamaica, you have to come to work clean, hair pulled back, no big gold jewelry, with respect for the profession. Here, the nurses and even some doctors have it all hanging out. Not professional at all." Like Arthaud, Tammy felt that asserting middle-class status was difficult for her. However, rather than placing the blame on the high cost of living in New York, she saw the inequitable distribution of wealth and resources to Black communities as the central problem. Tammy believed that Jews in New York enjoyed exclusive access to the city's vehicles of class and status mobility. "They get everything they need to get by in this country. It's unbelievable. I think the Jews get much too much." Tammy's views were deeply influenced by the riots in Crown Heights, Brooklyn, which erupted in 1991 not long after she arrived in New York. Yosef Lifsh, a Hasidic Jewish man driving in a motorcade escorting an important Chabad rabbi, hit two cousins, Gavin and Angela Cato, Black children of Guyanese heritage. Gavin died, and Angela was severely injured. The uproar over this event was fueled by preexisting tensions between the Black and Jewish residents of Crown Heights over access to housing, city resources, and local city boards; and unfair treatment by the police. Over the next three days, violence rocked the neighborhood, resulting in two deaths and numerous injuries.[1] These dramatic events left a lasting impression on how Tammy understood the city's racial, economic, and political environment. Tammy emphasized that while she worked hard "with no assistance" to become middle class, buy a home, and educate their children, the state has unfairly provided Jews in

New York with large-scale access to public assistance. When her niece applied for SNAP while a full-time student, her application was denied. From Tammy's perspective, New York's social welfare system is organized around ethnoracial categories, with Jews obtaining social services that help them to attain economic success while Black immigrants like herself toil to "make it" on their own. She saw herself as dignified because she did not to rely on food stamps or subsidized housing, but also felt racially excluded from government support in case she or her younger family members needed it.

Having lived in New York for just over twenty years and in Cascades for eight, Tammy struggled to make sense of New York's ethnoracial hierarchy and her place in it. New York's social order was obviously different from the one she left behind in Kingston, Jamaica. She grew up in an urban working-class home during the country's decolonization, became a nurse in an expanding educational sphere, and married her husband, Julian, in the 1980s before moving to New York. Tammy was one of the thousands of Jamaicans who migrated to New York after 1964. Although the majority of Caribbean immigrants arrived in New York through the process of family reunification, a significant number of Jamaican nurses and teachers were recruited to work in hospitals and public schools.

While Tammy was among those trained nurses, her move to New York was less about seeking greater economic opportunities for herself than about supporting her husband's move out of law enforcement in the increasingly volatile political atmosphere of Kingston. She presented the decision as a matter of going along with Julian's wishes. Tammy shared: "I never wanted to marry law enforcement. But I did. It was also never my plan to come to the United States. It was my husband's dream. We had more and more family living in New York, and he also wanted to pursue his career. And I said OK." In the late 1980s, Tammy's husband informed her that recruiters were coming to Kingston to hire recent nursing graduates for positions in New York's hospitals and suggested that she apply. "I was already working, doing nursing. I got promoted and everything was going well, so things were fine for me all over." Her husband had not had similar educational opportunities, however. If they moved to New York, he could earn a college degree and work in another field. At first, Tammy worked as a nursing assistant while earning her bachelor's degree in nursing to become a registered nurse. Julian earned an associate's degree and currently manages a small technology services company. Combined, they earn $130,000 a year.

Tammy has enjoyed living in Cascades. Her Tudor home had risen in value before the collapse of the housing market. She has also noticed signs of change in the neighborhood. Summer barbeque parties became more frequent. Increasing numbers of idle young men gathered along Cascades Boulevard, where they were subject to police surveillance under Bloomberg's "stop-and-frisk" policy. "I just try to stay away from that area. It's become too hot in the past couple of years," she commented. Tammy and Julian purchased their home with their savings and have no regrets. "We moved here because our family had all left Jamaica. Now they are nearby. I think we have reached some sort of dream." For her, the decision to emigrate was as much about family solidarity and political protection as it was about economic success (Clerge et al. 2015).

The journeys that Sarai, Authard, and Tammy made to middle-class diasporic suburbs illustrate the interconnected cultural, political, and economic positions of the post-Break Black middle class. They are related to the racial projects and migrations discussed in chapter 1 and the suburban inheritances discussed in chapter 2. In the rest of this chapter, I use demographic and ethnographic data to elucidate the diverse cultural economies of the post-Break Black middle class. Their socioeconomic status reflects the racial stratification of the economy. Racial capitalism sorts Blacks, whether native born or foreign born, into lower-status position compared to non-Blacks, even when they earn comparable salaries. This reality is just one side of the coin in the cultural economy of the post-Break Black middle class, however. As Black ethnic groups have expanded in number, so has their internal class diversity. They articulate different relationships with the neoliberal economy, which shape their cultural identities and encounters with one another in diasporic suburbs.

Like callaloo, the making of the post-Break Black middle class depends on its ingredients. Sarai, Authard, and Tammy's journeys reveal the heterogeneity of the Black middle-class experience today. Cascades and Great Park are crossroads of Black diasporas. These intergenerational migrants came from different locations of the Black Atlantic, moved to New York for a multitude of reasons, and occupy varying positions in the racialized and gendered economy. Simultaneously, movers and shakers and the products of epic migrations, they are a part of a long history of Black self-determination. This agency manifested in large-scale movements, set a flow by shifting global patterns of European domination and Black people's constant desires for family, kinship, mobility, community, and home.

Sarai, Authard, and Tammy's experiences, reveal many of the opportunities and challenges that Black Americans, Haitians, and Jamaicans face as they work to solidify their place in the middle class and transmit this status to their children. Their families' intergenerational journeys to suburbia arise from the desire for upward mobility in limited economic and educational systems in their places of origin. In the inner-ring suburbs where they live, they work to attain their own ambitious goals, always reflecting on the role that their Blackness, nationality, upbringing, and migrations have meant to who they are and who they hoped to become in New York. In the next section, we explore the larger socioeconomic patterns that are found among Black Americans, Haitians and Jamaicans.

HOME ECONOMICS

Income is a key indicator of class membership, but the appropriate thresholds for this assessment are continuously debated in public discourse as well as in the social sciences. The Great Recession has further complicated the definition of who is middle class and the incomes that constitute it. For the Black middle class in particular, the period between 2006 and 2014 represented the large scale undoing of the economic advancements made since the civil rights movement. The trifecta of predatory lending, the foreclosure crisis, and widespread job loss undercut homeownership. These realities make it difficult to talk about the Black middle class with any precision. Owning a home has been the primary vehicle of wealth creation for the Black middle class. Comparatively, Whites have a wider range of financial assets and in 2011, they had over $100,000 more in wealth than Black families (Hamilton et al., 2015).

The Great Recession revealed the dangers of neoliberal market deregulations that began in the 1970s. For example, rapidly increasing income inequality squeezed the White middle class but crippled the Black middle class. Between 2005 and 2009, Black's possessed less than $5,000 in wealth. This was a whopping 53 percent decline, and a gross disparity from Whites (Gottesdiener 2013). The racial inequality in the impact of the Great Recession economy is the result of White society's hoarding of power, receipt of financial inheritances that arm them with exceptional advantages, and their active exclusion of non-Whites from full political and economic power. Diasporic Black families, on the other hand, inherit histories of racial slavery, colonialism, and imperialism and must confront White-controlled labor markets that undermine their success, housing markets that segregate them, and financial markets that expand their debt (Addo, Houle, and Simon 2016; Conley 2010; Darity and Nicholson 2005; Hamilton, Darity, Price, Sridharan, and Tippett 2015; Massey 2007; Massey and Denton 1993; Oliver and Shapiro 2013; Wingfield 2007; Wingfield and Alston 2014).

Since the millennium, discussions of the Black and immigrant middle class have used household income to assess the middle-class standing of families of color in various ways. For example, Jody Vallejo's study of the Mexican American middle class in southern California uses the national median income in 2009 ($50,221) as the threshold for middle-class status (Vallejo 2012). Karyn Lacy argues that we must recognize the internal diversity of the Black middle class. A new middle and upper-middle class of Black families does not live in close proximity to poverty, wrestle with segregation, and face the risk of slipping into poverty themselves, Lacy argues. For example, Washington, D.C., in 2007, in order to be middle class, each person in a couple had to earn at least $50,000 annually in order for their household to qualify as middle class (Lacy 2007)—a level that is twice what Vallejo used in California. As income inequality rises, it also varies among cities and regions. It is, therefore, imperative that we adopt a place-specific definition of middle-class standing.

After 2008, as I walked past boarded-up, foreclosed homes and "for rent" signs in storefront windows in Queens and on Long Island, it became clear that time in addition to place make a crucial difference in how we should assess incomes and class status. Because this ethnography was conducted from the onset of the financial crisis through the protracted Great Recession to the uncertain and unbalanced recovery, the diasporic Black middle class was experiencing extreme economic uncertainty in real time. Earings that had seemed to purchase them a ticket to the middle class were disappearing. Partners lost their jobs; homes were underwater and short-sold. Meccas of Black homeownership received fewer social services and less recognition from their municipalities and the city writ large.

Income thresholds specific to the neighborhood, county, and region provided more precision when delineating who had sufficient means to lead a middle-class lifestyle.[2] In New York, the necessary income for a family of four to qualify as middle class was between $75,000 and $135,000 in 2006. Depending on where they resided in the metropolitan area, New Yorkers who were single needed to earn $45,000–$90,000 to live comfortably based on the cost of living (Bowls, Katkin, and Giles 2009). These figures are higher than the fluctuating national median household income of the first decade of the twenty-first century. Considered the "lost decade," the period between 2000 and 2010 saw a decline in national median household income (from $53,164 to $49,445).[3] The national median income, however, merges data from cities with high wage scales and rural towns where low-paid jobs and under- and unemployment are common. Instead, utilized the median household income of Queens and Nassau counties to create a middle-class threshold. In order to be interviewed, adults were required to have household incomes at or above the median of their county: at least $70,174 for Cascades and $82,315 for Great Park. These parameters for being middle class reflect local, regional, and national structures of income inequality during the research period.

The situations of middle-class people in these suburban communities vividly elucidate the complexity built into this assessment. Great Park interviewees' household incomes are well above the national median, but as Nassau County residents they pay some of the highest property taxes in the country. The impact of this gap between earnings and expenses was articulated by families like the Pattersons. Angel Patterson, a Black American real estate manager in his fifties, candidly remarked: "We make about $110,000, and with this house and our two kids in public schools, we are still struggling and praying we can keep the lights on every month." Although the Pattersons' household income might seem to place them in the upper-middle class, Angel and his wife think that their place in the middle class is tenuous.

Differences in income shape the structure and identities of the Black middle class. Nationally, average household incomes of the Black middle class vary by diasporic group. According to data from the Current Population Survey, in 2012 the Black foreign-born, who are comprised mainly of Caribbean and African immigrants, exhibit a higher socioeconomic profile than Black Americans (see table 1 in introduction). Black immigrants have higher median household incomes and a lower proportion of households in the lower-middle class than native-born Blacks. Much of this difference is attributed to the human capital that Black immigrants bring with them, as educated workers whose skills are in demand in the United States are recruited from countries such as Jamaica and Guyana. Black immigrants can be inserted directly into the middle class in cities such as New York, Miami, and Boston, where incomes are typically higher and more competitive. The relative good fortunes of educated immigrants is not universal, however: some Black teachers recruited from Caribbean countries have faced racial discrimination as employers' promises of equal wages and protected, long-term immigration status have been broken.[4] In general, Black immigrants' median household income is $11,000 higher than that of Black Americans, and a higher proportion of them are in the middle and upper-middle class.[5]

Black diasporic groups are also stratified internally, and intra-ethnic economic diversity shapes the social order of the middle-class Black diaspora, including their cultural identities and the places where they reside. José Itzigsohn (2009) argues that differences between and within nationality groups matter for how we analyze their incorporation into a racialized political economy. Complementary to racial capitalism frameworks, Itzigsohn contends that post-1965 immigrants of color experience "stratified ethnoracial incorporation"; that, is, they are inserted into different strata based on a host of socioeconomic and racial conditions and characteristics. These positions range from poor to affluent and are shaped by their human capital, finances, and social networks as well as by racism and colorism in America. Although all Black people confront a racially segmented economy, housing market, and educational system, the Black American, Haitian, and Jamaican diasporas have differing orientations to these systems. Moreover, cross-ethnic and intra-ethnic class heterogeneity affects how the members of the middle class see themselves and negotiate social inequality (Neckerman, Carter, and Lee 1999).

Black Americans' opportunities for upward mobility declined when New York's manufacturing sector contracted in the mid-twentieth century. They were largely excluded from the city's rapidly expanding and increasingly lucrative sectors, especially information technology and financial services. These shifts made unionized, public-sector employment a primary vehicle into the middle class for native-born Blacks. Many Jamaican immigrants were employed in the city's expanding education and health care industries. In a remarkable exception to the more prevalent gender hierarchy, many mothers, wives, and daughters led their families into the middle class through their employment as nurses and teachers. Many Black fathers, husbands, and sons confronted gendered anti-Black racism in the workplace from Whites and White ethnics. Some Haitians, too, entered the middle class through careers in the medical field. Compared to Jamaicans, they have had a more arduous socioeconomic journey, since they are not native English speakers. In addition, the Haitian diaspora faces higher barriers to mobility. They have had a poor context of reception from the state, the media, and private citizens in the United States, and a lower proportion of Haitians have been able to directly translate their human capital into corresponding jobs and earnings (Laguerre 1984, Portes and Rumbaut 2001, Stepick and Swartz 1998, Zephir 1996).

The historical and contemporary differences between the Black American, Haitian, and Jamaican groups shape how they are stratified by income. Jamaican immigrants exhibit higher median household incomes than Haitian immigrants and Black Americans with no recent foreign-born ancestry (see table 6). These immigrants' children and grandchildren inherit both resources and disadvantages across generations. The children of Jamaican and Haitian immigrants have higher median household incomes than those born abroad. Foreign-born Jamaicans and their US-born children have the highest household incomes. But the US-born adult children of Haitian immigrants exhibit greater intergenerational mobility, as their native English and US education enable them to escape the exclusion their parents faced in the labor market.

The differing socioeconomic profiles of Black American, Haitian, and Jamaican diasporas are reflected in the lives of Cascades and Great Park residents. Looking at distributions rather than averages reveals more nuances (figure 15). Compared to native-born Blacks with no recent for-

Table 6   Median Household Income by Ethnic and Pan-Ethnic Group, 2012

	Median Household Income	Mean Household Income	Managerial/ Professional (%)
African Americans	$40,425	$56,196	15.90
Haitian, 1st generation	$45,000	$60,078	15.80
Haitian, 2nd generation	$58,915	$67,316	25.49
Jamaican, 1st generation	$58,800	$72,745	27.16
Jamaican, 2nd generation	$63,484	$74,452	16.83
Other Caribbean	$43,000	$62,333	14.72
African Immigrant Groups	$51,512	$71,004	28.85

SOURCE: Current Population Survey (CPS) 2012.

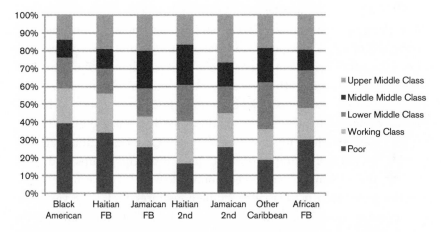

Figure 15. Class categories for Blacks by nationality and ancestry in the United States. Source: Current Population Survey (CPS) 2012.

eign-born ancestry and to Haitian and other Caribbean and African immigrants, US-born adults whose parents were Jamaican immigrants are also much more likely to be in the upper-middle class. Conversely, US-born Blacks and Haitian immigrants have the highest proportions of households that qualify as poor or working class. There is significant class bifurcation *within* the Haitian and Black American diasporas. They are both more bottom heavy than Jamaican immigrants. That disparity evens out in the next generations, however, as US-born adults of Jamaican and Haitian immigrant parentage are more evenly distributed across class categories. The higher concentrations of lower-income co-ethnics among Black Americans and Haitian immigrants may intensify intragroup tensions over class, and cross-class encounters may shape their cultural identities (Neckerman et al. 1999).

Although the differences in incomes across groups reflect the economic salience of nationality for Black people and have concrete implications for the identity work that happens during diasporic encounters, an intersectional analysis of their racial, gender, class, and nationality oppression is revealing (Collins 1999, Crenshaw 1990). For example, due to their labor force participation, West Indian women's earnings were similar to White women's, but the disparity between Black men and White men represented a severe racial-gender gap (Model 2008). This inequality reflects the continuing significance of racial and gender oppression in the economic life of Black diasporas and demonstrates that intra-Black and intra-ethnic socioeconomic heterogeneity exist simultaneously. The social construction of the pan-ethnic category "West Indian" is a misleading way to analyze socioeconomic experiences among the Black diaspora. Although this supra-national category is sometimes used to analyze quantitative data in studies that have too few cases of specific Caribbean ethno-national groups, the category lumps together quite different groups and thus obscures their distinct social and economic life worlds (Vickerman 1999). The disaggregation of this category demonstrates that class variation within and between Black nationality groups is key for understanding the cultural economies of their interior households.

Blackyards: All in the Family

The adults I interviewed spoke of homeownership as a sign that they had created stability and built a legacy for the families. Most of the homes I visited in Cascades and Great Park were owned by married couples, but a sizable proportion of households had a nontraditional makeup of single parents or multigenerational families. Incomes, resources, and wealth

were pooled and distributed differently based on the structure of my interviewees' homes.

The diversity of household types was an important feature of Black life
in diasporic suburbs. The structure and composition of family households
has long been a central factor in the debate over the influence of race and
class on the economic position of Black Americans. Many of these debates
have turned on entrenched images of Black social pathology, such as the
trope of the broken Black family.[6] In contrast to this culturally racist perspective and in keeping with analysis of Black family structures in the
context of global capitalism and migration (Chamberlain 2003, 2017;
Collins 1998), I found that diasporic Black middle-class households have
complex nuclear and extended family kinship structures that help, rather
than hinder, their stability. These household structures reflected the Black
families' experiences with global socioeconomic oppression; however,
they were also shaped by cultural beliefs about responsibility and love in
family settings brought forward from the common African roots of the
diaspora (Shimkin and Frate 1978). This finding challenges the conventional definition of the normative two-parent, heterosexual household
with children that is presumed to be the cornerstone of the suburban middle class.

Public and academic discourses often assume that middle-class families
who live in the suburbs are two-parent households and portray the Black
underclass as mired in poverty and stuck in "the ghetto" because these
households are headed by single mothers. However, almost one-third of
the families I spoke to were composed of unmarried mothers or fathers
with children. Their inheritances, incomes, and family organization facilitated middle-class lifestyles.[7] In Cascades and Great Park, single parent
families were most often headed by women, although I interviewed a few
single and divorced fathers as well. In many cases, single parents were living with their own parents or grandparents in addition to their children.

In light of the major demographic shifts that have taken place in the
late twentieth century, the culturally racist emphasis on Black family patterns as an explanation for their social immobility has been challenged,
yet the ideologies of Black pathology live on in public discourse and
assumptions about middle-class family patterns. The decline in marriage
rates that has occurred across racial groups should be attributed more to

the economic decline brought about by neoliberalism than to group cultural differences (Model 1991). Black women bear the burden of humiliation in these discourses on race, family and social policy (Harris-Perry 2011). Racial capitalism is gendered, and Black women across the diaspora have been segregated into service work in households and institutions. Since Emancipation ended unpaid labor, Black women's labor force participation rate has always been higher than that of White women, especially after they married and had children (Greenbaum 2015). When the women's liberation movement of the 1970s called for shifts in gender ideologies and the opening of lucrative job opportunities to women, middle-class White women, many of whom had been homemakers and relied on Black household help, entered the labor market and, for the first time in history, had labor force participation rates close to those of Black women (Cassiman 2007, 2008).

Black women in New York have long worked for low wages in service occupations for White households or institutions or engaged in entrepreneurial pursuits within the Black community (Goldin 1977). Since the mid-twentieth century, a number of them moved into higher-paying blue- or white-collar occupations, many of them fields in which women entering the labor force in unprecedented numbers predominated (Browne 1997; Tienda and Glass 1985). Coupled with the long-term rise in divorce rates and the recent decline in marriage rates, as well as shifting cultural norms around single parenthood, these trends are reshaping middle-class household structures. These family patterns are visible among the Black middle-class residents of Cascades and Great Park. When Haitian and Jamaican women arrive in the United States, they encounter Black American households with similar structures. While households headed by Black women in the Unites States have been subject to systematic attacks from slavery to current welfare policy, only recently are they attaining social legitimacy because of the labor of Black Feminists to resist White patriarchal ideologies about family structure (Collins 2002).

Black women enroll in and complete college at high rates.[8] Many educated middle-class Black women are independent, single, or divorced; they may or may not be raising children. These gendered dynamics were at play in everyday life in Cascades and Great Park. For example, Avril, a forty-five-year-old graduate of a historically Black college or university

(HBCU) and high school teacher who is the mother of a teenaged son, owns the Cascades home her parents passed down to her. Juanita, a forty-eight-year-old divorced, Black American tech manager, shares her Great Park home with her parents and three teenaged sons. Jean Michel, a fifty-eight-year-old Haitian scientist, is raising his teenaged children in the house he owns in Cascades. The assumption that all middle-class families have two parents is outdated, and perhaps has never been the norm among Black diasporic families. Like the concept of the middle class itself, this notion of the suburban family is a racial construct created by Whites to uphold their moral and cultural supremacy.

Intergenerational households, too, were common in Cascades and Great Park. Members of the Black diaspora have historically been more likely to live in extended family groups than Whites. The enduring legacy of slavery, colonialism, labor exploitation, and White tyranny are articulated through economic and housing discrimination to affect the composition and culture of Black homes. The presence of extended as well as immediate family members in households reflects Black kinship networks of emotional and economic support. Within diasporic suburbs, two-parent families lived next to mother-daughter pairs who shared a household and lived across the street from siblings who converted a single-family home into a duplex so they could live in separate households, but under one roof. These homes became transgeographical versions of the yards, lakous, and villages of the US South and the Caribbean. At the turn of the twenty-first century, over six million immigrants lived in multigenerational households.[9] Black and immigrant households tend to meet their needs for childcare and financial protection by pooling family resources (Model 1991, 2008). Even middle-class households were financially vulnerable, and cultural practices of shared familial support tended to make many Black households in Cascades and Great Park different from those of their White middle-class neighbors.

Household structure provides a glimpse into the home economies of diasporic suburbs. Antoinette, a Haitian nurse in her forties who resides in Great Park, flies her mother, Mary Paul, sixty-five, in from Haiti once or twice a year. When Mary Paul arrives, she lives in the finished basement of their Tudor-style home. Mary Paul is then able to go to the doctor for her annual checkup and watch over Antoinette's three children during school vacations while she and her husband are at work. In other households, adults share one- and two-family homes with their young children and aging parents year-round. The presence of grandparents shields the older generation from the financial stresses of aging and retirement, but it also serves the needs of parents whose long hours or multiple jobs require them to spend a significant amount of time away from home. Co-resident relatives are not only the most reliable source of childcare, but tend to share the parents' cultural values. Relying on a family member enables parents to avoid paying exorbitant childcare costs and gives them more income to devote to their children's other needs. Other strategies for maintaining household economic stability included renting out rooms or basements to family members or friends. Mr. Herbie and his wife, for example, rented a basement apartment from their cousins in Cascades while they saved money to purchase their own home nearby. Single parents, one parent and an adult child, siblings, and cousins from urban areas come together to purchase homes and improve their residential situation.

The other significant household pattern that existed among my respondents that calls for a rethinking of the dominant image of middle class suburban homes is the consistent presence of young adult children living with their parents.[10] The high costs of housing and schooling in New York mean that young adults who want to attend college or work in the city often stay at home well past the age of eighteen. After graduating, adult children continue to live in and contribute to the financial stability of the household. In other circumstances, their schooling or in-between jobs status make them adult dependents. Nationally, one-third of eighteen- to thirty-six-year-olds live in their parents' home; this arrangement is somewhat more common among Blacks than Whites.[11]

The diasporic Black middle class is characterized by a diversity of household arrangements, which are both a response to prevailing economic challenges and rooted in their cultural norms. Taken together, they require us to redefine how we understand middle-class families in twenty-first-century suburbia.

Location as Status

Neighborhood is as important an indicator of status as household income. In New York, saying that one lives on the Upper East Side or the South

Bronx conjures up distinct associations that are embedded in geographical racial and class inequalities. "Good neighborhoods" are equated with Whiteness and bad neighborhoods with Blackness and Latinx residents (Bonilla-Silva et al. 2006). The same notions are conveyed by living in urban versus suburban-like areas. Cascades and Great Park evoke images of elite and middle-class Black families living in large homes surrounded by manicured lawns. Black residents of other parts of the city perceive them as bona fide Black suburbs as do real estate agents who advertise homes in the area. Yet residents of these neighborhoods distinguish between Cascades, which is located in the borough of Queens and surrounded by diverse high- and low-income areas, and Great Park, which is in Nassau County and surrounded by predominately White middle-class and affluent suburban towns with peripheral pockets of low-income people of color.

In the imagination of many Black New Yorkers, Great Park is considered more elite than Cascades. Great Park's location on Long Island gives it a cache of both mystery and affluence. Often, the further east from the city center a neighborhood is, the more status and prestige it conveys. This ranking persists despite the fact that suburban towns in Nassau County are historically unequal and have some low-income enclaves. Manhattan's Upper East and West Sides and Brooklyn Heights are among the most affluent zip codes in the country, yet high-rise multimillion-dollar condominiums are located in close proximity to government subsidized, badly neglected housing projects in 'do or die' Bedford Stuyvesant and Queensbridge Houses. The ranking of neighborhoods has been complicated by gentrification of predominately Black and Latinx neighborhoods in New York since the 1990s, with the concentration of international investment in real estate development and the resulting displacement of Black residents to outer areas of the city and suburbs.

In a mental map of the Black residential hierarchy, lifelong New Yorkers and newcomers from the US South and the Caribbean have their own assessments of desirable places to live in a racially restricted housing market. Residents of Cascades, for example, see their area as a Black middle-class mecca. It's a desirable suburban place to raise a family within city limits. However, Great Park residents are more aristocratic in their renderings of their residential context. Their location in Nassau County helps them to define themselves as residents of a bona fide suburb, distant from the city and presumably the issues that plague it. They maintain this claim in spite of the fact that Great Park's population is now majority families of color, the result of the exodus of White residents since the 1990s. White ethnic communities on Long Island see Great Park's increasing racial heterogeneity as antithetical to the very reason why they and their parents moved to the suburbs in the first place: to create White-only spaces and uphold White power over resources and limit their children interracial interactions. This tension between Black people's desire to live in suburbs and White suburbanites' rejection of them is at the center of twenty-first-century battles over racial integration and my residents' everyday negotiation of race and status in Queens and Nassau county.

Certificates, Degrees, Diplomas?

A college degree is generally regarded as a vehicle to the attainment of middle-class status. In the information technology age, a bachelor's degree helps to secure adequate earnings, a career with benefits, and social stability. New York's job market is one of the most competitive in the nation. Entering a high-paying occupation requires advanced training with certified credentials or professional exams. Although a college degree may enable a person to find a secure foothold in the middle class, just taking college classes or obtaining formal (rather than on-the-job) training beyond high school can also be a ticket to the middle class for Black and Latinx individuals. They are more likely to have some college education than to have graduated with a four-year degree, and their educational attainment is reflected in their concentration in the lower- and middle-middle class.

The higher proportion of people with middle-class incomes than of people with college degrees indicates the discrepancy between educational attainment and earnings (see table 7). For example, just three-fifths of Whites hold a college degree, but more than two-thirds of their households belong to the middle class. This is also the case for Blacks: although two-fifths of Blacks have completed college, three times as many Black households belong to the middle class. Training past high school continues

Table 7   Socioeconomic Characteristics by Race and Ethnicity, United States, 2012

	Black	White	Latinx	Asian
Total Population	28,463,015	163,894,049	36,583,515	12,432,956
Median Family Income	$37,002	$63,550	$39,500	$65,606
Median Household Income	$42,000	$70,003	$46,420	$75,000
Lower-Middle Class ($30–$49,999)	19.5%	17.4%	23.9%	14.1%
Middle-Middle Class ($50-$99,000)	28.2%	32.9%	30.7%	31.7%
Upper-Middle Class ($100,000+)	14.7%	29.7%	15.5%	35.7%
Some College	30.1%	28.8%	22.1%	20.7%
College	18.0%	30.8%	12.1%	46.2%
Managerial/Professional	17.0%	25.9%	12.1%	29.5%

SOURCE: Current Population Survey, 2012.

to help Black families secure middle-class status. Nationally, almost one-fifth of Black people hold a college degree, while only one-eighth of Latinx people are college graduates. Asians and Whites have the highest proportions of college graduates and, correspondingly, the highest proportions of people in the upper-middle class.

Nationally, another 30 percent of the Black population have some college education. The proportions of native-born Blacks and Black immigrants in New York who have some formal education beyond high school mirror one another. New York's public higher education system has been a bastion of upward mobility for people of color. The City University of New York (CUNY) is one of the most expansive and affordable metropolitan college systems in the country and confers a range of associate's degrees. The CUNY system has been lauded for lifting generations of students and their families out of poverty and the working class. Children and grandchildren of the Great Migration and the Caribbean Migration who now live in Cascades and Great Park CUNY and the State University of New York (SUNY) as vehicles to higher education.[12] In the postindustrial economy, the attainment of an associate's degree or specialized training beyond

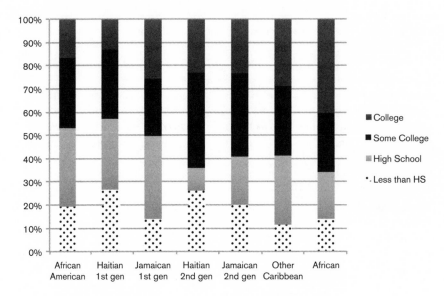

Figure 16. Educational attainment for Blacks by nationality and pan-ethnic group, 2012. Source: Current Population Survey (2012).

high school is an essential stepping-stone into decently paid professions. Although the leverage a two-year degree provides has decreased overtime, many Cascades and Great Park residents built middle-class lifestyles on the basis of these degrees in the 1980s and 1990s.

Educational attainment differs between Black Americans, Haitians, and Jamaicans. While a host of factors influence a person's ability to complete high school and college, these rates vary by both race and nationality. Barriers to education more acutely hinder Blacks' educational attainment, which in turn shapes their labor market outcomes. At the same time, group variations in educational patterns among Black New Yorkers also require exploration.

According to the Current Population Survey (2012), Jamaican immigrants are more than twice as likely as Haitian immigrants to have completed college. This disparity is in large part a result of the recruitment of educators and health care professionals from Jamaica since the 1960s, as well as Jamaicans' English-language skills. Some Jamaicans completed their education and began their careers on the island before moving to the United States. Haitians, by contrast, were less likely to have earned a college degree than US-born Blacks. Intergenerationally, the Haitian diaspora experienced an upward educational trajectory. While a smaller share of first-generation Jamaican adults have completed college compared to Jamaican immigrants, US-born adults of Jamaican immigrant parentage have lower proportions of college completion than the US-born adults of Haitian immigrant parentage.

More Blacks attain advanced training beyond high school than earn a college degree. For many families in this book, an associate's degree or training beyond high school has helped them gain access to desirable, well-paid occupations in accounting, nursing, teaching, and construction, affording them the opportunity to become middle class even though the quality of life for middle-class New Yorkers has sharply declined. A higher proportion of US–born Blacks have completed some college than either Haitian or Jamaican immigrants. The Haitian second generation, however, has a larger proportion of people who have completed some college than the other groups. A low proportion of US-born adults of Haitian immigrant parentage are in the working class; a relatively high proportion are in the middle-middle class. Differences in cross-ethnic and intergenerational educational attainment reflect the educational heterogeneity of Black Americans, Haitians, and Jamaicans. The status identities they articulate in their everyday interactions in New York shape and are shaped by these educational profiles.

Werk, Werk, Werk

Where people work and what job titles they hold are another key indicator of class position. White-collar occupations are seen as conferring middle-class status. Yet anyone who has spent time in Black communities knows that many people have developed multiple and creative ways of generating income and wealth inside and outside of the formal economy as a matter of sheer necessity. Racial and colonial capitalism in the United States and the Caribbean have historically suppressed Black mobility and wealth accumulation, requiring Black people to "make something out of nothing" or "make dollars out of cents." The diasporic Black middle class confronts these structural realities at multiple junctures. The governmentally mandated racial desegregation of the labor market since the 1960s and the shifts from a manufacturing-based to an information-based economy in the 1970s have reshaped the Black occupational structure. Black Americans sought new opportunities in a postindustrial economy where skilled, decently paid and stable occupations in communications, government, and business and finance required substantial educational qualifications for entry rather than training and promoting workers from within. The well-paid jobs that had created blue-collar aristocrats in nineteenth- and early twentieth-century Black communities declined, the number of high-paying professional and managerial jobs soared, and the lower-middle class found a precarious footing through white-collar occupations in the service sector.

New York's dominant global economic position makes it a place where astronomical amounts of wealth are accumulated and circulated, creating both opportunities and disadvantages for the city's Black middle class. As New York solidified its position as a "rich-tropolis" where $25 million is considered "economy-class rich," Wall Street financiers and entertainers have become superrich. Across the Brooklyn and 59th Street Bridges, the working professionals who comprise the city's middle class have incomes that have remained comparatively stagnant since the 1970s. This economic context has important implications for how we analyze occupation as a marker of status for the diasporic Black middle class. Although racial discrimination in the labor force has declined over the past forty years, the neoliberal economy has created new modes of exclusion along racial, gender, ethnic, and class lines. This process is matched by chronic poverty and the reduction of pathways to mobility out of poverty such as public education and redistributive public policies.

In this tricky context, Black diasporic groups have used different occupational and sectoral niches in order to get ahead in a racially constrained, anti-black, and anti-immigrant labor market. The Black American middle class relies largely on public sector employment. The "good government job" has provided the incomes and security that have given Black families across the country a solid foothold in the middle class. But this is largely the story of US-born Blacks; their birthright citizenship has given them access to civil service occupations that are closed to noncitizen immigrants. A combination of long waiting lists, the privatization of services and the attacks on unions decreases the prospects for public sector work for native-born and naturalized Black workers and their children.

The expansion of the private and nonprofit health care industry since the 1970s has offered significant employment opportunities for Black New Yorkers. Black immigrants have historically worked in schools, hospitals or homes (Foner 2001, Model 2008). Those working in hospitals have been able to secure well-paying, unionized occupations that allowed them to enter the middle class alongside their native-born counterparts (Greer 2013). In 1990, Suzanne Model (2008) found that among native-born Blacks in New York, one-quarter of men and almost one-third of women worked in the public sector. In contrast, over one-third of foreign-born Black women were clustered into health professions, and one in five worked in private hospitals as registered nurses, respiratory therapists, anesthesiologists, record managers, or chefs. By 2012, the proportion of foreign-born Blacks in health care had declined slightly. In terms of nationality differences, one-fifth of Haitians and Jamaicans compared to one-tenth of African Americans worked in health care (CPS, 2012). Others worked in the financial sector as accountants, bankers, executive assistants, and analysts. Some were information technology specialists. Still others were metro transit workers, small business owners, and church employees.

In the field, it became clear that the occupational patterns of married, cohabiting, and intergenerational households were also complex. Family members held jobs that might conventionally assign them to different classes. For example, in many cases women held white- or pink-collar jobs in gender-segregated fields, while their husbands clocked in and out of blue-collar jobs everyday (Vickerman 1999). For example, Paula, a Black American banker in her fifties, was married to Tony, a Black American school bus driver. Tony had worked for his bus company since the 1980s and recalled a time when the Irish dominated the occupation and Blacks in the city had a hard time "getting in." They have owned their home in Cascades since the 1980s and were close to paying off their thirty-year mortgage. They raised three children in their detached, single-family Tudor home. They planned to sell their house and move to Atlanta to join their eldest child in a couple of years, after their youngest was settled in college. Other couples included the following wife-husband combina-

tions: nurse and mechanic; counselor and foreman; and analyst and deliv-
eryman. Given the gender differential in wages, some of these men with
blue-collar jobs might have earned as much as or even more than their
female partners with white-collar jobs. In an intergenerational Black
American household, a grandmother was a teacher, a grandfather was a
business owner, and a daughter was a banker. Through my observations
and conversations with residents of Cascades and Great Park, I discovered
that white-collar employment was too simple a requirement for being
considered middle class. Instead, Black households gained middle-class
incomes through complex and varied pathways.

Side Hustles

Examining occupations alone conceals the various streams of income that
enable middle class families to survive and thrive. Many parents shared
that they had flows of income from outside their main occupations.
During my time in the field, I was invited to meetings that encouraged
multinational Black families to engage in entrepreneurship and investment in order to liberate themselves from debt and gain financial freedom
from their full-time jobs. For example, people had one regular job that
provided a regular income and benefits, but they also had "side hustles"—
economic activities that generated additional income to pay for the needs
and wants of the household. Home improvement projects, a newer car,
private school tuition, sports or music lessons, summer camps, travel back
home, or remittances were often supported by side hustles.

Mary-Josette, a Haitian woman in her fifties, owned a beauty salon but
was also a part-time social worker. Other parents held one full-time and
another part time job, worked multiple shifts at the same job, or engaged
in seasonal work. One Haitian father of two was employed as a hospital
manager but also prepared tax returns from January to mid-April for family and friends. Some nurses worked their regular hospital shifts but conducted visits to homebound sick and elderly patients during the weekend
through private agencies. Teachers taught summer or night school to
upgrade their kitchen cabinets or to "bless" their grandchild with a formal
first communion celebration. Full-time home contractors did projects for
friends or family during the weekends. Financial managers hosted invest-

ment meetings in their living rooms to advertise lucrative schemes (some-times pyramid schemes) to potential investors. I met a Black American social worker who spent her evenings and weekends preparing cakes and catering desserts for birthdays, christenings, anniversaries, graduations, and showers of relatives, church family, friends, and a growing clientele in Brooklyn and Queens. The Black diasporic middle class responded to the limits of their take home pay from formal work by harnessing their talents to earn more income in informal settings. This strategy was in part a response to the economic squeeze imposed by the Great Recession, but it also belongs to a long tradition of "making ends meet" by Black families who have been historically locked out of a White-dominated economy.

This middle-class hustle was acutely apparent when I attempted to sched-ule interviews with working parents whose availability was limited. At a local church, one young adult shared her father's contact information with me but commented: "Good luck reaching him. He ain't never home, him and my mom, they always working." This pattern is different from the stereotype of the White middle-class family, in which both parents hold nine-to-five jobs and are home in time every night to eat dinner with their children. The eight-hour workday has vanished in the highly competitive, constantly con-nected work environment created by the neoliberal economy if it ever existed in large scale at all. For Black diasporic families in particular, who have always had to do the "patchwork" necessary to survive in an anti-Black econ-omy, the Great Recession required them to "werk, werk, werk" in order not to fall out of the middle class.

Western Union, C.A.M., and Moneygram: Domestic and International Remittances

An important feature of middle-class lifestyles in Black diasporic suburbia is the transfer of money from one's home economy to family, friends, associ-ates, and institutions both here and in their hometown or country. Although US-born Blacks with no recent foreign-born ancestry and those born abroad employ similar systems of extending support to their lower-income counterparts nationally and internationally, this activity is seldom recog-nized as a symptom of the economic constraints that are systematically imposed on Black families. The need for Black migrant and immigrant families to provide domestic and international remittances to the villages they have left behind demonstrates the cultural duties and expectations that they negotiate in everyday life. The diasporic Black middle-class experience mirrors that of Asians and Latinx immigrants, who also send large amounts of money home to support families and communities.

These practices of helping low-income family members are conventionally separated into two categories, international remittances and domestic social support. US-born middle-class Blacks have a higher proportion of family members who need financial assistance than Whites. "Informal forms of social support are important in the Black community. . . . Extended family members serve as key bastions of psychological and economic assistance, providing emotional support, money, childcare, housing, and food to their relatives when necessary" (Chiteji and Hamilton 2002, 9). The data on Black immigrants is less clear. Remittances to the Black Caribbean amount to billions every year, which suggests that Black immigrants provide economic support to family and friends in much the same fashion as Black Americans. The White American portrait of the middle class hinders us from seeing the true colors of Black family economic interdependence, as love, support, and obligation are transferred between and within the households of the middle-class Black diaspora and siblings, parents, aunts, uncles, and cousins in need.

The culture of social support that characterizes the diasporic Black middle class is reflected in the neighborhood institutions found in Cascades and Great Park. The vitality of kinship and ethnic ties expressed through remittance centers is shared across native and foreign-born groups. The Jamaican and Haitian diasporas' provision of family support is especially visible, while the exchange of money by Black Americans within the nation-state is a more covert transaction. For example, Ricky, a Black American educator and Great Park resident, deposited money into his Aunt Beverley's bank account to pay for his nephew's football camp in Virginia. For immigrants, financial transfers to family members take on different forms. In Cascades and Great Park, residents frequent local supermarkets or storefront businesses that specialize in transporting goods and transferring capital to their home country. Billboards on Cascades Boulevard advertise "Send Money Home." At bus stops, colorful Caribbean themed Digicel posters offer immigrants the chance to "send minutes" to the cellphone of family members back home.

On a Saturday afternoon in Cascades in June 2011, a six-foot-tall brown skinned man with dreadlocks down his back and wearing tan construction boots carries large blue cargo barrels to his White Escalade SUV. He has a red-and-black Trinidadian flag hanging from his rearview mirror. He will likely fill the barrels with food and clothing items that his younger siblings, nieces or nephews in Trinidad need for the new school year. These barrels are widely used by Caribbean immigrants to ship goods to loved ones in their home country, where crushing rates of inflation make them too expensive to purchase. Supermarkets across Cascades and Great Park sell barrels; sometimes they are sold out during the holiday season. The Haitian-run Marianni's Market sells Haitian spices, calling cards, music CDs, and *paysans*-style clothing. The market is certified by C.A.M., the quintessential moneygram business for the Caribbean. C.A.M customers pay a nominal fee to wire money back home.

The blue plastic bins and money transfer businesses in Cascades and Great Park facilitate a social and economic support system by which the diasporic Black middle class assists lower-income family members. These remittances make them entirely distinct from the White middle class. Therefore, it is not only how people make money, how much money they make, their accumulated wealth, or the prestige of their neighborhood that define them as middle class. In this Black diasporic community, one's ability to use the money they earn to support others in their networks in New York, the US South, and the Caribbean abroad attests to their status. Providing support to others in their kin and social networks is a form of altruism that is both more intimate and more demanding than the charitable donations that yield tax deductions to the White middle class.

Some researchers say that members of the Black middle class evade association with poor Black people and neighborhoods in an attempt to assert their class standing. This conclusion is, at best, incomplete, since many Black families are economically diverse and those who have higher earnings provide financial and material support to those who do not. In addition to taking care of their aging parents, siblings who are college educated share household space, ideas, responsibilities for children, and hopes for the future with those who did not fare as well socioeconomically. I observed the intimate interdependence between the Black middle class and their cousins, nieces, and nephews who needed a financial boost, near or far. This cross-class connection among kin requires sociologists to reorient their thinking about the relationship between the Black diasporic middle class and lower income individuals in their social network.

My interviwees were not seeking escape from poorer people who shared their ethnoracial background, nor were they worried that assisting their relatives would threaten their social status. In communities characterized by tightly knit networks of social support, someone like Tara, a fifty-two-year-old Black American lawyer from Great Park, would alienate loved ones if she withheld assistance from her grandmother. Tara's parents were absent from her life, and her grandmother had raised and supported her in Harlem. Now that her grandmother needs help to make ends meet on her fixed income, she says, "I will do everything to help her. I would not be where I am today if it was not for my grandmother." Peter, a fifty-three year old Jamaican Cascades teacher believed it important to help his little brother Jeffrey finish school in Jamaica since it was going to take over a decade for him to be considered for residency in the United States. Peter sends Jeffrey money every semester so he can complete his education.

The pervasive notion that the Black middle class wants to rid itself of ties to low-income Blacks ignores the interdependence that exists between family members who have long and deep intergenerational ties that bind them socially, morally, and economically. While escaping financial responsibility might allow individuals to accumulate money, fulfilling what were regarded as the obligations of kinship and friendship earned them reputations as a person who "gives back" or who hasn't "forgotten where they come from." This inevitably also leads them to be taken advantage of, for petty jealousies to arise and strained relationships to emerge. These cultural and emotional expectations animate the lives of Black Americans, Haitians, and Jamaicans in ways that are important for understanding their cultural identities and encounters with one another.

CALLALOO ECONOMIES

A diasporic lens on the cultural economies of Black middle-class households elucidates the complexities of status among people who have been shaped, both similarly and differently, by the long history of slavery, colonialism, and imperialism in the United States and the Caribbean. Exploring the cultural diversity and class stratification among the ethnonational groups that comprise the Black diasporic groups in this chapter has demonstrated that peoples with deep historical commonalities of slavery, empire, and colonialism have heterogeneous cultural economies. Utilizing Itzigsohn's framework of stratified ethnoracial incorporation, this chapter has analyzed both the intra-ethnic and cross-ethnic diversity of middle-class Black Americans, Haitians, and Jamaicans.

On income and education indicators, Jamaican immigrants consistently had more favorable positions than Black Americans and Haitian immigrants. Jamaican professionals were often recruited from the island nation and inserted into the American middle class as nurses and teachers. They are not only tokenized by White employers, but are also shown preferential treatment compared to Black Americans. The concentration of Jamaicans in major cities like New York may also contribute to their higher incomes. Black Americans' middle-class occupations are largely in the public sector, although they work in a wide variety of fields ranging from education and law enforcement to transportation. Haitian immigrants, too, attained middle-class status through health care occupations, but they did this from the bottom up because English was not their first language. Many of the people I interviewed did not have a four-year college degree but, instead, became middle class at a time when their postsecondary training could help them attain middle-class earnings, a home and comfortable lifestyles. My observations in middle-class homes demonstrated that multigenerational and single-parent households were important features in the mosaic of the Black suburban middle class. In all ethnonational groups, too, Black middle-class families patched together multiple sources of income from regular jobs and side hustles to maintain their position in a fluctuating global economic market. These characteristics shape how these groups articulate culture and negotiate their racial and class situations.

Space was an important incubator of class and status, as Great Park had a higher concentration of middle- and upper-middle-class families than Cascades and its residents ranked it above Cascades in the status hierarchy. Yet, amid the racialized economy that generated constant change in suburban as well as urban spaces, families of color have become the majority of its population. That trend, coupled with the insecurity created by the Great Recession, may put its future social standing in jeopardy, affecting the Black middle-class families for whom buying a house on Long Island epitomized success.

Despite the stratification within and between ethnonational groups, all participated in the culture of domestic and international remittances. Beyond their income and consumption patterns, strong systems of financial and social support for loved ones near and far were a key part of the Black diaspora's middle-class cultural repertoire.

In the next chapter, we move from a social-structural analysis to a more phenomenological exploration of how Black Americans, Haitians, and Jamaicans articulate belonging in New York's middle-class suburbs through the prism of their migration histories. Theoretically, the Black middle class uses place as well as class identities to assert their belonging (Feagin and Sikes 1994, Lacy 2007). However, the lived experiences of class and status for diasporic Black people on the move is less clear. How does class identity take shape for Black migrants and immigrants? Their trans-geographical definitions of status and color impact their class identities, therefore, the subsequent chapter employs a longitudinal approach to understand how social class is articulated among Black migrants who come from different systems of racialized and neocolonial capitalism. In tandem with remittances, they influence the culture of stratification systems in their places of origin as well as bring transgeographical politics of mobility to their suburban pockets of the New York.

5 Fish Soup

CLASS JOURNEYS ACROSS TIME AND PLACE

Immigrant life may be interpreted in terms of continuity
rather than disruption, and rerootedness rather than
uprootedness.

Michel Laguerre (1998)

I became acquainted with Fritzner, an elderly Haitian man, during one
of my first weeks as a volunteer at the Caribbean Center for Change
(CCC) in Cascades. He had a striking appearance, as his mocha-colored
complexion contrasted sharply with his salt and pepper hair. People
affectionately called him NeNe. Judging by his wrinkles and crisp dress
pants, NeNe was in his seventies, but his energy level, sharp mind, and
wit were those of a much younger man. He was referred to as the "Granpa"
of the organization and the neighborhood block. When the afterschool
children rushed into the office, they would stop to greet NeNe. Hugs
around his waist or small hands tugging at his leg or arm were met
with his smile. He would tap the children on the head or put both of
his hands on their shoulders and ask them in a warm accent: "Did you
do good in school today? Are you going to listen to your teacher,
Mrs. Janvier?"

One Thursday afternoon I walked into the office to prepare for elementary school students that would soon be running in the door. The afterschool program started at 3:00 and officially ended at 5:30, but most days
the last parents picked up their children at 6:00. NeNe was engaged in
bay blag as he fixed the constantly jammed copy machine. The women

who worked in the office were his audience, hyping him up with their laughter and responses. *Bay blag* is a Haitian term for playful storytelling. It can range from the dozens, gossip, and jokes to metaphors, proverbs, or tales that teach moral lessons. These stories often stem from real-life encounters and experiences but can also be fictional. Today's topic was the role of social class in the Haitian diaspora.

I walked in as NeNe was sharing his perspective on the class condition of the Haitian diaspora. He had been fired up by *nouvèl dirèk*, direct news from a family friend. The first story was of a middle-class woman who had migrated from Haiti to Queens. She was from a prominent family in Haiti and had studied law. Like many well-off households in Haiti, she grew up with servants who ranged from women who lived in the house, serving as nannies and cooks, to young boys who were *jeran lakou*, or yard keepers.[1] This woman fell on hard times in New York because she could not find adequate work. She eventually married a Haitian man who abused her. After years of mistreatment, the husband told his wife that he abused her because he was a yard keeper for her family when he was a young boy. Abusing her was revenge for his exploitation by her family. The fact that this woman did not recognize her partner as someone who once worked for her family suggests that he and his work had been invisible to her. The continuation of this invisibility placed her in the way of his revenge. Back home, community and family networks uphold the class and status hierarchy. Migration both disrupts and intensifies this class stratification system, leading to complicated identities and interactions within the Haitian diaspora.

CCC staff were from across the diaspora, but NeNe spoke to three Haitian women employees who sat at their desks shaking their heads and saying "*Ki Sa?*" (What?) to the surprising developments in the story, NeNe firmly stated:

> *Ayitian c'est un poisson craze nan un bouillion.*
> *Nan NY, C'est comme ci. Bam di nou.*
> *C'est un respe nou te gayan ayiti.*
> *Te gain un distinction.*
> *Icit pa gen sa mem.*
> *C'est plusiers poisson craze lan bouillon.*
> *Un soup de poisson*

Ou pa konnen ki pwason ki oubyen sa k' pa bon
Ou pa konn ki moun ki bon, ki moun ki pa bon
Tout moun al travay, y'ap fè lajan, youn pa gen respè pou lòt.

Haitians are mashed up fishes in a soup.
In New York, it's like this. Let me tell you.
There was a level of respect that we had in Haiti.
There was distinction.
Here, there is nothing like that.
It's all these fish mashed up into the soup.
It's fish soup.
You don't know which fish is a good fish, or which fish is a bad one.
You don't know who are the good people, or who are the bad people.
Everyone goes to work. They are making money. One doesn't have
    respect for the other.

Yon soup pwason, fish soup, is a metaphor for the class heterogeneity of Black diasporic suburbs. They are comprised of people of different qualities, flavors, and desirability from the perspective of people who see themselves as part of the Haitian bourgeoisie but now live in a middle-class community that they believe is not comprised of *their kind of people*. Haitian immigrants grew up in diverse and segmented class worlds on the island, but the bourgeoisie, *petit bourgeoisie*, working class, peasant class and *pòv* intermix in unorthodox ways when they arrive in New York. The migration and upward mobility of agricultural or domestic workers alongside members of the elite and middle class has led to complicated class distinctions within the Haitian diaspora. NeNe's aristocratic critique offers a glimpse into the perspective of those who considered themselves elite and desired to remain separate from people in lower class categories. The same attitude is expressed in the respectability politics of Black Americans who are considered "uppity" and Jamaicans who are regarded as "hitey-titey" by those who belong to groups they regard as their social inferiors. To them, class is not something you can buy with household incomes, homes, cars, or nice clothes. Activating French-style colonial beliefs, Haitian elites in the diaspora believe that class is "breeded,"—that is, it is inherited, passed down, acquired over multiple generations. This was a process of creating a closed circle of self-interested elites who were indifferent to the *noir* masses (Nicholls, 1996; Trouillot, 1990). The politics of class belonging are shaped by the evolution of Haiti's stratification structures and their families' position within it. Their understanding of belonging in the middle class in New York reflects their class origins in their home country and the colonial stratification structure that prevailed during their coming of age process.

NeNe described the process by which fish soup is created in diasporic suburbs.

> Let me explain how you make this fish soup. It's a French soup. You go to the market, and they will have all kinds of fish there. They take the fish and then they fillet it and sell it to the people. But people who want to make this fish soup, this is what you do. You go to this market and they will have the fish head and other pieces people don't want. If you are a chef, you will buy it. You boil it, then you strain it, take the fish head out. Then all you have is the broth. You put a square bread piece on it, then cheese, put it in the oven. There, voila, *soup de poisson*. But the customer, when they drink the soup, they don't know what fish you used to make the soup because they are all mashed up and boiled together and then taken out. This is what the Haitian community is, a mélange of people but you don't know where they are coming from.
>
> The fish are mashed up in this soup. Let me give it to you exactly. In Haiti, there were people who did domestic work. They were illiterate, people who were poor. You would have maids and property overseers. Haitians had a *grad* (status). Then that person takes a boat, and then they come here; they enter the U.S. These are people who sweep the yards. They start making money and they think it is everything. You are working, and they are working now too. They become arrogant. You can tell when they are in the area over here, talking loud for everyone to hear them. They don't have class, but they have money now. They are *verbale* 'cause they are lower class and illiterate. They think because they are making money now, that we are all the same. We are not the same. Even the Haitian people who come here and are making minimum wage, they look back at people who are struggling in Haiti with pity. They think they can do whatever they want because they have money.

NeNe continued explaining how a colonial dish symbolizes the class remixture of the Haitian diaspora just as children shuffled to the back room where the afterschool program was held. What had started off as a humorous story became a heated exchange. A debate erupted as two of the social workers contended that, although NeNe had a point, he was too harsh in his judgments of Haitians who transcend economic hardship through immigration.

NeNe represents gatekeepers of the Haitian middle class, benevolent in his desires to serve the diaspora through community engagement, but drawing harsh, bright boundaries between social classes. He was speaking from the perspective of someone who has been in the United States for decades; many like him were political exiles during the Duvalier regime. They were successful business owners, educators, and politicians in Haiti; they became nurses, social workers, entrepreneurs, nonprofit administrators or bankers in New York's Black middle class. NeNe's metaphor for diasporic suburbia drew from his experiences and those of other Haitian middle-class people who lament that their country's class stratification system does not define social relations here. NeNe moved to New York in the 1970s, when the Haitian diaspora consisted mainly of the country's elite. The bourgeoisie was composed of mulatto, fair skinned, French-speaking, and educated people. NeNe saw himself as a member of this cohort. They had the resources to purchase homes in Queens, and a number of them also managed rental properties in Brooklyn (Laguerre, 1984) to generate income. Over four decades, NeNe has watched as newer waves of Haitians have arrived in New York, become middle class and bought homes in Queens and on Long Island by pooling resources, saving money in local banks, participating in a sou sou (savings club), obtaining credentials, and finding niches in the labor market. Cascades and Great Park are suburban soup bowls of many fish as waves of Haitians from different class strata have redefined what it means to belong to the diaspora's middle class. They also restructure Haiti's class, gender, and color hierarchies through circular migrations, media communication, and remittances.

The fish soup metaphor for the heterogeneous class origins of Haitians in New York mirrors the identities and boundary work of my Black American and Jamaican interviewees. Based on interviewees' self-described childhood socioeconomic characteristics (parental occupation, household size, availability of resources, and schooling) I derived general categories of growing up poor, working class, middle class, or bourgeois. This chapter takes us deeper into the lived experience of class and status across time and space for my interviewees. In this context, the term *diaspora* is both a descriptive label and a process of class and status renegotiation. Coming from the class stratification system of New York, the US South, Haiti, or Jamaica to that of New York requires migrants to manage class and status norms here and there in tandem and reconcile the tensions between them. The diverse class origins of the Black residents of middle-class suburbs shape identity and boundary work in their encounters. An individual's class identity is colored by their childhood status and the changing classes and statuses they occupied during their arduous journeys to middle-class suburbs.

NEVER SEE, COME SEE: POLICING MIDDLE-CLASSNESS TRANS-LOCALLY

It is no secret that middle-class Black people create and challenge class boundaries in everyday life. They are pressured to convey their status in their interactions with White society in order to lessen the likelihood of racial discrimination (Anderson 1999, Feagin and Sikes 1994, Lacy 2007, Pattillo-McCoy 1999). This boundary work allows them to create important class distinctions in their cross-racial interactions with Whites and assert cultural and moral identities. How are these class distinctions articulated by the myriad of nationality groups that are a part of the Black diaspora? How have their migrations reshaped their sense of class status? How do they articulate class identities in their encounters with co-ethnics and other Black ethnic groups?

At the turn of the twentieth century, Du Bois elucidated the class heterogeneity of Philadelphia's Black community. In *The Philadelphia Negro* (1899) he identified a four-strata class system. Less than fifty years after the emancipation of nearly four million Black people, Du Bois believed it his mission to build knowledge about the racial problems diverse groups of Blacks faced and to heighten the sense of urgency and moral responsibility among affluent Blacks for the progress of Black society. These debates within Black civil society intensified during the Great Migration, when the old Black aristocracy in cities such as Chicago, New York, and Philadelphia felt ambivalent about the large number of Black southerners who were arriving from the rural and urban South whom they perceived as having lower levels of education, lacking usable skills, and displaying unrefined manners. The Black middle class built educational and social institutions to "uplift" the rapidly expanding Black migrant population. At the same time, racially segregated and barred from political and economic power in the White world, the Black middle class created sharp class distinctions between themselves and the very people who were the clientele of their businesses and the target population of their benevolent organizations (Chatelain 2015).

After the 1960s, the relationship between the Black bourgeoisie, the middle class, and the poor continued to be marked by both interdependence and insidious distinctions, but in more complex ways. The Black middle class expanded beyond the fair-skinned bourgeoisie with inherited money to include those who gained upward mobility through education and jobs in the public and financial sectors. This shift was compounded by the outmigration of the Black middle class to peripheral areas of cities and the suburbs (Wilson 1987). As the Black population became increasingly bifurcated between the truly disadvantaged and the middle class, it also became more geographically segregated than ever before.

The suburbanization of the Black middle class led to its eventual reincorporation into an apartheid residential structure (Pattillo-McCoy 1999; Massey and Denton 1993). As members of the middle class interact with low-income families in proximal low-income Black neighborhoods, they construct sharp class boundaries. The Black middle class is also stratified internally, with elite middle-class people creating social distinctions between themselves and core middle-class families (Lacy 2007). These boundaries are based on the racial composition and quality of their neighborhood, how they maintain their properties, their comportment, and their approach to childrearing. Although Black elite middle-class families engage in strategic assimilation by limiting their interaction with the White world and immersing themselves in the social activities of the Black world when possible, they feel that they have a superior social status to Black people who earn less than they do (Lacy, 2007).

Members of the Black middle class are constantly engaged in asserting and defending their claims to social status. Although Whites in the United States think of their society as a color-blind meritocracy, countless examples in everyday life demonstrate that most Whites assume that Black people are poor, criminal, and from ghetto environments until they prove otherwise (Anderson 2011, 2015; Feagin and Sikes 1994). Black people who want their status to be recognized must perform and display the markers of middle-classness as they traverse White and multiracial spaces.

These markers include styles of dress and speech patterns that the White middle class approves of. This strategic display of middle-class identity is an effort to protect themselves from White racism and fit in. Black people's middle classness is unstable and vulnerable, highlighting the long standing and peculiar position of Black people in racial capitalism (Feagin and Sikes 1994, Robinson 1983).

Stratification within the Black middle class is further complicated by the fact that it is comprised of various diasporas who have heterogenous class backgrounds, histories, and experiences with racism (Feagin and Sikes 1994). Black Americans, Haitians, and Jamaicans come from societies that have distinct racial formations and class stratification systems but now live within a common, racially segmented economic, occupational, and residential spaces. How do they negotiate class and status in light of their trans-geographical experiences? What aspects of class matter to them? How do they reconcile their class past, present, and future? This chapter shows that people both create continuity and renegotiate status across space and time. Their class repertoires are fundamentally transnational and transregional, and they forge class identities and boundaries that help them make sense of their place in hierarchies both here and there. The cultural codes around class and status shift across time and space. Migration transforms their class relations both in their suburbs and in the places from which they come (Laguerre 1998, Levitt 2001).

One of the important and hidden ways in which migrants engage in constructing class boundaries lies outside of the tensions within the middle class and between them and low-income groups. Important fault lines are based on whether their childhood status matches their present occupation and income. A person's class upbringing, not their income or ability to purchase a home, is a key marker of middle-class belonging. Having money, nice cars, or fancy clothes is not enough. Those who consider themselves gatekeepers of middle-class status argue that a middle-class upbringing is required, and it takes generations before a family is recognized as accepted members. This distinction is enforced by those who see themselves as born and bred in upper-middle-class networks. Many of these people are from the Black bourgeoisie in the United States, Haiti, and Jamaica. They seek to maintain the privileged status they enjoyed in their childhood. Others seek to create themselves anew by transcending or entirely erasing their class origins. This strategy sometimes helped those who generated their wealth from criminal activities to quietly blend in with people they may have persecuted in their places of origin.[2]

Migration is a tool of the politically and economically oppressed. It's used by Black migrants to temper the devastations created by a racialized neoliberal global economy. Upper-status migrants may choose to conceal their affluent background in order to protect themselves from scrutiny, ridicule, or discomfort. Those of bourgeois, middle-class, and low-income origins work both to uphold and to dismantle a transgeographical class system based on their social and cultural needs in Black diasporic spaces. Boundaries are not passively maintained or straightforward. Instead, the system is constantly challenged and contested by those who have "moved on up" but were deemed outsiders within (Collins, 1986). This process is also complicated by the loss of status as a result of migration and entrance into the American brand of racial caste. In the next section, we explore the class journeys of Black Americans, Haitians, and Jamaicans and unpack the boundary work involved in re-rooting and re-creating their class and status norms and positions with co-ethnics in diasporic suburbia.

CLASS JOURNEYS

Movin' on Up

Ernest's journey to middle-class suburbia followed a trajectory known in the hip-hop community as "starting from the bottom." If judged by NeNe's standard, Ernest would be considered a poor fish in the soup bowl who has blended in. By Ernest's own standard, however, he was deserving of respect and recognition despite being a new member of the middle class. Now a community organizer in Cascades and a married father of two, Ernest, forty-eight, recalled that during his childhood he did not have as many toys or clothes, or even as much food as some of his friends. His struggles as a child were layered by the physical and emotional absence of his parents. "Our mother walked out on us. And my father was drowning in alcoholism," Ernest explained. Ernest's paternal grandparents stepped in to raise him, his six siblings, and two adopted cousins. His grandparents, who were in their sixties at the time, had five grown children who had fallen prey to alcoholism or abandoned their own children. He, his siblings, and their cousins shared three bedrooms in an ordinary house in rural South Carolina. "My grandparents . . . had built the house, which was nothing fancy," Ernest commented.

In retrospect, Ernest revealed that the most challenging part of his upbringing was his longing for parental bonds, not their lack of adequate food, clothing, shelter, and financial resources. His grandparents struggled to provide for their grandchildren in the stagnant economy of the rural South, which many of their relatives and friends had left behind to seek better lives in New York, Chicago, and Philadelphia. Ernest's memories of his grandparents elucidate the racial barriers that confined them to a perpetual state of economic insecurity and deprivation.

> My grandmother was a cook and a homemaker while she had to, as was necessary because of segregation, she cooked for Whites basically. And she kept her own home. My grandfather was a handyman in the true sense of the word. He knew how to do everything. He knew how to do gardening, he knew how to do some auto mechanics, electricity, plumbing, carpentry. . . . I think, in an ideal set of circumstances things could have been different for my grandfather. If it wasn't for his circumstances, he would have owned a farm, or he would have been a Baptist preacher. Or a combination of both.

South Carolina's racial caste system denied Ernest's grandparents any possibility for mobility and prosperity; it also destroyed his father's life. It was rumored that ongoing abuse by White men on the other side of town where he worked traumatized Ernest's father and pushed him into a downward spiral of alcoholism. Ernest's memories of his grandparents' struggle to raise their grandchildren left a lasting impression on his understanding of class, status, and his place in the social hierarchy, as well as his conviction that Black people's potential was often thwarted by their racially constrained circumstances.

Ernest grew up during the civil rights movement, and his journey from rural poverty in the South to the middle-class suburbs of New York was partly the result of generations of Black political struggle for desegregated schools. Through extra-familial networks in his town, Ernest went to an elite boarding school and later attended an Ivy League college and graduate school. In boarding school, he always felt like the "poor Black kid in rich White places." One of the few Black children who integrated the school, he befriended his White classmates. One year, his White room-mate invited him to Thanksgiving dinner in his family's large, thickly car-peted, lavishly furnished apartment in Manhattan. It was during this visit that fifteen-year-old Ernest had come to terms with his humble begin-nings. He could not afford a flight to New York, so he spent the entire day traveling there on a bus. The visit helped craft Ernest's repertoire around class. He rejected status distinctions and repudiated people in higher-income positions who sought to place him in an inferior category because of his upbringing.

> I knew we were poor compared to the way friends of mine lived in the South. But I had no idea how poor we were. Until I came to Manhattan and I saw wealth. But even in seeing the opulence, . . . I still just didn't know my place. I took literally, and I take literally, that I am a child of God and that that is enough. And I do not bow to any man. That's why if I have to face the Prince of Saudi Arabia and Kuwait today, and I have something to say, then I got to say what I got to say.

Ernest's upbringing in a deeply religious community helped him develop spiritual tools for negotiating socially constructed class distinc-tions. His coming of age was marked by class ascent and constant expo-sure to the life of the "other half." Ernest made sense of this class mobility as meaningful only in the material world. However, he believed it was irrelevant in the spiritual world. He repeatedly stated that he "didn't know his place" and refused to be categorized as less than others simply because he was the first in his family to enter the middle class. His belonging to the middle-class suburb he lived in and worked to improve could not be questioned. It would, perhaps, be easy for gatekeepers of middle-classness in diasporic suburbs to see Ernest as an imposter. He did not have the right family background, skin color, or pedigree. However, Ernest "talks back" to those who try to police the boundaries around class and status by using his identity as a child of God as the ulti-mate equalizer.

Education and occupational status may be indicators of class position, but people's journeys into the middle class shape their class identities and belonging in ways that affect how they interface with middle-class and affluent Whites and Blacks. Emerging from a poor or working-class childhood often meant that Black people challenged the bright class lines set before them by White, Latinx, Asian, and other Black people, and instead evoked more democratic ideals to claim their belonging and sometimes delegitimize class categories altogether. This repertoire was shaped by a sense of being outsiders who made it into the middle class and evoked desires to challenge the power of the bourgeoisie village that did not accept them.

In contrast, some who came from humble beginnings acted as gatekeepers. Walter, sixty, a retired law enforcement officer, Great Park resident, and the adult child of Jamaican immigrant parents, despised Jamaicans whom he regarded as "imposters" or those who tried to conceal that they grew up poor in Jamaica by "acting like they are better than Blacks in America who have less." Walter explained:

> Now when I go to Jamaica—let's say you go to Kingston. Right where the Pegasus Hotel is in Kingston, everything there is affluent. You go six blocks away from there, there is a tent city there. And these guys come over here battling African Americans for living in housing projects, saying, "See, that's the complacency of people who live there." That is just something I don't understand.
>
> You know what I do? Because I bring the Jamaicans that say this and that out. I let them hang themselves. I ask them, "Wait a minute, where do you come from?" They will say "Manchester." And I say, "Oh, OK." Then I come to find out, guess what? They are ashamed of telling people that they grew up there and grew up poor. That's why they are over here in New York. You come over here and act like you are better than me. "Why didn't you stay where you were?" How many times have you heard that?
>
> Haiti the same thing. You know. Barbados . . . their currency is more like US, but they still have those poor areas. But a lot of them have that, they have a "I'm a proud West Indian" attitude. But they've benefited from a lot. A lot of them got to the United States with the help of Black American leaders. . . . They were the majority over there, not the minority. So, they never felt the real oppression. Pretty much they were in control in their own countries. But here in the United States, like I was telling you about the laws and about the lynching. The whole system of law that we gradually had changed. But guess what, they benefited. And just like the Jewish people, they came here poor, but they benefitted.

Walter believes that members of different Caribbean diasporas need to do some soul searching. He especially despises Black immigrants who use class-based rhetoric to criticize Black Americans in order to enhance their own status. Of Jamaican parentage, Walter was able to access educational enrichment programs in New York and became a public servant on Long Island. He uses his knowledge of the stratified residential structure in Kingston to demonstrate the diverse class origins of the Jamaican diaspora and undercut the class and moral boundaries that he argues they assert between themselves and low-income African Americans. He exposes a hypocrisy among some Black immigrants. He himself has been able to ascend the class ladder from growing up poor with immigrant parents to the upper middle class in New York. He makes it clear that his socioeconomic mobility would have been impossible without the highly organized racial protest and resistance practices of Black Americans to White supremacy. Therefore, Walter challenges Jamaicans, Haitians and other Black immigrants who attempt to remake their class selves after migration, while disparaging Black Americans who have been systematically barred from mobility. He calls on Black immigrants to remember the "shantytowns" and "yards" where they come from back home. A firm grounding in "where they come from," he believes will be the moral compass needed to create the political pan-ethnic Black identities necessary to eradicate the structural racism that continues to subjugate and segregate Black Americans.

Stepping Back to Step Forward—and Judging Those Who Do Not Climb (Back, Back, Forth and Forth)

The second type of fish in the soup of diasporic suburbs are those who *cross a bridge over troubled waters* to reclaim their status in the middle class. For some of those who came from a working-class background, the voyage to New York suburbs meant not the realization of a dream but recurrent nightmares that made them consider return migration. Those with comfortable upbringings experienced twists and turns in their journeys to middle-class suburbia. Lloyd came from a well-to-do family in small-town Jamaica. He came to New York in 1998 "kicking and screaming." His wife, Michelle, had been recruited to work as a nurse in a hospital in the Bronx, along with a quarter of her graduating class from nursing school. They had been in a long-term relationship when she migrated to New York in 1990. The hospitals in Kingston were cutting back on staff because of a budgetary crisis. Nurses had more patients than they could handle and were underpaid. Disappointed by the declining urban health care system in Jamaica, Michelle sought a career in New York instead.

Lloyd and Michelle married and had their first child in the 1990s. Michelle returned to New York with their young son. But soon she was calling Lloyd in tears. She was overwhelmed by stress at work and raising their young son alone. "Michelle would call me, completely hysterical, and then I would hear my kid in the background. I said to her, come home, it will be fine here, I'm fine here. But she didn't want to work in the hospitals in Kingston. You know, it's a developing country so the facilities don't compare. So, I said OK, I will come to New York."

Lloyd was a reluctant migrant. He was "making a good salary, worked for a good company, and had a good car" in Kingston. His father was a successful agronomist and prominent community leader. When Lloyd turned five, his father told his mother to stop working as a store clerk and to take care of their four kids and home while he worked. Lloyd describes his upbringing as middle class. They had a modest home, a car, and a steady stream of income from the farm. Their neighbors saw his family as respectable and influential. Lloyd recalled his father's status as a central political player in community affairs:

> They would come, and they would be outside—the people in the town. So, my mom would be the one that would say, "He is sleeping, you are going to have to wait till he wakes up." By the time we are leaving for church on Sunday, they are knocking on the gate to speak to my dad about their . . . problems. So that's what they used to do. He met with the people. If somebody needed water piped into their home, or they needed help to get a job for their son, or a recommendation, he was the one they would come to. He was looked highly upon, and because of that I got to meet, like, prime ministers. They would be at my house, at functions. When we grew up, he was being groomed for higher office. I remember his dad begged him to stop being in politics. . . . Because back home it's different. It can be dangerous to be in politics. He feared that that was going to happen to him.

I remember when I went to college, back home, in those days, the 1980s, college campuses were hot beds of political radicalization. That's where they, like the outbreak on Wall Street now, it would have started on a college campus. So that's how it was. I remember when I was in college and I lived on campus. I remember my dad came to visit me one Sunday. A guy saw him. This guy from the rival political party saw him and he came to me and said, "Oh, that's your dad?" He shook my hand and he said, "You and I are on different sides of the political framework, but that is one guy that we all respect for hard work, your father." And that's just who he was. We grew up with a little privilege.

Lloyd's father was well known in the local political scene, which gave Lloyd the sense that he was coming of age in a family that had status, money, and influence.

Lloyd's new life in the Bronx came as a shock. It was the direct antithesis of his class upbringing and adulthood repertoire. He lived under economic strain and felt alienated in a poor and working-class urban community far away from the middle-class comforts he had become accustomed to in Jamaica.

I remember for the first two years, I would cry every night. I wanted to go home. Looking back, it was the right decision. Long Island is great, but it took a while. We were living in an apartment in the Bronx, near Grand Councourse. Our car was broken into and the neighbors look at us like we broke into our own car. No one would help us. I was there for, like, five years. I could not deal with that. Noise and all that. You lived in an apartment and you don't know anybody. You saw them, but I couldn't tell you anything about one person in that apartment building. I couldn't tell you a single name. You saw them and said hi and that was it. When we moved over here, I remember we moved in on a Sunday and by the Tuesday, Wednesday, all the neighbors were coming over. I mean, "welcome to the neighborhood," "if there is anything you wanted."

Lloyd's journey from the rural middle class in Jamaica to middle-class suburbia on Long Island required that he travel a bumpy road. The first years in New York were characterized by spells of unemployment, hardship, and heartache. He and Michelle were disconnected from the community that supported them in Jamaica and were engulfed by the sadness that accompanied migration and isolation.

Lloyd had completed an associate's degree in Jamaica, but in order to work as an engineer in New York he had to return to school. "Going back to school was the last thing I wanted to do at the time. . . . But my wife said it was the only way." Lloyd went to a local community college and remembers sitting in classrooms with eighteen-year-olds. He was in his thirties, married with a child. He went on to earn a bachelor's in engineering from a public university and held internships where he experienced racial isolation. Yet within a decade of his arrival in New York, he and Michelle purchased a home in Great Park.

Like Lloyd, many people in the diasporic suburbs had experienced setbacks, but they eventually translated their middle-class childhood into a middle-class suburban lifestyle well into adulthood. Access to affordable education and social networks were the bridges over difficult circumstances and vehicles to mobility for the diasporic Black middle class. This group is concerned with erecting class boundaries between themselves and those who earn less money and continue to struggle to move out of poverty. They postulate that their hard work earned them access to the middle class. Yet they often downplay the enormous amount of human capital and educational resources that gave them middle-class status in their hometowns and allowed them to join the middle class in New York. Jamaicans and Haitians who came from middle-class backgrounds were activating the class distinctions of their home country in their new suburbs. Some failed to appreciate the enormous amount of work others had put in in order to "move on up" in New York or the fact that they themselves had been helped by external institutions to which not everyone had access. They erected boundaries between themselves and lower-income Blacks who did not ascend the class ladder as rapidly as they did. Like Tammy, the Jamaican nurse I discussed in the previous chapter, those who came from Jamaica's Brown middle class and walked on bridges over troubled socioeconomic waters in New York felt a sense of pride for not "relying on the system" during hardship, and they snubbed Black and Jewish families who used government assistance. They saw Black Americans and Jews as exploiting government programs. Therefore, the meritocratic narrative among Jamaicans was often based in anti–Black American cultural racism they consumed from White media sources and political pundits.

African Americans who had grown up middle class but fell on difficult financial times before reentering the middle class expressed fewer criticisms of co-ethnics and other Black people who were unable to move out of poverty or the working class. Translating a middle-class upbringing into a middle-class adulthood is an arduous task for Black people in the United States. Children of Black middle-class parents are more likely than Whites to descend into the working class or poverty because of setbacks and missteps.[3] Instead of securing stability, Black middle-class Americans experience economic vulnerability, which leads to downward intergenerational mobility. Those I interviewed commented that the unpredictability of the economy during the Great Recession and their lack of access to financial knowledge blocked the transmission of their parents' class status to them. This was particularly the case for Black Americans, who because of their longer history in the country, inherited their homes from their parents.

Fallen Bourgeoisie

The combination of Haiti's bifurcated class structure and political attacks on the country's middle class and bourgeoisie led to the mass exile of affluent Haitians from the island beginning in the late 1950s. The Duvalier regime left no family untouched by violence, political repression, or economic constraints. The *petit* and *grand* bourgeoisie experienced a dramatic decline in status when they fled the terror and humanitarian crisis in Haiti. The children of exiles who now live in diasporic suburbs recount the stark differences between their affluent lifestyles in Haiti and their struggle to enter middle-class suburbs that offered far inferior homes, neighborhoods, organizations, and social connections than they had enjoyed growing up. These fallen aristocrats saw life in middle-class suburbs as a step down from their previous social standing. They were maladjusted, disgruntled, and resentful that they were forced to join a diaspora that many felt was beneath them. However, they are dependent on this same diaspora for social networks, information, and opportunity.

Regine requested that we meet in her salon on the Boulevard for our interview. When I opened the door, a glamor headshot of a blond, curly haired Beyoncé circa 1998 stared back at me. The scent of hair sheen and Jean Naté greeted me. When she heard the bell ring, she looked up at me and I waved hello. Smiling and bending her knees to demonstrate excitement, she gestured for me to take a seat in the first salon chair. She was on the phone with a client. In addition to owning her own salon, Regine also helped Haitian immigrants who were new to the city with their immigration concerns. She had many new clients who were applying for Temporary Protected Status (TPS) after the 2010 earthquake and needed assistance with translation and documentation. "It's been so busy busy. Everyone is calling me; they need this and that. They are getting all this wrong information. I have to help them," Regine explained with a large grin after hanging up the phone. She put her hand on my arm as she kissed me on my left cheek, my right, and then my left again. I was a bit startled by the greeting and almost dropped the folder with my consent forms and the interview questionnaire. Regine sat down on a black leather loveseat directly across from me, crossed her legs, and laughing asked me, "So, what do you want to know about my big crazy life?"

Regine owned a hair salon in Cascades but lived in Great Park. She came to New York as a teenager and was reunited with her mother and father, who had left Haiti four years earlier. In Haiti, her parents had a profitable textile business. During her adolescence, they spent a brief period island hopping before Regine's parents migrated to New York and Regine and her brother Marcus were sent back to Haiti. Family lore says that Regine's father had made a business deal that put him on the wrong side of the Duvalier regime. While Regine's parents were in political exile, she and Marcus lived in their plush Petionville suburban home in Port au Prince where they were cared for by grandparents and servants.

Regine was raised with the accoutrements of the bourgeoisie, so when she arrived in Queens to join her parents she felt she went from "riches to rags" and experienced a significant decline in status. Her parents purchased a home in Cascades in the 1970s and entered the middle class suburbs a few years after their arrival in the United States. Then they sent for Regine and Marcus. Before Regine boarded the flight from Port au Prince to JFK airport, she had reservations about the lifestyle that was waiting for her. She explained:

> I grew up in a class where we had maids, drivers and everything. I am spoiled, so coming here I don't want it to be any less. Without having come

here, I never like it. You know what? When my mother come to visit us, she always talking to my grandparents about where she had to work and what she had to do. I remember looking at her, and asking "What? I don't want to be there!" Because when my mother start working in New York, she was a nanny. And then after that she went into elderly [care]. And the abuse that she used to take from other people because she didn't have her green card. So, I was like, "What? I don't want to be there." . . . "You don't have a maid?" That is the first thing that I ask her. "Who cooks the food, who does the laundry?" She said, "I have to do it." I said, "You do? And your nails are like that?" She has beautiful hands. I said, "Your hands are beautiful." I'm like, "Oh, no! This place is not for me." She said that they have good education. You learn to speak English. I said, "Ma, I am learning English here, I don't like it, I like Spanish better." I find English to be the worst language ever that anybody have to speak. Up to now I still feel the same way. I don't like New York. I don't like the United States period.

Regine's perspective on life in New York was solidified long before she arrived. Her transnational consciousness of status was informed by her mother's reports of the labor and humiliation she endured while serving Whites and White ethnics in the city's childcare and elder care industry. In her job as a home attendant, the elderly Jewish woman shouted racial slurs at her daily. Regine's mother was a savvy businesswoman back in Haiti, but now she had to swallow indignities and insults from White employers in New York. This was the ultimate fall from grace in Regine's eyes. Her mother was now performing onerous tasks she had paid servants to do at home. The exploitation her mother faced on the labor market was compounded by the fact that she did not have a green card, so she had little leverage in the workplace. Regine's parents never received proper political refugee status, but instead overstayed their visitor visas. The complicated web of political and economic problems they encountered in the United States came as a great shock. In the diaspora, Regine had to reconcile her previous status as an upper-class person who attended elite schools, traveled, and never did arduous housework with the reality of living in a Black middle-class community where you have to work, cook and clean your own home and attend public schools. This was a tragedy for Regine's younger self.

The transnational rupture in class status and Regine's inability to enter the American upper class left an indelible mark on her sense of class identity and how she negotiated class relations within diasporic suburbs. In her social circles and spaces, Regine performs bourgeois cultural repertoires. She wants people to know that where she is now is not where she comes from. She found it difficult to connect with peers in high school and college because they "wanted to wear their pants big and low, and dance nasty." She didn't "have time for the other business people on the block" because they didn't know how to do business as well as she did and didn't "respect people" (as in clientele) the way they should. She said it was difficult to make friends because people perceived her to be overly optimistic; she is often accused of not "living in the real world." In addition to struggling to build friendships and social ties because of her sense of status and superiority, Regine had to negotiate an additional blow: her brother Marcus's departure from New York to avoid deportation. Regine lamented that after moving to Cascades, her brother became entangled with the wrong crowd. Because he did not have citizenship, his criminal record made him a target of deportation sweeps, which spiked up after the 1996 IRRIRA (Illegal Immigrant Reform and Immigrant Responsibility) Act and went into high gear after 9/11. His move abroad strained the close sibling bond they had nurtured while coming of age in Haiti and New York together. This rupture added to Regine's sense that she had lost more than she had gained by migrating to New York. This experience of decline, loss, and downward mobility permeated Regine's sense of belonging to the middle class. She felt that she was above an "average middle-class American," but her financial worries were a sobering reminder that she was no longer part of the Haitian bourgeoisie and struggled to secure that status in her current life in New York.

The journey to middle-class suburbs is fraught with legal, social, political, cultural, and economic complications for migrants of bourgeois upbringings. Their inability to transfer their status from their places of origin to New York sheds light on the slippery class slope the global Black bourgeoisie must negotiate in order to remain middle class in the metropole. As an entrepreneur, Regine was unable to recapture the elite status her parents held in Haiti, although she has become a business woman in their tradition. Because of the risks involved in starting and sustaining a salon in Cascades, Regine engages in such "side hustles" as real estate, notarial services, and immigration assistance.

This is a far cry from the upper-class life she and her brother were being groomed for before they were forced to leave Haiti, but this was the destiny of many children of the bourgeoisie during the Duvalier dictatorship and post-Duvalier era.

For the adult children or grandchildren of Black migrants from the US South, their life course demonstrates that their parents' upward mobility did not translate into intergenerational mobility or even stability. Those brought up in affluence took several steps backward, partially reversing the class advancement that the generation of the civil rights movement had attained as a result of the decline of racial discrimination in education, employment, and housing. Their inheritance from their middle-class parents is complicated and hindered by an assortment of private and public problems. Anita, an educator and Cascades resident in her forties, lives in the colonial revival house she grew up in. Her parents had a successful trucking company in the 1980s, in addition to owning multiple rental properties as well as gas stations and liquor stores. Anita described them as "well off—just below rich." She did not recall wanting for anything during her childhood. She had the best bedroom furniture and bedding, stylish clothes and sneakers, toys, hairstyles, accessories, and makeup. She credited her father for her love of large SUVs; she shuttled between her job, her son's school, activities, and home in a Black Suburban SUV. When her father passed away unexpectedly, her mother sold the gas stations but kept the rental properties and the liquor store. When their business partner decided that he wanted to move back down South, they sold the majority of their investments.

After her mother passed away, Anita was unable to control and retain the assets her parents left behind. Anita explained:

I sort of regret it, but I sold that piece of property. Because I just kind of was finished with it. [It was] a money maker or rental property; I should have kept it. At that time, and it was kind of harsh too, after my mother had died, I didn't know what I had to do to keep it. And then again there was another person involved. And he said, "We're moving out of state." You know, so . . . yeah, and at the time I didn't feel that I was ready to do that, so I let it go. Obviously, I was younger. And I was not savvy. As a matter of fact, the house that I have, I had an equity house. I didn't buy my house, so I had never bought a house. Didn't even know if I was going to be able to keep or afford the house. So, I was like, okay. And that's a reward. I have one more house, it is prime real estate in New York City. And I keep telling myself, don't let it go.

Anita's downward journey into the middle class involved losing the wealth that her parents toiled to accumulate. A series of setbacks, including the dissolution of financial partnerships, the premature deaths of her parents, and financial misinformation as a young woman led to her loss of status. Yet, because her parents provided her with an education from a historically Black college and she inherited a home to reside in and a lucrative rental property, Anita has landed on her feet in the middle class as an adult. Anita's parents migrated to New York from South Carolina and North Carolina to ensure that they could maximize their earnings, become entrepreneurs, and provide for her. Anita's difficult descent within the middle class is part of the long story of her migrant parents' aspirations colliding with the challenges of class transmission to their daughter.

For Richer, for Poorer: When Intimacies of Status Collide

In diasporic suburbs, Black American, Haitian and Jamaican men and women are actively managing their class identity through the prism of dating, romantic relationships, marriages, and partnerships. Romantic relationships are the most intimate space within which the diasporic Black middle class reconciled their past and present class identities. The meeting of two partners who came of age in households with different financial and social resources requires significant cultural and emotional work and entails substantial vulnerability. Here the cultural work around class status moves from an individual repertoire to a relational matter. The most salient conflicts around class status among my respondents occurred within marriages.

Within the Black diaspora's middle class, heterosexual men and women settled into the suburban lifestyle largely in family units. Cascades and Great Park were social spaces where traditional and nontraditional family forms both dictated and were dictated by class journeys. In this social fishbowl, some partners who were currently middle class had emerged from disparate class backgrounds. Their different class origins created contestations that sometimes ended with the dissolution of the relationship. The promises that spouses make "to have and to hold, through sickness and in heath and for richer or for poorer" crumble when men and women have divergent sensibilities of their belonging to the middle class and are not able to translate them into a unified plan for their future as a couple.

Joyce, a technology manager, and Robert, an entrepreneur, had a typical love story, but years of tensions over their class differences ended in divorce. They were college sweethearts and married after Joyce completed her degree. Both of their families had moved to Great Park when they were in high school. Joyce's parents had lived in an apartment in Queens, but were originally from Tennessee. In the 1960s, they purchased a home in Great Park amid the White backlash to desegregation that was sweeping New York City and Long Island. Robert came to Great Park to live with an uncle, leaving his immediate family behind in South Carolina. Joyce and Robert connected over their love for the arts, culture, and learning. Joyce wanted to be a teacher, and Robert was an aspiring artist. They had two children and bought a house within blocks of Joyce's parents in Great Park. Robert's vision was to return down South and start a family business in South Carolina. Joyce had a different vision for their future. Looking back at the age of fifty-two, Joyce described how the difference in her and her ex-husband's class journeys contributed to the demise of their marriage:

> There was no way I was going to move to South Carolina to a town which I couldn't find on the map. I was lost, I couldn't find my bearings. All I kept thinking of was the town where my parents were from in Tennessee. There is only one street light in the entire town! Because it was either there, or he wanted to live in a cabin in the sticks. It just wasn't me. When I was younger, sure. I was a Girl Scout when I was in school. I liked going camping. But I didn't like the primitive life, like "let's make a dream come true" type thing, so that was when we started to have really our differences.
>
> My husband went through a lot of the class distinction between Blacks and Whites. He actually lived on a farm down South. His grandfather was educated up to the third grade. He actually talked about seeing a cross being burnt on his lawn, and the Ku Klux Klan. So, it was a whole different distraction with him because he was a Black man, educated, very talented, had very good jobs. But still seemed very low class, very insecure about his class. I was really surprised about that. And he tended to be impressed with me

because of all my accomplishments and where I had gone to school and everything. He was impressed I could speak French, and that I had the exposure. We came here . . . the same exact year. But our past was different. I understood that it was very different.

I wanted a spouse who was family oriented. Had Christian beliefs. Christian in a sense of nurturing and understanding that people are different. Loving. I have to admit I wasn't really looking for a provider. I believe in being a team. That was a really big thing for me, to be more of a team. I didn't want somebody to have to take care of me. I always felt that it would be me and him.

If he constantly worked trying to provide, and being the sole provider, I thought that he would die earlier, and I would be alone. So, I wanted to be of help. And it's interesting that both my husband and my last son's father, I felt were kind of intimidated by that. They wanted me to be a "stay at home mum." And again, stay at home was OK but I felt it limited me.

Joyce and Robert were middle-class adults, but had different class pasts and divergent future aspirations. Robert desired to return to the rural South, where their family could have the simpler working-class lifestyle he had experienced in his youth. He heard that the post-civil rights movement South was different from its Jim Crow past. The new South had become less dangerous for Black families. Joyce, however, had cosmopolitan desires. She wanted to live in New York's suburbs, with access to a city that would expose their children to a global arts and culture she revered. Robert, although an educated and accomplished entrepreneur, was intimidated by Joyce's cultural exposure and career ambitions. His attempts to dissuade her from returning to the workforce and convince her to move to the South were strategies to make Joyce's socioeconomic achievement secondary to her family. Seen through Joyce's eyes, he had never adjusted to life in New York and felt like a fish out of water. Moreover, Robert interpreted the freedom that Joyce enjoyed as an ambitious middle-class suburban Black woman as threatening, creating a high level of masculine insecurity and conflict between them. His dream was to replicate the male-dominated family life in which he had been raised. Joyce wanted an equitable gender dynamic in her marriage. Their relationship did not survive this tension.

In the fish soup of diasporic suburbs and inside the homes of some residents, people's differing origins prevented some from mixing and blending with others. Their class and gendered expectations are sometimes so divergent as to become irreconcilable. In Joyce and Robert's case, return migration to the South is a strategy of male resistance to the freedoms, mobilities, and liberations that many Black fathers and mothers left the South in order to give their daughters (Chatelain 2015). On the other side of gendered return migration, women rejoin their mothers and sisters and assume a central role in the sustenance of close-knit communities and the upbringing of the next generation of children (Stack 1996). These intrafamilial dynamics shed important light on the intimate gendered experiences of racial capitalism, demonstrating that a life-course perspective deepens our understanding of how class status is negotiated across time, space, between individuals and within families. Black migrants from the US and Global South confront systems of stratification in their diasporic settings that lead to dissonance, insecurity, and challenges as they seek to fulfill their desires to found families and create communities.

In this chapter, I've argued that members of the Black diaspora who live in middle-class suburbs occupy complex class positions that require us to expand how we understand the micropolitics of social stratification. Cascades and Great Park are nodes in a larger transregional and transnational Black migration network. Black migrants must negotiate multiple systems of racialized capitalism as they traverse New York, the US South, and the Caribbean. Their changing relationships to these systems encourage articulations of class identity that reflect their pasts as well as their current situations. This life-course, cross-spatial analysis encourages scholars to reconceptualize class status and identity in Black middle-class settings. Immigrants of color are inserted into the American class and racial stratification system in varied ways. These processes result in intragroup and inter-group class diversification (Itzigsohn 2009) that require further sociological study. Black Americans, Haitians, and Jamaicans do not make sense of their class status only or mainly in social interactions with lower-income Blacks; their diverse class origins and various journeys to middle-class suburbia matter at least as much. Their experiences across time and space affect how they interact with the other members of their diasporas, see themselves in the social hierarchy, and challenge, or reinscribe existing class categories.

Migration is an important mediating factor in incorporation into the middle class. As these groups have moved up, down, or laterally into New York's *class moyenne*, their class origins manifest in how they negotiate intra-ethnic, cross-ethnic, and cross-racial interactions. Since childhood, Black migrants have been conscious of their class positions relative to groups above and below them, both here and there. Time and space restructure norms around social class, which results in Black migrants continuously building and articulating class identities and boundaries that allow them to negotiate their place in multiple stratification systems simultaneously. This cultural and emotional work is sometimes expressed as regret by those who have lost status and as pride among those who have gained status over time.

Contrary to the assumption that individuals who grew up in affluent families would reside in Great Park rather than Cascades, I found that class origins did not map on to one's residential location; what mattered most was the status people attained in adulthood. This variability exacerbated tensions within diasporas, where those of higher-class origins sometimes resented neighbors, coworkers, friends, and even relatives who were born into a lower income or caste position but had radically altered their class standing through migration and mobility. For members of overlapping diasporas in the suburbs, migration had generated a seeming class revolution and crises of subjective perceptions of status. The class consciousness of the contemporary Black middle class marks a new chapter in relations within Black civil society that has implications for their racial political solidarities and collective action against economic inequality. In the next chapter, we explore their Black identities. This chapter introduces a new framework, the racial consciousness spectrum, which elucidates the histories and social interactions that shape the cultural politics of racial belonging within diasporic suburbia.

6 Vanilla Black

My Negro consciousness does not hold itself out of lack. It
is. It is its own follower.

Frantz Fanon (1952)

Vanilla enhances the flavor of homestyle favorites like candied yams
and banana pudding. We have the genius of Edmond Albius, an African
boy subjected to slavery, to thank for vanilla spice. In 1841, the twelve-
year-old Edmond discovered the pollination technique in the French colony Réunion. Before that, the technique of hand pollination was kept
secret by the Totonacs and Aztecs in Mexico to undermine Spanish colonial interests in developing the crop. The plant's restricted range, its
inability to self-pollinate, and the many months required for its seedpods
to mature made it rare and, true to capitalism, expensive. After Albius
figured out how to pollinate it by hand, a nearby slave owner asserted that
he had taught Albius this technique. Historical accounts say this is false.
The irony of a White slave owner seeking credit for the scientific break-
throughs of an enslaved boy resembles the twisted image of vanilla in our
popular imagination. Vanilla represents Whiteness, chocolate Blackness.
Yet the vanilla bean and its seeds are the color of chocolate and was once
referred to as the "Black flower."

Similar to the attempts to strip Albius of recognition for his revolutionary discovery, White society erases recognition of Black people's ways of
knowing their world and themselves. Albius traveled the island doing

workshops to share his technique, making Madagascar and Réunion the world's main vanilla exporters. Yet he died in poverty. Today, vanilla production profits continue to be based on the exploitation of child labor and the poor. This chapter reclaims vanilla's silenced Black history in order to push aside the veil that obscures the breadth and depth of the Black diaspora's knowledge production and micro-practices around race.

How do the cross-national histories and migrations of those who are now part of the Black middle class in New York's suburbs shape how different diasporas conceive of Blackness? Racial identity is both imposed and self-defined. Race is a socially constructed category used to differentiate people on the basis of skin color, physical features, and ancestry. Europeans created and deployed it to separate themselves from African and Indigenous peoples and justify their total domination in the expanding capitalist system (Omi and Winant 1994, Winant 2001). Racial categories continue to be imposed by White society. The contents of this category propagate racist ideologies of Black biological and cultural inferiority to non-Blacks. These anti-Black tropes are embedded in institutions and communities, serving to suppress the economic and political development of Black communities in America and abroad (Marable 1983, Rodney 1972).

Racial identity is also internally defined by racialized groups who share common histories, cultures, and political interests. These categories have a life of their own among racialized groups in search of emancipation, freedom, and true self-determination. The members of the African diaspora have historically resisted the White supremacist renderings of Blackness. They've determined the contents of Blackness from the inside out. Transformative political movements such as the New Negro, Negritude, Back to Africa, Rastafarianism, Noirisme, and Black Is Beautiful were radical cross-national political campaigns of Black self-definition and liberatory practice. In this chapter, we explore the contemporary philosophies of racial identity among middle-class Black people who are from cultural systems in the U.S., Haiti, and Jamaica.

Two decades after Albius passed away, W. E. B. Du Bois published *Souls of Black Folk* (1903). In an analysis of his lived experience as a Black boy in a White world, Du Bois gifted us with penetrating insights into the structural and individual dimensions of racial identity formation (Du Bois 1903, Itzigsohn and Brown 2016). He eloquently describes the development of racial awareness through the life course from childhood to adulthood. As a small child, he lived as a free being, unaware that the world was racialized. When he encountered rejection from White children and adults because of his race, he sought to challenge their assumption of his inferiority by proving his intellectual, spiritual, and moral worth. Du Bois learned that his rejection by the White world was not simply about interpersonal contempt; racial exclusion is built into the fabric of institutions, hindering Black social, economic, and political progress. He describes his awakening as double consciousness: an awareness of his innate capacity and dignity, and of how Whites see him, as they deny his belonging and humanity. "Why did God make me an outcast, a stranger in mine own house?" Du Bois inquires on behalf of Black boys forced to live in the shadows of the veil in a country that their ancestors built. Acutely aware of the irreconcilable conflict between being Black and American under the prevailing racial order, Du Bois committed himself to liberating his own people and oppressed peoples globally in the early twentieth century.

In a process of racial identity formation reflective of our so-called colorblind, post-racial era, members of the post-Break Black middle class formulate what I call the racial consciousness spectrum, a continuum of cultural definitions of Blackness. This spectrum is at play in a wide range of everyday situations. A walk through diasporic suburbia displays the internal diversity of the Black world produced by migrations from the US and Global South, in all of its local, diasporic, generational, religious, transnational, gendered, classed, and sexualized forms. Women dressed conservatively in pantsuits and penny loafers go door-to-door to spread the message of Jehovah's Witness. Private school students wearing yellow, green, and blue uniforms play-fight en route to the handball courts. Young Black men and women crowd around Five Percenters, as group leaders dressed in Black and purple regalia spread the message of the Nation of Gods and Earths. According to their beliefs, the Black man is the personification of God. "Don't believe what the White man tells you," one man exclaims.

Kevin, a twenty-three-year-old student dressed in large, rounded, thick black glasses; suspenders; and skinny jeans, walks past the crowd. His style is a hybrid of 1960s Malcolm X and the counterculturalists of Williamsburg. Kevin is Diana's youngest son. Diana, sixty-one, a Black American woman, moved to Cascades in the 1980s. She had accumulated enough savings to purchase a home from her promotions working for the US Postal Service. Kevin is on his way home to grab dinner before going to his evening nursing classes at a local college. He passes young Black teenagers waiting at the bus stop whose complexions range from light caramel to dark chocolate. They sport handbags by Michael Kors and Coach on their shoulders and hold the latest iPhones and Androids. Their parents, older siblings, or boyfriends buy them fashionable attire from Lucky Brand, PINK, Timberland, and the House of Dereon. Others work part-time in retail to pay for their luxuries. Their hairstyles range from long cornrows with blonde highlights to Senegalese twists, natural coils, and sewn-in hair extensions. A couple of blocks away Dante, twenty, a Great Park resident whose parents are Haitian immigrants, parks the used Honda Civic his parents purchased for him. He is heading to Golden Crust to pick up beef patties on his way home. He sports a fraternity jacket he brought home from the historically Black college he attended. He returned home after three semesters; his parents encouraged him to return home and enroll at the local community college because he struggled with his coursework.

That evening, a group of Black American and Jamaican community leaders held a meeting at a center on the Boulevard. They meet biweekly to discuss how to promote entrepreneurship in the community. This week's speaker was a Black lawyer who was promoting a legal insurance program. "If you want to make sure that you and your family get adequate representation, especially with all the problems we have with police in this city, when the time comes, all you have to do is pay a small fee each month, and we can get you the right legal support." The group was led by Clive, fifty-four, a Black American small business owner who was invested in supporting Black entrepreneurs and their families.

During the meeting I sat next to Carrie Ann, a friendly and outgoing Bajan woman who enjoyed track and field, the arts, and dance performances. She shared her excitement that her son would be taking her to see a Broadway play for Mother's Day. She arrived in New York at the age of nineteen during the Black Power Movement, when, she said, "life in New York City was affordable." Shortly after the meeting ended, Carrie Ann and a couple of others gathered around the television to watch the coverage of the wedding of Prince William and Kate Middleton in London. Carrie Ann expressed admiration for their "royal ways." She explained: "Barbados and the other British colonies received a fine, fine education as British subjects. Britain is just more sophisticated than New York. If I could have, I would have went to England." Jeffrey, fifty-eight, a Jamaica-born retired accountant, looked at the wedding procession and, with his arms crossed against his chest, said to Carrie Ann, "I could not agree with you more."

Seen from a Du Boisian perspective, this scene demonstrates that this small group consists of a range of cultural repertoires around race, however White society renders this heterogeneity invisible through the color line they have created. Du Bois's double consciousness model of racial identity development focuses on the self-society dynamic between Blacks in a White-controlled nation. I propose a neo–Du Boisian perspective on Black identity formation that extends his analysis of racial consciousness. Identity develops in social interactions between Black people and White society. However, racial identities also takes shape during encounters among different national and regional groups within the African diaspora in tandem with the color line. I submit that middle-class Black Americans, Haitians, and Jamaicans are in conversation with one another not only about how the White world sees them. Central to this chapter. This is what Blackness means to them in relation to one another. The scenes observed above move us well beyond sociological inquiries into what box individuals check off when they are asked to identify their race.

To understand the social life of race inside the African diaspora, we must examine how people racialized as Black define the cultural contents of Blackness and their relationship to it. This snapshot of life in Black diasporic suburbia displays a wide range of articulations of Blackness. The Five Percenters show us the strong religious connections to Black people and their ancestral continent. Benevolent association members Carrie Ann and Clive share postcolonial attachments to the British Crown. This is represented by Eurocentric ideals that are often in opposition to Afro-Jamaican Blackness. This is all occurring as they are consuming advice on how to legally protect their Black families from their encounters with White authorities. Kevin and Dante, like other millennial youth of the post-Break Black middle class, display urban, Afro-punk, hipster, and couture aesthetics and have affiliations with historically Black institutions, expressing their belonging to various segments of the Black community.

All these suburban residents are in conversation with a larger Black culture and express their desired positions within it.

Behind the veil of New York's racially heterogenous, yet segregated environments, the diasporic Black middle class builds identities that reveal new patterns of trans-geographic Black identity-making. Like Du Bois's model of double consciousness, the racial consciousness spectrum provides us with a paradigm of how the Black diaspora comes to understand, negotiate, and challenge constructions of Blackness across time and space. This continuum reflects the *evolving* nature of Blackness and its cultural articulations among the diaspora. It allows us to look at the subjectivities that are hidden behind the category "Black," which is imposed on people of African descent in order to classify, control and surveil them. It demonstrates the fluidity and movement that occurs as Blackness is renegotiated as a source of empowerment amid its stigmatization. Because the Black diaspora hails from nation states and regions with varying histories and cultures around racial and color stratification, understanding the cultural work behind racial identity provides us with an understanding of Black identity within and beyond the borders of neighborhood, region, and nation. Next, I describe the three main cultural forms of the racial consciousness spectrum.

RACIAL CONSCIOUSNESS SPECTRUM

The *racial consciousness spectrum* consists of cultural viewpoints and characteristics that Cascades and Great Park residents constructed to describe their own and others' relationships to the subjective, ideological, and social articulations of Blackness. There are three main social positions on the racial consciousness spectrum: *pro-Blackness, selective Blackness*, and *post-racial Blackness*. These cultural categories reflect the shared language that my respondents used to articulate their identities. A person's place on the spectrum is defined by their racial subjectivity. Specifically, my respondents' definitions of *being* Black—that is, as an identity—and of *belonging* to a Black world—in terms of their practices— created the parameters of the racial consciousness spectrum. The spectrum consists of *fluid* social positions that describe the varying intensity

Table 8 The Racial Consciousness Spectrum (RCS)

	Pro-Blackness	*Selective Blackness*	*Post-racial Blackness*
Identity	Both being and belonging	Either being or belonging	Neither being nor belonging
Definition of Blackness	Core identity, anchor	Accepted, but tangential	Avoided; seen as retrograde

of identification and participation that make up the dynamic cultural and political landscape of Black middle-class New York.

The racial consciousness of the Black diasporic *class moyenne* ranges from accentuating a heightened level of racial consciousness to explaining away racialized encounters. The development of racial consciousness and where individuals fall on the spectrum of Blackness are informed by the crosscurrents between their own diasporic histories of race, nation, and empire and their present encounters with other communities in New York's racial landscape. Careful analysis of the range of racial consciousness people express and their cultural pathways to them demonstrates that Blackness is not a static, agreed-upon identity, but is defined and acted upon differently within and across Black diasporas.

Black Americans, Haitians, and Jamaicans occupy each of the cultural spaces in the racial consciousness spectrum. However, each diaspora travels along a distinct cultural pathway to arrive at the same position. For example, Sheila, Derrick, and Rony articulate a pro-Blackness viewpoint. They each had strong attachments to their Black identities and engaged in practices that inserted them into Black social spaces. Since they had different national origins, however, they articulated the contents of pro-Blackness from varying historical perspectives. Sheila espoused a racial identity and expressed a sense of belonging that was informed by the "Black is beautiful" movement in the United States. Derrick adopted the cultural messages about global Blackness that he enjoyed on the reggae scene in Brooklyn in the 1980s and appreciated Jamaican reggae musical artists' affirmation of pan-African identity. Rony's pro-Blackness was inspired by Haiti's radical Black liberatory history. The "Black is Beautiful" movement in New York,

the Rastafarian cultural politics of reggae music in Jamaica, and the intellectual history of Black revolutionaries in Haiti exemplify different cultural
pathways that lead to pro-Blackness for Black Americans, Haitians, and
Jamaicans. These pathways reveal the complicated processes of transnational and transregional cultural work around racial identity occurring
among New York's Black middle class. I will now discuss these cultural positions in greater detail. I first demonstrate the middle position on the racial
consciousness spectrum, selective Blackness, then pro-Blackness and post-
racial Blackness. Selective Blackness, I argue, is considered a balanced,
modern and strategic subjectivity by interviewees. I unravel its contents first
because they are demonstrative of the social boundaries that define pro-
Blackness as an outdated political repertoire and post-racial Blackness as an
out-of-touch positionality yet to be realized.

SELECTIVE BLACKNESS

Blackness is defined in a myriad of ways depending on the racial subjectivity of each member of the African diaspora you meet. Those who are
engaged in selective Blackness claim a Black identity, but disengage from
intensive attachments to Black communities and social circles. Selective
Blackness is the cultural space on the racial consciousness spectrum
where more moderate forms and expressions of Black identity operate.
Selective Blackness means that individuals see themselves as Black, they
embrace it as a descriptive identification, but actively avoid participating
in expressive practices that seem to endorse what they regard as racial
extremes. This ideological perspective includes two seeming opposites:
being hyperaware of race, and trying "not to see race" at all. Selective
Blackness entails a tension between not wanting to be perceived as "too
Black" in the White world and trying to avoid being regarded as "not Black
enough" by others in the Black world. In their interactions across the
color line, those who are engaged in selective Blackness are aware of anti-
Black structural discrimination. Yet, they strategically employ moderate
responses to these encounters.

Among Jamaicans and Haitians who adopt selective Black consciousness, their initial experiences of racism in the United States made them

acutely aware of how Whites disparagingly perceive and mistreat Black people in daily interactions. Their diasporic encounters with Asian and Latinx immigrants in New York's multiracial milieu also exposed them to anti-Black racism from other people of color. These experiences led them to identify as Black in ways that are specific to the conditions of Blackness in America and to understand a collective racial struggle.

Simultaneously, selective Blackness entails rejecting solidarity with other Black people, families, or communities and the eradication of racism politically. Jamaicans who perform selective Blackness generally tend to value the respectability paradigms of the multiracial creole class in their homeland, but were confronted with White domination in the United States. Others arrived in New York with memories of the civil rights and anti-Apartheid movements but were caught off guard by present-day racism. Coverage of these global antiracist and anticolonial social movements was channeled through local radio stations and newspapers as my respondents were coming of age, and their understanding of racial inequality evolved with each breaking story in the United States or South Africa. They straddled the fence between being conscious of, and not paying too much attention to, Black struggles.

Black Americans engaged in selective Blackness saw themselves as success stories in the face of racial discrimination. They understood the collective plight caused by anti-Black racism, but still believed that Blacks could "make it if they try." Haitians who espoused a selective Black consciousness were equally aware of the racial obstacles White society imposes upon Black people. At the same time, however, their dual sense of being racial outsiders to White society and of being on the margins of the Black diaspora because of their distinct colonial, anticolonial, and postcolonial history; their native language; and their poor reception in the United States meant that they disassociated from additional markers of stigma.

"I'm Black. I'm not African American; I'm Black," Tracey Benedict, forty-eight, declared. As she took a sip of her chamomile tea, her burgundy nail polish contrasted with her mocha-colored fingers. Her husband, Anthony, a fair-skinned man in his fifties, sat to her right at a round dining table that looked like a floor model from a Pottery Barn store. The table was near a large bay window overlooking their fenced yard. They had an all-White kitchen with shiny stainless-steel appliances. Their Yorkie dog sat barking at the back door. The Benedict family was the "it" couple in Great Park. They hold advanced degrees, make $200,000 a year, take "nice" vacations where they "do it big," and host fancy dinner parties. Their eldest child was a star athlete and the youngest an artist. Tracey and Anthony were fit and healthy, and they looked ten years younger than their actual ages. Tracey, an educator, was an active participant in her children's Parent Teacher Association. They shared a similar philosophy about raising their family: "We do what have to do. We do everything we can do to support our children."

Tracey and Anthony were in lockstep about the role that race, and racial identity played in their life. They both approached their Black identities judiciously. Racism was made clear to them through interactions in the White worlds of their children's school, extracurricular activities, neighborhood, and workplace. Yet they came from different diasporic worlds.

Tracey was born in Harlem and raised in a Black suburb on Long Island. Her mother worked in social welfare services; her father was from Alabama, but he was in the military and played only a marginal role in her life. She grew up with younger siblings in an extended, intergenerational household. Her grandmother lived with the family after she retired from her job as a domestic worker for a White family in the city. The household also included two of Tracey's mother's nephews. In contrast, Anthony was born to what he defines as a lower-middle-class family in Jamaica; his father was an engineer and his mother worked in a bank and did editorial projects. His family lived in a rural area during his childhood, and his wife joked that Anthony "discovered plumbing" only when he left Jamaica. He completed high school and college on Long Island. After graduation, Anthony was introduced to Tracey by a mutual friend. They fell in love, married, and moved to Great Park to raise their children. Tracey exemplifies the variation in how Black Americans engage with Blackness. She and Anthony incisively identify as Black and chastised Whites who purported to have a color-blind ideology. At the same time, they resented being seen as the "Cosby couple" and rejected the idea that they raised their children as "Black parents."

ANTHONY: [They say] we're the power couple or we're the Cosby couple or, you know. You hear that stuff all the time.

TRACEY: Which was interesting, and we never thought of it that way. We just thought that here we are doing our thing. Doing what we do with our kids because we're parents and that is what we are supposed to do. Anthony makes my life easy because he understands life. When we're out, we don't profess to know it all or show off in what we do for our children or anybody else. We only do what we can do, and we do [these things] as parents, not as Black parents. We don't say, "This is what a Black parent would do." It's interesting because some people would say, "Oh, that's what White people would do."

I cooked for the football team, right, here's a classic [example]. I cooked for the football team every Friday, just macaroni and cheese. I didn't do a whole lot because they always had food. So, the coach's wife, they are White, says to me in front of all the other White women that she hangs with and says, "Tracey, my gosh, how do you do it?" and I said, "Do what?" She says, "I mean you cook for the team every Friday; you have a full-time job and you're raising your kids and I mean you look fabulous, how do you do it?" I said, "I'm not doing anything that you don't do." Now I thought it was a nice compliment.

Now here's my thing, though. Do you say that to the White lady who's your friend who does the same thing for her family that they do? Do you understand what I mean? So, I didn't take it negatively but, as we're discussing it, it's kind of interesting to think, what did she think I would do? My son needed me to be there. We're there. We pick up the kids. We drop them off, whatever we have to do. We buy things. If we have money, we can pick up things. We can do certain things for them. We don't think in terms of this is the Black thing to do or we are breaking the Black mold, this is the way Black people should act but because we are acting more White, or rich, or this . . . We're just doing things we can afford within our means to help our children be successful, period. I've never looked at it any other way.

ANTHONY: Yeah. So no, it's not a Black thing. To us it's a family thing, it's a kid thing. It's doing everything to get them where they need to be. It's as simple as that.

In their interactions with White parents, the Benedicts encountered racially exclusionary slights and aggressions. The White mother, who was stunned by Tracey's level of involvement with her children's extracurricular activities, reveals how White parents view Black parents, especially Black mothers. Tracey's response to this skewed perception was to invoke a colorless perspective on parenting. When she was racialized, she responded with an antiracist stance. She rejected the assumptions made by Whites that Black parenting is generally inferior and that her mothering strategy makes her an exceptional Black woman.

The Benedicts resented being perceived differently than White parents who engage in similar practices, and posit that being seen as "breaking the Black mold" is more of an insult than a compliment. White adults and youth in their neighborhood attempted to categorize their childrearing or family practices as a performance of a special type of Blackness, but the Benedicts disagreed. They rejected both the idea that their motivations are based on their racial identities and the idea that they are different in their interests and comportment from the White families in their neighborhood. The Benedicts are conscious of racial discrimination and actively reject labels that reduce and humiliate them.

The Benedicts do not participate in Black social circles or see their own practices through a racial lens. Instead, they seek equity in White society so that who they are and what they do are not perceived as a "Black thing." They do not engage in any practices that reinforce a Black identity and, while aware of the discrimination that mandates conversations with their children about the realities of racial discrimination, they seek to be seen and treated equally by White families in Great Park. In order to challenge being underestimated by the Whites they interact with, Tracey said, "We live our lives as people who happen to be Black."

The Benedicts' detachment from participation in Black life is shaped by their interest in being seen through a non-racialized lens. Their solution to being racialized by White parents is to deemphasize the role of Blackness in how they conduct their life. Selective Blackness means that a person takes on individualistic repertoires. Those who espouse selective Blackness actively identify as Black but dissociate themselves from the Black community to avoid being racially stereotyped. Selective Blackness involves a reluctance to be seen as a part of a collective Black group because of the negative associations that Whites attach to the group. The cost of this identity work, however, is that it validates instead of undermines White norms.

Esther expressed a similar position. The forty-five-year-old, light-skinned Haitian woman with two children, was a health care worker and small business owner. She had been living in New York for twenty years, and since her arrival had moved up the nursing ranks. She earned a six-figure salary, and she and her husband, led an upper-middle-class lifestyle. Esther explained her sense of identity: "In my job, I always tell people that I am a Black person but I am not . . . Black people. I don't want to be labeled as people; I want to be labeled as a Black person. Because to me, this is what I've realized, once you say Black people, they attribute it with, like, very bad things, and they are scared of us. This type of things, you know, I don't want to take part of these things. I want to live my life as a Black person, honest, respectful, you know."

Esther identifies as a respectable Black person but refuses to identify with "Black people" as a group in order to dissociate herself from the stigma placed on Black people by Whites. Esther understands that Whites harbor racist perceptions of Blacks. She walks a fine line between identifying as a decent Black person and being associated with the negative images Whites have of Black people by erecting symbolic boundaries between herself and the Black community. Demonstrating her selective engagement with Blackness, Esther claims the positive attributes she confers on Blackness, such as being "honest" and "respectful," but in the same breath avoids the negative labels attached to Black people by White society.

Esther's cultural pathway to selective Blackness is shaped by her status as a Haitian upper-middle-class woman. Her racial consciousness is informed by her awareness of how Whites view Black people in America. In addition, Esther negotiates a particular outsider status that disrupts any positive connections with Blackness. She recounted many instances of anti-Haitian discrimination she has encountered from Jamaican and Black American coworkers. Her accent is a clear indicator of her Haitian nationality in the hospital settings she works in. Her selective Blackness is informed by the desire to mitigate the layers of ethnoracial disadvantage that she experiences as a Black immigrant who speaks English as a second language. Her reluctance to identify with "Black people" allows her to minimize her ties to racial categories that she feels pull her further into social stigmatization. This type of racialized cultural work signifies the complexities at play for middle-class Haitian immigrants who strategically limit their ties to Black communities in order to minimize the fear and rejection from Whites that they believe a more amplified expression of Blackness would evoke.

FINDING A MIDDLE GROUND

An important feature of selective Blackness is expressing moderate views about the politics of racial identity and solidarity. On a cold winter evening, I sat at the Brathwaite family's IKEA kitchen table. Claudia Brathwaite, who migrated from Jamaica to New York twenty years ago, had settled in, changed clothes, and started cooking dinner after coming home from her shift as a registered nurse at a hospital in Queens, where she worked from 7 a.m. to 3 p.m. Her three children were circling around their ranch-style home in Great Park. Her eldest son, Jeremiah, a brown-skinned teenager with a high top fade parted with two strand twists, was on his smartphone texting friends about a party at school the next week. He listened in on our discussion, interjecting every so often when Claudia retold a family story that he thought misrepresented the facts.

Upon arrival in New York, Claudia moved directly to Great Park to join one of her six siblings, who had migrated from Jamaica long before. She was a part of the flow of immigrants who since the 1990s have bypassed the city and settled in the suburbs. Claudia and her younger sister, May, were the last to enter the United States. Their mother told Claudia and May that they both had to finish high school first before boarding a plane to come to New York; one sibling could not leave the other behind. Claudia's experiences in the suburban job market sparked her journey to selective Blackness. She recounted many instances in which she encountered anti-Black sentiments and practices on the job.

> It was tough. When I came in the first time, my sister helped me to get a job. We looked in the papers and my only experience was doing bookkeeping. I started working for this Jewish lady in Queens and she was very nasty. I hated the job. She treated everybody just horrible. It was a shock to me because we weren't accustomed to the racists. Even if it was a class thing [in Jamaica], it was not because you are Black. If you are minority here, they treat you bad. I couldn't stay at the job, and I didn't.

Claudia then found a job closer to home for another Jewish-owned company. After working there for almost a year, Claudia had had enough. She received the news that Solomon, who had been at the company for about three months, had received a promotion. This was the second time that Claudia had trained a Jewish employee who had recently arrived from Israel only to see them promoted over her head. When she complained to her manager, she was given a $2 raise. Claudia went on maternity leave from this job and never returned.

"When you come here, you learn that you should stick to one thing, and that is your Blackness," Claudia stated. She learned very quickly that White ethnics regarded her as Black and decided that she should align herself with the group to which she was now assigned.

> My Black identity, I don't know, it didn't matter before I came here. Like I said before, nobody ever told you that you are Black or whatever back in Jamaica. There are people in Jamaica that have light skin but it wasn't that deep. . . .
>
> I know when I came here you have to stick to something and you stick to your roots, your Blackness more here. Even at work, I tend to gravitate to minorities more. I have some of my coworkers that are White that I speak to and somebody come on board that is a minority, I get closer to that one.

The stark ethnoracial divisions Claudia encountered in the workplace, which were imposed by White ethnic business owners, were encountered by most of the adults I interviewed. Middle-class Jamaican immigrants' racial consciousness developed through these experiences. Coming from Jamaica's color hierarchy to New York's racial and color stratification system shaped the development of Claudia's racialized self-understanding. This is similar to how middle-class Black immigrant racial consciousness is typically understood. In *Crosscurrents: West Indian Immigrants and Race* (1999), Milton Vickerman argues that Jamaicans reluctantly develop a racial consciousness. Jamaica's political landscape and majority Black demography socializes its citizenry to downplay the role of race in everyday life. Colorism and class are considered more salient fault lines. The Jamaican diaspora, however, repeatedly encounters anti-Black racism from White and sometimes lighter-skinned Latinx and Asian coworkers, classmates, and neighbors. Claudia's heightened sense and expectation of White racism on the job helps her negotiate racial slights and develop a deeper understanding of how racial exclusion works.

Claudia's ties to the Black community elucidated something that many Black people are acutely aware of: Black identity is defined differently depending on the social location of the Black person you ask. Claudia identifies as Black. Her ties to Black people and other minorities are meaningful; they nurture bonds that help her navigate the racism she encounters. She learned from personal experience that the promises of upward mobility were not extended to her because she was a Black woman in New York city where WASPs and White ethnics control the job market. Her encounters with discrimination were so severe that she left her profession in business administration after being passed up for multiple promotions; she entered nursing because "the medical field did not care about race. You have to just take and pass the test and that's it, you're in."

PRO-BLACKNESS

The racial consciousness spectrum consists of categories of Black identification and practices defined by my interviewees. Claudia's construction of her moderate position in the racial consciousness spectrum relative to others became clear when she compared her ties to Blackness with those of her husband, Winston, and their children; especially their eldest son, Jeremiah. Claudia explained: "Winston, their father, is *pro-Black* and that is how he raised them [their children]. Sometimes I think he goes overboard. And now that they are older, they see it. You can't be too extreme at anything. You have to be in the middle; there has to be a gray area. For my husband there isn't one." Claudia erected a clear boundary between what she saw as her husband's *extreme* pro-Black political position and her more moderate Blackness. She defined her Blackness by outlining the type of Black cultural repertoire she does not embody. Her husband's practice of instilling reverence for Black cultural traditions of roots reggae, Afrocentric arts, and pan-African radical politics into his children was far left on the spectrum of Blackness and out of her comfort zone. While she saw herself as Black and learned its importance as a category of difference and solidarity in White Jewish spaces, her Blackness read as less direct or militant than that of her Jamaica-born husband. Although the Black population in general and the Black middle class in particular is seen as rallying behind a particular expression of Black identity, being Black and affiliating with a Black social sphere and adopting Black-identified cultural practices is only one position along a spectrum of cultural repertoires of

Blackness. Selective Blackness enables people to differentiate themselves from others they see as either "too Black" or "not Black enough." Claudia's selective Blackness is crafted through the clash between two important yet competing realities: her own moderate views on race relations and her husband's radical Black identity and practices. The contrast between Claudia and Winston's cultural repertoires illustrates an alternative position on the racial consciousness spectrum: *pro-Blackness*. Pro-Blackness is defined by espousing strong attachments to Black identities and promoting pan-African politics. Unlike selective Blackness, pro-Blackness involves engaging in active Black empowerment to advance the social, political, economic, spiritual, and cultural life of the Black world.

Rachel exemplifies this position. A forty-two-year-old Black American, she works as an office manager during the day and spends some of her evenings attending meetings or organizing events for the Parent-Teacher Association at Cascades High. She is the mother of two sons and has been married to her husband, Joseph, for almost twenty years. They were high school sweethearts and have lived in Cascades for most of their lives. Rachel enjoys living in an all-Black neighborhood and is especially drawn to the community feel of her block. Her husband's Bajan parents sold them their home before returning to Barbados to retire. "This area is so serious about being close-knit. Like when Mr. Hendrick died last year, they drove his casket down this block. They do it for everyone who passes away. They bring them back to the block. They do things a little different over here." Rachel and her family live in the same house that her husband was raised in. Their residential continuity deeply connects them to the history and culture of their block, and they engage in practices such as collective mourning, which passing on Black traditions of honoring the dead intergenerationally in Cascades.

Rachel grew up in a section of Cascades about one mile away from her current home. She was a child of the civil rights movement. When her mother purchased their Cascades home, there were only a handful of Black families living on the block, shaping her understandings of race and difference during her formative adolescent years. Like many other Black families in Cascades, Rachel's family moved there from a lower-income section of the city. As she came of age, she saw the rapid racial changes caused by White fight and flight and the entrance of families from across the Black diaspora.

Rachel described her Black identity as strong, upfront, and unapologetic. When I asked her how important her Black identity was to her, she said, "Very important. 'Cause it's who I am. When you see me, you see I am Black. But there is so much about us as a race that helps with your identity. That saying that "you have to know where you come from to know where you going." Like I said earlier about Whites being racist, that's how it has always been. Yes, times have changed and people are politically correct, but I think that when you don't know your culture, the history of your people, then you are missing something."

To Rachel, having a firm grasp of her own history as a Black woman gave her an important blueprint for her children's consciousness. She feels strongly tied to the Black world, which she sees as specifically Black American. The tensions between Black Americans, Jamaicans, and Haitians lead them to define boundaries around whom they consider authentically Black. For Rachel, the southern diaspora held the keys to the Black collectivity she felt most comfortable with. Her Bajan in-laws were the only Black immigrants with whom she shared strong, personal ties, making them the exception to this social boundary.

Because dominant discourses on Blackness center on the conflicted relationship between Blacks and Whites, we miss the opportunity to understand how Blackness is culturally defined, revered, and respected by people of diverse origins. Researchers have found that positive attitudes toward a person's Black racial identity serve as a protective factor that supports positive social development and gives them the strength to resist daily racist assaults on their character (Sellers, Copeland-Linder, Martin, and Lewis 2006). When we peel back the layers of the Black racial category, however, we see the enormous cultural work that defines it. Blackness and the institutions that Black people organize around it are a source of joy, comfort, desire, and solidarity (Lacy 2007; Neckerman, Carter, and Lee 1999). Yet it is rarely seen as an identity that brings pleasure to those who identify with it, indicating the historically pejorative manner in which White scholars and popular culture simplify dynamic definitions of Black identity, politics, and culture (Kelley 2001).

Most Black American respondents in this study espoused pro-Blackness. For them, being Black was of central cultural importance, not simply a protective mechanism for negotiating the assaults on their racial identity from non-Blacks. Rachel's pro-Black consciousness is shaped by her strong symbolic and material ties to Black culture and by her active interest in practicing and participating in Black life. Rachel preferred to remain rooted in an all-Black neighborhood to teach her children about being Black and building cohesive relationships within the Black community. Rachel cultivates this complicated and sensitive aspect of belonging: "I teach my sons that they are Black and it's something to be proud of. I am always giving them assignments when they come home from school. I have them write biographies and reports on Black famous people. Like, get a book, do some research and write it up. They need to know who they are and be proud of that. They can sit here and watch all these Black things on television and think that that is Black people." For Rachel, her definitions of being Black are in direct contradiction to the media's representations of Black people. Moreover, she "tells it like it is" and is constantly engaged in conversations and debates about the merits of Blackness with Whites and Latinos whom she interacts with on the job.

For those who adopt a pro-Blackness stance, being and belonging to Blackness is not simply about negotiating structural constraints; it centers on community, pro-social identities, and pride. This makes them distinct from those in the selective Blackness cultural positions. Pro-Blackness is a cultural space where the full range of skin complexions from light to dark are appreciated. In our interview in Great Park, Teresa went on for ten minutes about how "Black is beautiful" and that she had come to love her family members' various shades of brown. The coiled texture of their hair, the support of Black neighborhood traditions, and southern-style soul food constitute sites of shared community. Rachel's and Teresa's practices reflect the conviction that instilling knowledge and appreciation of Black history, culture, and politics is vital for Black youth, families, and communities.

Jamaican middle-class people in this category expressed distinct pan-African pathways to pro-Blackness. Rich, a fifty-year-old realtor, believed that lifting up the Black community starts with fortifying the Black identities of children. Rich was born in Brooklyn to Jamaican immigrant parents in the 1960s. He grew up working class when, as he described it, being a mail carrier was considered a steady, middle-class occupation. Rich's Jamaican heritage and his encounters with Black radicalism in

Brooklyn shaped his entrée to pro-Blackness through Afrocentric views of history and culture. His cultural pathway to pro-Blackness was heavily informed by Rastafarian political thought.

Rastafarianism is a social and religious movement firmly based in Marcus Garvey's pan-African agenda of global Blackness. Although it began as a response of poor, Afro-Jamaican labor communities to British colonial rule in the early twentieth century, the Jamaican diaspora in New York has infused its philosophies of antiracism and Black empowerment into their communities. Rich came of age during the rise of Rastafarianism in decolonizing Jamaica, as well as the civil rights and Black Power movement in New York. The meeting of these global antiracist social movements is at the core of his racial subjectivity. He argued that civilization began in Africa and that a shared memory of being the descendants of God's first and chosen people is central to uplifting Black people. When asked how he describes himself racially, he stated:

> Just a Black man, I'm just a Black man. [It is] very important because that's who I am. We don't realize this but, one day I'm looking at the Bible and reading the Bible. I'm reading Genesis and I'm reading about Adam and Eve and they talk about that they were in the garden. They start to describe the setting in the garden. The rivers Euphrates, Pishon, and Tigris. And it goes over everyone's head. Adam and Eve, they were leaping around Africa! It's just weird. Nobody ever says "Oh, I want to go back to Africa." Nobody does that. When you look at that, that's important. It's like, man, I know who I am. I am a prince. You know, a child of the most-high king. We don't realize that, so it's very important. You know you start to have *a conscious[ness]*. You see things, you just see things politically. You know, it's like why, why, why is it that always, they got to get the Black man? Why do you got to do that? We got to step up. We got to know who we are. I don't want to be conceited, but we need to realize that we're it. We don't realize that we're it, but we're it. Not to say I'm better than anybody, but I'm it.

Rich sees Black identity as conferring deep spiritual and cultural rewards across time and space. In his view, Blackness is at the heart of being a child of God, and being chosen holds the keys to a promised land for the Black diaspora.

From this perspective, selective Blackness is an internalization of Whites' negative opinions of Black people and avoids ties that would demonstrate Black solidarity. Pro-Blackness, in contrast, encourages the transcendence of racial fictions about Black one-dimensionality and promotes biblical and spiritual constructions of the superiority of African civilizations and their descendants. As a second-generation Jamaican immigrant, Rich embodies historical and cultural expressions of Blackness, but also questions why such a revered population is constantly being "got," or captured, penalized, tortured, and oppressed by White people. He is making sense of the collision between his positive constructions of Black Africanness and the persistent criminalization of Black people. Rich demonstrates similar orientations to Blackness as African Americans like Rachel who are trying to make sense of how their protective and validating notions of being Black collide with the messages and practices of an anti-Black society. Rich articulates a pan-African political and spiritual repertoire. This cultural stance is informed by Rastafarian and Garveyite politics that were born in Jamaica, but whose ideas and practices traveled with the diaspora to New York and have been spread throughout the Black urban and suburban communities since the mid-twentieth century.

The path to pro-Blackness for Haitian immigrants reflects the nexus of their national histories of Black revolutionary politics and their contemporary encounters with Black diasporic cultures in New York. When asked how he identified, Carlo Baptiste said: "Black, I'm a Negro." Carlo, forty-five, who was born in Haiti but grew up in New York, is employed as an administrative manager. He is married to Charlene, a Trinidad-born corporate manager; they have children ranging from the ages of two to sixteen. Carlo resides in Cascades and works for a predominately White corporation in Long Island, where he encounters constant racial insults. He has a gregarious personality, and throughout our conversation he pointed to his Black identity as being important to how he sees himself and carries himself in everyday life.

The Baptiste family purchased their home in predominately Black Cascades intentionally. They had the option to purchase a home in Nassau County but wanted to raise their children in a Black neighborhood. The family lives in close proximity to lower-income households and busy commercial streets, and Carlo joked that things "can get a little strange around this block." But he saw the neighborhood as a racially protective one for his children. He stated: "I don't want them to be the only ones. That's not

good for them and it's not good for their self-esteem. No, it's not for us."
Carlo and Charlene send their children to predominantly White private
schools in the city, and Carlo believes that they need a reprieve from their
constant engagement with the White world (Lacy 2007).

Carlo's pro-Blackness is also evident in his cultural consumption of
Black diasporic music. He shared: "We know we are Black. We fight everyone—we are proud of our color, our skin. *Noir* is Haitian, you can't separate that thing. Some people think they are French. But our music is
African, our religion is African." Carlo's consumption of Black music demonstrates his strong attachment to Black culture and art forms. He listens
mostly to hip-hop and rap—which he prefers to Haitian kompa—and the
Afro-Haitian roots music known as rara. However, he also consumes a
mix of pop, country, and soca music, which his Trinidadian wife plays regularly at home on the weekends. He identifies as Christian but believes in
the cultural power of voodoo, a spiritual practice bought to the Americas
by enslaved Africans. Carlo's pro-Blackness is strongly shaped by his
understanding of the cultural and intellectual history of Afro-Haiti.

POST-RACIAL BLACKNESS

Located at the opposite end of the racial consciousness spectrum from pro-
Blackness is post-racial Blackness. Post-racial Blackness involves a cultural
repertoire that is antithetical to Black identification and practices and, in
label and form, expressed the contradictions resulting from the tensions
between the political/economic progress of Black people since the 1960s
and persistent racial inequality. While pro-Blackness centers on people's
memories of Black history, cultural expressions, and the struggle against
White supremacy, post-racial Blackness is based on a denial of structural
racism and an avoidance of potentially stigmatizing cultural ties to
Blackness. The political climate of the twenty-first century is characterized
by contentious debates about whether American society is "beyond race."
Among the people I interviewed, the pervasive tension between their socioeconomic mobility into the middle class and spatial mobility into the suburbs, on one hand, and their continued individual and collective encounters with White racism, on the other, was a troubling feature of their lived

experience. Those who neither wanted to identify as Black nor participated in activities, social positions, and ideologies centered on the Black community articulated post-racial Black consciousness.

The term *post-racial* is undoubtedly controversial. The gains made by the Black middle class since the civil rights movement have been used in public discourses and in sociology to demonstrate the increasing significance of class in social relations. The election of Barack Obama is portrayed as the nail in the coffin of White domination. "My president is Black" conjures up the misguided belief that we are somehow beyond race in the United States. Despite the data demonstrating persistent racial stratification and the lived experiences of racial terror embedded in American political culture, some Black American, Jamaican, and Haitian interviewees espoused post-racial politics as their core identities.

As a cultural repertoire, post-racialism denies the continuing significance of racial oppression that continues to hinder social progress and democracy for many. Instead, it emerges from the desire of the successful few to imagine a world that has moved beyond race as social fact and identity. Post-racialism takes two forms. The first reproduces notions of White domination through anti-Black discourse (the pejorative terms *Uncle Tom* and *sellout* demonstrate the transgression of expectations of Black solidarity), often expressed through naivety or deliberate ignorance of the existing racial order. The second is an antiracist stance that seeks to undermine racial categorization in interpersonal interactions. Post-racial Blackness inevitably involves contradictions for Black people who operate in predominantly White settings. In the company of other Black people, they recount life events that reflect how race and racism shaped their social experiences, yet they chose to espouse the myth of post-racialism as a cultural identity to deny the power that White racism has to restrict their mobility.

Post-racial Blackness is not necessarily post-racism, however. Similar to the term *New Black* espoused by hip-hop artist Pharell, post-racial Blackness emerged from community critiques of Black celebrities who, because of their wealth, disconnect from the Black community, detach themselves from a collective Black identity, and decline to use their economic power to advance a racial justice agenda. Post-racial Blackness helps people unsubscribe from Black cultural identifiers unless it benefits them (usually in the form of profit). Post-racial Blackness creates a world where they proclaim that they "do not see" race, chastise people who recognize racism and speak truth to power, and disengage from Black solidarity projects.

Instead, those who espouse post-racial Blackness proffer anecdotes of their own or others' individual success to deny the existence of structural racism on the local, national, and global scale. This cultural repertoire was highlighted among the Black bourgeoisie described by Franklin Frazier (1957). In a scathing critique of newly monied Black families in the postwar United States, Frazier argued that middle-class Black society suffered from racial unconsciousness. Their obsession with status, consumption, and emulating a White world they could never break into came at a high cost. Their disengagement from the plight of the Black working class was construed as a moral transgression of the social expectation that the Black elite is called to lead the charge of Black progress. Instead, their pursuit of social status deprives them of a soul.

Post-racial Blackness, however, demonstrates that a segment of the Black diasporic middle class is not racially unconscious, but is instead hyper-conscious of racism. As a result, they seek to disassociate themselves from Blackness, ironically fortifying the color line that they seek to wish away. The twenty-first-century cultural repertoire of post-racial Blackness reflects the historical debates around Black solidarity, political mobilization, and progress that have occurred in the diaspora ever since slavery.

Jamaicans who espoused post-racial Blackness manifested the racial unconsciousness they brought with them from the island to New York's suburbs. These Jamaicans came from segments of Jamaican society that either benefitted from or aspired to the creole middle class. Central to the cultural repertoires of this brown and Black middle class is the belief that Jamaica is a post-racial, postcolonial, racially democratic nation (Thomas 2004). The Jamaica-born Black and British social theorist Stuart Hall (1990) argued that Black consciousness among Jamaicans was awakened only during their pan-African fight for independence from the British Empire in the early 1960s. Yet the remnants of colonial race relations and identities persisted. The Jamaican diaspora that emerged from these citizenship and nationhood narratives remakes these post-racial identities and belief systems into tools they use to navigate their lives and mobility in New York suburbs.

Phillip, a forty-six-year-old Great Park resident and engineer, migrated from Jamaica to New York to join his wife in 1998. With a light complexion and the build of a professional athlete, he exemplified the transnational migration of ideas of race, identity, and inequality that were the building blocks for Jamaicans in these post-racial cultural spaces. When asked for his perspective on race in the United States, Phillip asserted, "We took care of that Black-White problem a long time ago in Jamaica. We don't have that issue anymore." Phillip explained: "Growing up in Jamaica, it wasn't about race. Never. Because our motto [is] 'Out of many, One People.' Because we have a lot of interracial marriages, relationships and all of that. So it was never about your race. It was just about class. You know, you have the upper class, the middle class, and the poor. And everybody get along. Nobody looked at you because of the color of your skin or stuff like that, no." Phillip adopted a repertoire of post-racialism. His cultural pathway to post-racial Blackness in diasporic suburbia was informed by his consumption of national discourses of racial democracy as he came of age in postcolonial Jamaica, where his middle-class family enjoyed the power and privileges conferred on lighter-complexioned citizens. He uses this cultural repertoire to interpret racial encounters in the United States. He pointed to his economic success as a testament of American opportunities. He remarked that if he had been born in the United States, he would be "living in the Hamptons by now."

Post-racial Blackness is informed by an unwillingness to recognize Blackness as a positive attribute, participate actively in the Black world, and engage in racial justice struggles. Phillip harshly critiqued Black people in Jamaica and in the United States for using racism as an excuse for their own economic stagnation. It emphasized individuals' shortcomings as the main barrier to their upward mobility. He held very good jobs in the engineering industry and was well educated. Phillip recounted several questionable encounters with White peers, managers, and coworkers. In one instance, his White manager failed to give him a promised raise. But Phillip was adamant that the problems he experienced were not race based and used examples of positive encounters with Whites to deemphasize systematic racial discrimination.

Post-racial Blackness involves complicated boundary work. Postracial Blackness relinquishes its belonging to a Black community and highlight their interest in erasing racialized indicators and solidarities. For example, Nadege, thirty-four, was born in Haiti but came of age in New York. She argued that racial discrimination "is history," but she strategically minimized markers of Blackness to avoid discrimination today. Herein lies the contradictions of post-racialism and post-racial Blackness. Her family arrived as political exiles during the coup d'état in the 1990s. She described her upbringing in Haiti as a "fairy tale," surrounded with all the accoutrements of affluence. Nadege displayed a bourgeois persona and was hesitant to recognize race as a factor in her diasporic experiences in New York. Deeply uncomfortable with identifying as Black, she employed many strategies to cross racial boundaries. I met Nadege during my fieldwork with a community organization in Cascades. A single mother, she had pronounced facial features, mocha brown skin, and a subtle smile. She was a public health specialist who canvassed communities of color across the five boroughs for health screenings. On this particular day, she was organizing free dental checkups for uninsured neighborhood residents.

Nadege recounted:

> I don't really like when people keep asking your race. Because I feel like, somehow there is a . . . [long pause] on applications because I feel like, as if, you know, sometimes things can become . . . [long pause] I would say I think sometimes it can, how do I say? People judge you based on your race without knowing your sources. But I don't like to put stigma on myself. Yes, I know my history; don't get me wrong. But I also feel like it's [a] different type of generation. There is opportunity given to people and you can still do something. You can still do something, and not use excuses.

Nadege adopted an attitude that racism and mobility cannot coexist and that Blacks' reliance on "excuses" keeps them in a subjugated position. She used her nationality to demonstrate her non-Blackness and to avoid the stigmas attached to Black people.

Later in the interview, Nadege indicated an allegiance to post-racial Blackness through her son's name selection. She named her son Jack, which she believed would make him more acceptable to Whites with whom he may interact in everyday life.

NADEGE:	That's why people may not like what I'm going to say but . . . that's why even some names I don't believe in giving to a child.
INTERVIEWER:	Okay, like what types of names?
NADEGE:	You know, I will really not say.
INTERVIEWER:	Like the types of names now that . . .
NADEGE:	You know, I feel like college application; they are going to look after a child and then, oh, he's Black.
INTERVIEWER:	Yeah, right. So, what's your son's name?
NADEGE:	His name is Jack.

In an attempt to break down potential barriers to upward mobility, Nadege stripped her son of characteristics that would indicate his ancestry.

Names are important signifiers of status. In Haiti, surnames act as passports to status recognition. Particular surnames indicate what family one belongs to and can reveal a person's social class in a neighborhood or town. Therefore, a family name can indicate one's place in the country's spectrum of bourgeoisie to proletariat classes. Perpetuating this tradition, first names that signify status are a part of the culture of mobility post-racial Haitian immigrants activate as they try to move up in the socioeconomic system.

Surnames have been especially malleable among immigrants. Family names often indicate national origin. Historically Southern and Eastern European immigrants have changed their names in an effort to become indistinguishable from WASPs and avoid ethnoracial exclusion. For Black Americans with creative first names, this process has become even more complex, as Black job applicants with a "Black name" are less likely to be called back and interviewed than those with White-sounding or racially ambiguous names (Lavergne and Mullainathan 2004). The problem in the labor market lies with the White gatekeepers who prefer to hire other Whites (and even favor White offenders over Black non-offenders; see Pager 2003). Nadege skirted around this discriminatory preference; instead of giving her son a name that affirms his ethnic or racial background. She disapproved of those types of names and Black parents who chose them. Highly sensitive to potential attacks on her racial identity, Nadege participated in race-aversive behaviors and tactics.

The racial consciousness spectrum in general and the cultural repertoire of post-racial Blackness in particular reflect the transcultural negotiation of race, racism, and nation happening among the Black diasporic
middle class. Many use their clothing, hairstyles, and material resources
to dim bright racial boundaries they encounter and to display their class
status to Whites (Feagin and Sikes, 1996). The common interest of post-
racial Blackness is the intense interest in preserving class and status for
themselves and their children in an anti-Black society.

SPACE AND SPECTRUM

Residential context mattered for the patterns of being and belonging to
Blackness as it was defined by the adults I interviewed. While Black
Americans and Jamaicans who expressed pro-Blackness were distributed
fairly evenly across Cascades and Great Park, Haitians who espoused pro-
Blackness resided mostly in Great Park. This difference points to several
important themes. First, residential settlement in the more affluent,
racially mixed suburb is paired with upward class mobility. However, it
also entails frequent interracial interactions and confrontations with
White society and racism. Racial awareness and socialization are stimulated by suburban residence, leading to stronger attachments to a Black
identity in conjunction with ties to a smaller immigrant community. This
process marks an integration into the Black American middle class of
experiences and subjectivities that have yet to be considered. African
Americans were the first Black families in predominately White ethnic
areas. They came of age in contested environments where school desegregation was met with widespread White retribution, White friends disin-
vited them to social events, and they adopted the "Black is Beautiful"
campaign as a way of stating their belonging in suburbia. Haitians and
Jamaicans who were new to the United States and suburbia inherited
these histories and learned how to negotiate contemporary problems of
continued racial exclusion.

Haitians and Jamaicans, however, exhibited some differences in their
location on the racial consciousness spectrum when we examined their
experiences in Cascades versus Great Park. For example, Joseph Duvivier,

a Haitian immigrant who grew up in New York and resided in Great Park, articulated a pro-Black identity and practice. He and his wife, both high-ranking health professionals, owned a modest home and sent their children to elite private schools. They felt that their son was missing quality connections with Black children. They decided to join Jack and Jill. The day of our interview they received an invitation to a local Jack and Jill orientation meeting. "I think it's good for him. . . . It will expose him to good things and people," Joseph shared. The Duvivier family values and actively engages with the Black community in their professional lives. They also do this as a respite from their constant social engagement with the White world (Lacy 2007). In their upper-middle-class community, the Duviviers and Great Park Jamaican families use an historically elite Black American organization to reinforce an exclusive version of Black community formation. What was most striking, however, was that the Stephensons, a core middle-class Jamaican family living several blocks away in Great Park, pursued Black diasporic church spaces in the Bronx that were class heterogeneous, while the Duvivier family selected Jack and Jill social groups on Long Island, which are likely to only have upper-income, elite Black members. For them, strategically joining elite Black communities demonstrated class-specific identification and ties to the Black world. This allowed them to immerse themselves and their children in an upper-middle-class Black community while limiting their interactions with the White world, and lower-income families in Black New York.

The Black world consists of different and dynamic cultural worlds. The identities of the Black bourgeoisie hinges upon their peculiar position in racial capitalism. Because "middle class" in the United States is a construction designed to ensure Whites' full access to economic resources, upwardly mobile Blacks are often caught amid tensions between racial and class solidarity. When we unpack the nationality heterogeneity of the Black middle class, we see that the colonial and postcolonial histories of Black Americans, Haitians, and Jamaicans shape their consciousness of these conflicting solidarities and the intersectional ways in which they see themselves vis-à-vis a rigid global and local racial structure. The racial consciousness spectrum provides us with a paradigm to begin discerning the cultural work involved in identifying as Black and to explore how it is challenged and redefined in everyday life across ethnonational groups, space, and time.

The portrayal of racial identity in the Black middle class by social scientists and other outside observers argues that they employ a range of public, racial, class, and ethnic repertoires to negotiate their encounters with White racism in everyday life. Middle-class Black Americans are said to strategically use visible markers of status in order to convey their middle-classness, but also seek Black spaces of refuge from anti-Black workplaces, schools, and neighborhoods. Middle-class West Indians, on the other hand, are believed to be reluctant to accepting race as a social fact in their everyday life and cling to their nationality and accents to demonstrate that they are a different type of Black people. Upon repeated experiences with racism, however, they develop a racial consciousness. I pick up where other studies have left off by analyzing how middle-class Black Americans, Haitians, and Jamaicans in diasporic suburbs articulate variable relationships to individual and collective Black identities.

This chapter moves beyond the distancing framework, which dichotomizes the Black American and West Indian middle classes' approach to Black identity. This chapter has argued that these diasporic groups experience and articulate Black consciousness along a continuum. This racial consciousness spectrum is comprised of different cultural positions that represent people's ties to Black identity and their affiliations with Black communities. Examining how people articulate and enact their racial consciousness reveals variations both within and across ethnonational groups. Although Black Americans are portrayed as adopting intense Black identities because of their long exposure to the American brand of White supremacy, some members of the Haitian and Jamaican diasporas also adopt this stance. Yet Black Americans and their Haitian and Jamaican neighbors have different cultural definitions and pathways to Blackness that are shaped by coming of age in the post-colonial and post–civil rights era and the movement of ideas about Black progress and people across regional and national boundaries in the Caribbean and the United States.

The notion that Black immigrants come from societies that deemphasize race is an ahistorical depiction of Jamaican and Haitian societies. These nations have centered the *presence Africaine* (Hall 1990), the African presence, of their country's formation from the revolutionary period through the decolonization epoch. Intellectual and political communities in both countries espoused pan-African political consciousness alongside Global South politics that ranged from reformist to revolutionary. These cultural repertoires have been amplified globally through the media and the migrations of their citizens to diasporic cities such as New York. This chapter has demonstrated that there is a wider historical range of histories of antiracism and anticolonial movements before migration to the United States and racial consciousness among Black Americans and Black immigrants than generally recognized. The racial consciousness spectrum is shaped both by the histories of these diasporas and by the politics of their encounters in the United States, New York City, and the suburbs in which they reside.

In the previous chapter, we met Black middle-class people who grew up as aristocrats at home and reasserted trans-geographical class distinctions in suburbia. This chapter shows that many members of this class strata follow a similar pattern of engaging with post-racial Blackness as a tool to assert their class superiority to other Blacks. In contrast, people who "moved on up" the economic ladder from poverty to the middle class articulated stronger attachments and belonging to Blackness. Residential context also played an important role in people's cultural attachments to Black identities and practices. In Great Park, heightened exposure to racial exclusion from White neighbors meant that more residents expressed a strong attachment to pro-Blackness. However, their ties to Black communities were either with elite or economically diverse social groups. Residence in the elite suburb meant that Black immigrants in Great Park were invited to join Black Americans' elite organizations on Long Island, which they saw as a way of solidifying their class status and passing it on to their children. This diasporic perspective on racial identity negotiation across position, space, and time among the Black middle class allows us to see how the cultural identities around race reflect multifaceted and changing orientations to Black identity and community in the twenty-first century. The spectrum in racial consciousness demonstrates variability within the Black racial category as much as it shows conver-gence between Black Americans, Haitians, and Jamaicans who occupy the same cultural position. They all traveled different journeys to arrive there. In the next chapter, we turn to how these overlapping diasporas make sense of their place in racial capitalism by creating local ethnic hierarchies within diasporic suburbia.

7 Green Juice Fast

SKINFOLK DISTINCTION MAKING

All my skinfolk ain't kinfolk.

Zora Neale Hurston

I met Pastor Jenkins in Cascades in the spring of 2011. He lived in a house adjacent to the church congregation he served. Before being selected as their senior pastor a couple of years earlier, he had pastored a church in Georgia. Pastor Jenkins, his wife, Justine, and their children were still getting adjusted to the mundane challenges of daily life in Queens. The pastor was very busy during the morning I interviewed him in his large office in a wing of the church building. He answered multiple calls from his wife, who needed his help unloading the groceries she had purchased for the church's afterschool program. Justine was also carrying the fruits and vegetables they needed for the new juicing diet initiative organized by the church, which had both spiritual and medicinal purposes. A number of people I met were changing their diets, requesting that Village Market carry organic products, and establishing groups to address health problems such as diabetes and high blood pressure. An aerobics afterwork program was organized by the women's ministry. Pastor Jenkins' new regimen made him more exhausted than usual, he said.

> This is exactly what I think our community needs. And I am going to tell you why. I have worked for the past couple of months on the Boulevard. You think

about lunchtime and you think about where you gonna go, where you gonna get some food. There aren't too many options about where you are gonna go. Are you gonna go to McDonalds or spend money on the local restaurants like the Jamaican spot or the Haitian spot? The Chinese food spot? And the food is not healthy. It's a greasy spoon; Jamaican is high in fat. See, that is my issue. So where is our Panera Bread? Where can I get a decent salad? You know, we have to watch our diet—high blood pressure, hypertension, diabetes. I'm trying to get my congregation to do a Daniel fast with me, just fruits and vegetables and prayer for a week.[1] Just one. We can't eat yams and bread all the time.

While Pastor Jenkins stepped out to help his wife with multiple grocery bags, I noticed that he had earned his master's degree from an elite school. He had also received a number of awards recognizing his community service. The plaques were hung next to pictures of President Obama, Malcolm X, and Martin Luther King Jr. Together, these framed awards and images decorated an entire wall between his expansive office windows.

Pastor Jenkins had quickly inserted himself into the public life of Cascades. He served hundreds of parishioners in a Protestant church that has historically consisted of families of the Great Migration, but now a growing number of worshippers were from Jamaica, Trinidad, Panama, and Barbados. He was involved in the civic association, local task forces, block associations, and the community board that addressed the needs of Black, White, Asian, and Latinx groups in and beyond Cascades. When he arrived from the South, he relied on parishioners and neighbors to learn the local culture and social codes of Cascades. The combination of his associational affiliations and interpersonal interactions led to his assessment that Cascades was ethnically heterogeneous and that, albeit predominately Black, people interpreted and used these differences across nationality in ways that forged interpersonal and institutional divisions. Pastor Jenkins stated: "The tension is there. I have not seen anything overt, but the tension is definitely there. You can tell how the lines are drawn relationally and when you conduct business and take care of all things political." He had discovered that nationality was an important fault line that organized social relations. "You know when I moved here, a person in the community made a comment to me that 'there are only a few of us Blacks, you know, southern Blacks, African American Blacks left in the neighborhood' because of the number of Caribbeans and more specifically the Haitians who moved into the neighborhood."

Migrants from the South and their adult children who have built their lives in Cascades see themselves as Black, southern people. These identities have been strengthened through their direct contacts with Black immigrants who have entered Cascades in increasing numbers. Black Americans demarcate a subjective and cultural boundary between themselves and Black immigrants from the islands in the Caribbean Sea, often using the pan-ethnic term *Caribbeans* to refer to them.[2] Among themselves, Black southerners discuss the ethnic transformation of their neighborhood namely that Great Migrants and their children were being replaced by Black immigrants who are purchasing homes and renting spaces to family members, friends, and strangers. For Black Americans, their sense of cultural incompatibility with the Black newcomers has solidified a southern Black regional identity.

At the same time, some southern migrants and their children were leaving New York and returning to the South, with which they had retained strong familial, psychic and cultural ties (Griffin 1996). For some Great Migrants, indeed, the desire to return "home" someday was an important anchor (Cromartie and Stack 1989, Pendergrass 2013, Shannon 1997, Stack 1996, Wilkerson 2011). Famous African American playwright August Wilson, a child of the Great Migration, articulated the belief that Black southerners lost more than they had gained by migrating to the North, Midwest, and West, for they had forfeited strong Black communities and a sense of "who we are" (Shannon 1997, 659).[3] Forty years after the Great Migration, when Black southerners had become middle class New Yorkers, questions of community and identity still permeated their lives. The long-term decline of manufacturing, the metropolitan and fiscal crisis, and the rising cost of decent housing prompted them to retreat to thriving southern cities such as Atlanta and Charlotte. Sections of Cascades were inhabited mainly by people of retirement age, and some left for the South's warmer climate and cultural comforts. For Black Americans, the entrance of Black immigrants into their neighborhoods reshaped their ties to community, and sense of belonging. Their concerns about the loss of community prompted the desires of some residents to return to ancestral lands their families had left behind half a century ago.

When introduced to the culture of Cascades, Pastor Jenkins became aware of the boundaries between Black Americans and Caribbean immigrants. However, he also discovered that divisions existed between various groups of immigrants, as well as between them and Black Americans: "Even in terms of marriage, you have a lot of people who are of a Caribbean ethnic group who want their children only to marry within that group, who would not necessarily want their children to marry someone outside. You don't see a lot of marriages of Jamaican people and Haitian people. You know, and then there is some African Americans who don't want either as in-laws, so, it's there. The challenge is, can we find some unified purpose? So we can actually work together?"

Heterosexual cross-ethnic marriage and romantic relationships, the most intimate of relations between people from different nationalities, were features of interior life in middle-class suburbs. Black neighborhoods and institutions in New York have historically been the meeting places of men and women from various countries and regions. As a result of these encounters, they build friendships and romantic relationships across ethnic and sometimes racial lines. Yet these relationships often meet social resistance. I interviewed married couples who were Jamaican and American, Haitian and Trinidadian, and American and Guyanese. These interethnic marriages witnessed tensions between the partners' families (See Ostine, 2007 for counternarrative). For the Benningtons, with a Jamaican father and a Black American mother, holidays spent with one or the other side of the family were marked by cultural learning, missteps, and sometimes insults, which they and their children learned to navigate over time. The sentiments that underlie the private and public encounters among Black diasporic groups evoke the words that the inimitable anthropologist, author, and activist Zora Neale Hurston used to describe divisions in the Black community: "All my skinfolk ain't kinfolk."

NATIONALITY NARRATIVES AND THE LOCAL DIASPORIC HIERARCHY

In this chapter, we are concerned with the meanings of diaspora, nationality, and region in Black suburbia. Distinctions within the Black diaspora are nothing new. Before Black people were stolen from their tribal lands in West Africa, they were from different linguistic, cultural, religious, and territorial ethnic groups. The slave trade made them into "Africans," and European's racial capitalism imposed the Black racial label on them. Whites racialize members of the African diaspora, using this singular classification to continuously subjugate them. Since the end of racial slavery and colonialism, however, important and varying relationships to the ethnoracial power structure and nation-state identities have emerged.

Race is a dominant feature in Black-White life chances, experiences, and relations. Nationality among the Black diaspora presents an additional layer of inequalities. For example, the relationship of Black Americans to Whites is characterized by ongoing White domination over those who are the descendants of enslaved African people. Black Jamaicans, however, are interpreted differently by Whites and White ethnics who engage in divide-and-conquer cultural politics. White employers, for example, report preferring Jamaicans for employment because they have a "better work ethic" and do not challenge White American domination over Black Americans in the workplace. Middle-class Jamaicans, in particular, are interpreted by Whites as a model minority (Waters, 1999, Ifatunji, 2017). They are English speakers with British cultural repertoires. White employers' preference for Jamaican white- and blue-collar workers reinforces the larger racial status quo: the incorporation of small numbers of Black people born outside the United States into what had been exclusively White occupations creates false narratives of racial progress, while allowing Whites' power in the labor market to remain unchallenged (Winant 2001). Haitians are interpreted as a low-status group by White American society. Their foreign-language, French colonial legacies, *presence Africaine*, and fraught relations with US imperialism and immigration policy make Haitians categorical outsiders as Black immigrants and non-English speakers who are deemed to be poor, uneducated, and from a politically volatile society.

Beyond the limited perspectives that Whites have on the Black diaspora, the encounters and interactions between Black diasporic groups have historically been characterized by both cooperation and conflict. Studies have demonstrated that national identity is a salient marker of difference in relations between Blacks from different corners of the diaspora who meet in international cities (Watkins-Owens 1996, Stepick and Swartz 1998, Zephir 2001). Often the tensions between these migrant and immigrant groups are seen as resulting from economic and social competition, and the spokespeople for these problems are often their political leaders. Researchers argue that Black Americans feel that immigrants have come to take jobs and opportunities that should be reserved for Blacks with a history in the United States that dates back to slavery (Gay 2006, Marrow 2011). These claims lead many working- and middle-class Black Americans to see Black immigrants as "others." Black immigrants, on the other hand, engage in *ethnic projects* whereby they strategically emphasize their ethnic distinctiveness from Black Americans in order to improve their position in the racial hierarchy and chances for social mobility (Treitler, 2013). This strategy has been a failed attempt to escape racial discrimination. This distancing is regarded as mainly occurring among middle-class West Indians (Waters 1999) and amounts to a native-born versus foreign-born divide that has been referred to as the "diaspora wars."[4]

Reducing intergroup tensions to a matter of economic competition does not account for their cultural basis and their persistence within the Black middle class. This chapter explores the meanings of ethnicity, region national origins in the subjectivities and worldviews of everyday middle-class people of the Black diaspora. Through their social interactions with one another across ethnonational lines in suburban New York, they create what I call a local diasporic hierarchy. Nationality is an exceedingly complicated terrain for peoples of the Black Atlantic, who were first Africans, and then Americans, Haitians, Dominicans, and Cubans when nation-states solidified along with modern racial capitalism. After emancipation, large numbers of Black people moved across the Atlantic in search of economic and political liberation, crossing and recrossing the boundaries of empires and nation states.

Encounters between middle-class adults of different nationalities give rise to *nationality narratives*, sets of identities and lore about how each person's own ethnic group stacks up against others culturally, morally, socially, and economically. These narratives are shaped not only by the rootedness of these groups in national histories of race, nation, and empire, but by their new encounters with other Black ethnic groups in everyday life in New York. These narratives congeal into a local diasporic hierarchy. While it is shaped by ideological understandings of the past, it is dynamic rather than static, as it is reshaped by continuous interactions between different Black nationality groups who overlap in New York's diasporic suburbs. This perspective goes beyond structural or economic notions of intergroup competition, it recognizes the complex ways in which the encounters between Black middle-class diasporas elicit confusion, suspicion, conflicts, and cooperation inside and outside their suburban enclaves.

The nationality narratives of the African diaspora are different from those of Jews, who also came from many nation states, and those of Germans or Italians, who left before their nations was unified. For the Black diaspora, the transatlantic slave trade complicated allegiances to any one nation. The continuous trading of slaves throughout the Atlantic; post-emancipation migrations throughout the Caribbean, the United States, and South America; and the rise of postcolonial nation-states in the wake of revolutions and decolonization make the relationship between nationality, ethnicity, and Blackness exceedingly convoluted. This chapter unpacks the continuity of these phenomena in twenty-first century suburbia by examining how nationality narratives organize cultural relations within and between middle-class Black Americans, Haitians, and Jamaicans.

Their nations and regions of origin are important points of reference for Haitians, Jamaicans, and Black Americans in Cascades and Great Park. Today immigrants from the African continent, particularly Nigeria and Ghana, are also growing in number in these communities. These groups have common histories of colonialism, but different experiences with national liberation, contestation over racialized dictatorships and democracies, and imperialism that define their variegated relationships with "home." Their strategies for upward mobility are characterized by strong ethnic boundaries and us-versus-them politics.

The sum of these interactions is a local ethnic stratification system. The identity posturings of Black Americans, Haitians, and Jamaicans are intra-Black ethnic projects. The goal of nationality narratives is to demonstrate that a group deserves to climb the local diasporic hierarchy. The process of making one's national-self occurs across multiple groups in various spaces, contains cross-national and interactional boundary work, and constitutes an important fault line that New York's Black middle class learns to navigate in diasporic settings in addition to, and simultaneously with, divisions of race and class.

In response to nationality narratives that scaffold the local ethnic hierarchy, some people form pan-ethnic or racial solidarity projects. The hierarchy of nationality groups in Cascades and Great Park is created through a set of relationships that emerge as diasporas encounter one another as neighbors, schoolmates, coworkers, and organization members. In a system of cultural stratification created by beliefs about one's group vis à vis others, nationality groups subscribe to and enforce a locally designed system of normative rules of interpretation and interactions. A range of subjectivities and boundaries animate the structure and durability of this diasporic hierarchy.

The local ethnic hierarchy and its contents complicate how we think about the Black middle class. Karyn Lacy's model of the Black middle-class toolkit model (Lacy 2007), outlines the social identities and practices that help people navigate their movement between the Black and White worlds. But the Black world consists of many smaller ethno-national worlds. I extend the Black middle-class toolkit to reflect the identities that residents of Cascades and Great Park create in order to navigate the multiple ethno-national worlds that exist inside their homes, neighborhoods, and workplaces and in their outside worlds. Important cross-ethnic identity work is being done in diasporic suburbs. Recognizing this work broadens our understanding of race, class, migration and immigration. Cultural work is involved in making and unmaking diasporic ties among the Black *class moyenne*, and elucidates that suburbs are important sites for navigating multiple forms of racial and ethnic inequality in daily life. As various Black diasporas come together in private and public settings, sets of identities and practices emerge that help them navigate these diasporic spaces, assert their belonging to them, demonstrate status and build solidarity relative to the other Black people whom they meet. With this framework in mind, the chapter turns to the interactions and everyday talk that expose how members of distinct but overlapping middle-class Black diasporas make sense and meaning out of one another and themselves. The next section discusses the social processes by which nationality narratives build up a local diasporic hierarchy, group by group.

BLACK AMERICANS: DISOWNED AND REJECTED VERSUS MARTYRS AND GATEKEEPERS

My Black American interviewees painted, a portrait of Cascades and Great Park as having disjointed diasporic figures. The harsh judgments and ridicule they receive from Black immigrants collide with their self-perception as the descendants of generations who toiled, marched, and died for Black liberation. They argue that they are owed respect, loyalty, and reverence from immigrant newcomers, who owe the opportunities they now enjoy to Black Americans' protracted struggles. Instead, Black Americans feel that they are social rejects in the eyes of Caribbean immigrants. Through a combination of verbal and nonverbal slights from neighbors and associates, they have developed a dual consciousness of encounters between Black ethnic groups as distinct from cross-racial interactions. They recognized that how Haitian and Jamaican immigrants viewed them as a group was in direct opposition to how they viewed themselves. The attitudes they encountered in their neighborhoods, workplaces, churches, and organizations came as a shock, leading to intense disappointment among many of the Black Americans. When they saw themselves through the eyes of Haitians and Jamaicans, Black Americans did not like what they saw and were troubled by the ways these perceptions paralleled the rejection they encountered from Whites and Latinx communities.

How They See Us and How We See Ourselves

The social interactions between Black Americans and immigrants in their neighborhood taught them more about how they were viewed among the Black diaspora than about the actual interior life, culture, and mores of each immigrant group. They said that many Black immigrants whom they met as neighbors, coworkers, church congregants, organizational members, service providers, and sometimes friends or family members expressed an attitude of superiority that was palpable in social interactions. Kim, forty-five, Black American office manager and Cascades resident, said that when middle-class Black Americans interact with people from Asia and the Caribbean, they are made acutely aware that these newcomers feel like they are "above us."

KIM: I believe everyone is racist. I believe that when, like, okay, this is going to sound so horrible. I believe that when people look at me, they only see my color, and I only see theirs. And even if they're Chinese, Haitian, Jamaican, umm Trinidad, I believe that everyone—especially when it comes to us Americans—feels like they are *above us*.

OC: So you think the immigrants, they come and they think of you like that? So they can look at you and will think you're American? They wouldn't mistake you for being from, say, Jamaica?

KIM: Maybe until I open my mouth. Most Jamaican women know right off the bat I'm not Jamaican, because I'm a "pushy little American." I don't find Jamaican women take to me too well. My girlfriend was Jamaican; I met her mother, and her mother didn't like me. But there was something about my presence that rubbed her the wrong way. And it was 'cause I was a "pushy American." There is a West Indian lady up the block; she doesn't care for me either. She is very *screw face* when she sees me. And I'm like, OK. My girlfriend said that, "You are a pushy bossy American woman in their eyes." And I was like "OK, oh well." I did notice that there is a cultural difference, and I don't know what that is. That's where one of my racist comments will come in and I will keep that to myself.

Kim's Jamaican girlfriend provides her with insight into how she is perceived by older Jamaican women. In the cross-ethnic friendship, Kim is alienated from her friend's family.

Kim routinely encountered nonverbal expressions of disapproval from Jamaican women in her neighborhood and in her friendship network as well. She has come to rationalize this interaction with Jamaican women as a product of her nationality as American, her gender as a woman, and her outspoken personality. She believes that the combination of these characteristics makes her unpalatable to Jamaican immigrant women in Cascades, who see her as an "overbearing Black American." In saying that "everyone is racist," she also emphasized the salience of nationality as a marker of difference and distinction within her public and private interactions in Cascades. The Jamaican women with whom Kim has contentious interactions came of age under the strict social codes of respectability in Jamaica. Disseminated by the mulatto and Black post-colonial middle class, this respectability politic is highly gendered, as women are expected to behave in a way that is proper, quiet, and "classy." This cultural script of Jamaican femininity has historically been defined by White, British, middle-class womanhood and imposed upon Jamaicans through the assimilationist cultural practices of colonialism. The image of respectable and upright middle-class Jamaican women who speak the Queen's English in a genteel tone is in direct conflict with rural and urban proletarian women, such as higglers, who sell goods in the market and use their bodies and voices to contest and disrupt the race, class, and gendered hierarchies that restrict their social and spatial mobility in Jamaica (Brown-Glaude 2011).

When these daughters of postcolonial Jamaica who belong or aspire to the middle class migrate to New York and make their way to middle-class suburbs, they bring gendered ideologies about class and propriety with them and reshape it to interact with the gendered racism found in the United States. These repertoires are reflected in their interactions with multiple diasporas in New York, producing transnational hierarchies of race, class, and gender. Kim encountered a Jamaican system that marginalized and restricted poor Afro-Jamaican women by constructing their voices and bodies and actions as low status and illegitimate. These conceptions are compounded by gendered racism in the United States, which seeks to silence and subjugate Black American women who are deemed too loud and aggressive because they assert their humanity and speak truth to power in White and Black spaces (Fordham 1993).

The politics of Black women's respectability and silencing in Jamaica is compounded by the cultural and structural war White people and institutions have waged against Black women and matriarchal or mother-centered households (Greenbaum 2015). The gendered racism that constructs Black American woman as unfeminine reflects established interests of White hegemony in repressing Black women who resist White and Black patriarchy and White feminism as they seek to claim their liberation, rights, and respect. The nationality narratives that Kim encounters in her interactions with Jamaican women is a product of the racial, class, and gendered inequalities both here in the Unites States and there in Jamaica. Inscribed into the micro-level social interactions of Kim and her Jamaican women neighbors are boundaries created through a web of multiple cross-national hierarchies of racial, class, and gender stratification.

Kim's experience with Jamaican women exemplifies the hypervisibility of Black Americans to Jamaicans in the local diasporic hierarchy. This hypervisibility, however, coexists with the social invisibility of Black Americans in Black middle-class spaces. Deidre, a Cascades resident in her sixties and a technology specialist, is one of the few people I interviewed who was the child of Black bourgeois parents. Deidre is educated, fair skinned, and vocal about her admirations for the "high culture" institutions in the city, such as the Alvin Ailey Dance Theater and the New York Philharmonic Orchestra. Although Deidre's education, skills, and community leadership roles make her generally middle class, these characteristics led her to be misrecognized as Jamaican by Jamaicans in Cascades. They believe that her political public identity makes it impossible for her to be Black American. Deidre explains:

> It is interesting. Like Janelle, I think her husband is Haitian. I think that is what Kendra said. But she told Kendra that she thought Americans were lazy and Jamaicans were hardworking people. And when Kendra told me what this woman had said, "Oh I thought Deidre would be Jamaican," you know. She is like, "No" (laugh).
>
> And there was a woman who is a board member of my community organization that I had offered to give a ride home to. And she asked Kendra, where was I born. "You mean she is not Jamaican?" she asked. She figured that I was Jamaican because they have this notion that Americans are lazy. "Because she is well spoken and she seems educated so I figured that she must be Jamaican" is what she thought. And Kendra shared that with me. She said that to her: "I thought Deidre would be Jamaican cause she is so well spoken and she seems educated."

Jamaicans' assumptions that influential middle-class Black Americans are immigrants created awkward interactions that they had to learn how to negotiate. The popular culturally racist assumption in academic and public circles is that to be Black in America is to be poor. This viewpoint elucidates the significance of anti-Black cultural racism in the post-civil rights moment: the prevalent assumption that Black people occupy lower-class positions in the socioeconomic hierarchy because of deficiencies in their culture that prevent them from taking advantage of the opportunities they are now offered.[5] Jamaicans reproduce these scripts in encounters with Black Americans in their own middle-class neighborhoods. This view reflects the narratives that fuel the engine of an economy and culture based on racial capitalism. Yet this myth does not match the demographic or cultural realities of Black Americans who have no recent foreign-born ancestry. Despite the countless barriers to Black mobility, Black Americans occupy a myriad of class statuses ranging from poor to working class to middle class to affluent. Black immigrants and their children enter into a Black stratification system that may be exceedingly complex, depending on the occupational opportunity structure of the metropolitan area where they live. When Haitian and Jamaican diasporas first entered the United States, they resided in low-income, predominately Black and hyper-segregated neighborhoods. Therefore, their encounters with Black Americans were often with low-income families.

When Black Americans and Black immigrant families acquire enough capital, they often follow intra-metropolitan migration patterns to middle-class Black American suburbs. However, the notion that all Black Americans are poor travels with Black immigrants. It is compounded by Black immigrants' desire to create narratives that bolster the image of their own group at the expense of the image of others. Even in interactions with Black Americans in the middle class, persistent culturally racist labels remind us that White domination continues to infiltrate relations within the Black diaspora. Black immigrants buy into these racialized narratives and use them in order to climb the local ethnic hierarchy. Combining racist tropes and national hierarchies, these narratives structure the local status hierarchies of diasporic suburbs. Indeed, even in the presence of middle-class Black Americans, Jamaicans continue to evoke culturally racist views of Black Americans. In addition to the Black-White color line, the Black American middle class negotiates ethnic fault lines in diasporic encounters, which undermine their ability to successfully convey their status and belonging as they traverse the diasporic Black world.

"You Don't Know Our Struggle"

What cultural work do Black Americans do to offset the devaluation of their culture during encounters with "skinfolk" who are not "kinfolk?"

Black Americans use moral and cultural boundaries to assert their desired social status among the diaspora. One strategy involves demonstrating that the success of Black immigrants as well as Black Americans is the legacy of the civil rights movement. They argue that they have a powerful and unique heritage of advocating for democracy, justice, and equal citizenship in the United States and that their long struggle for freedom and equality has pried open the doors for immigrants. Identifying themselves as heirs of this moral tradition, Black Americans use this history as a marker of their moral superiority and to establish their claim to honor and respect for the sacrifices they and their ancestors made so that Black, Asian, and Latinx immigrants can experience moderate levels of social success today. In this process, they assert a sense of deservingness to a status above that of Black immigrants, who, they argue, overlook, minimize, or are ignorant of the political labor of Black citizens in this country and are benefitting from an opportunity structure they did not work to create. Sheila, fifty, Black American, Cascades resident, and an office manager, explained:

> Well I have heard that it's been said that the Jamaicans come here and talk about African Americans. You don't know the struggle that the African Americans been through. There were people who allowed this to happen. It's not the Jamaican or the Haitian history. They don't know that history. You can't come here and say some of the things that you say about the African American. A lot of times to get along with people, you have to meet people where they are. You gotta get along with your neighbor. You have to make an effort to.

Sheila argued that Jamaicans and Haitians are newcomers to the racial landscape of the United States and the struggles for Black liberation. Therefore, Haitians and Jamaicans wrongly judge the condition of Black Americans in America, painting them with a broad brush instead of seeking cooperation and collaboration. Sheila thought that Black immigrants believed that Black Americans had "sold out" to White people and allowed them to define standards of beauty and aspiration. Sheila's response is to stand up against what she regarded as an anti–Black American smear campaign.

Anne, forty-seven, a Great Park resident and information technology manager, stated:

They're very forceful about their beliefs and speak their language. And it's interesting to see that comedy because they do feel that you've sold out. You're American, but you've allowed someone else to tell you how to be and live and what's beautiful to you. Whereas in our country, we know where we're from, and we know our ancestors. We know how important we are. I don't feel like I'm, I know I can be a little bit quieter, but I still feel very strongly about what I believe and I'm not going to let too many people step over you or say negative things about me or my culture or my people, Black Americans.

Anne felt that Black Americans are constantly maligned and repudiated by Jamaican and Haitian immigrants in her neighborhood. She refuted the culturally racist tropes that weigh on Black Americans. While Black immigrants perceive them as "selling out" to White American culture, she emphasized Black Americans' moral history of collective struggle for liberation and citizenship. This disjuncture between how Black Americans see themselves and how they are perceived by Jamaicans and Haitians creates tensions and conflicts over position and power in diasporic suburbs. As these identity clashes generate antagonism and defensive responses within the Black diaspora, they fortify ethnic boundaries between groups. Paradoxically, these patterns demonstrate that ethnonational identities and narratives are reinforced as well as challenged in multiethnic spaces of the Black diaspora.

How We See You and Ourselves: Not (Southern) Black Like Us

The second theme in Black Americans' descriptions of their encounters with Jamaican, Haitian, and other Caribbean immigrants is the drawing of boundaries around who is truly Black. Black Americans define themselves as "authentic" Black people and create boundaries that exclude Black people who are not from the South from this cultural space. Immigrants and other ethnic groups in the African diaspora are considered outsiders and allocated a lower status in the local ethnic hierarchy. Black Americans frequently argued that foreign-born Blacks are "not really Black." Acts of social rejection are launched by Black Americans who, because of their long history in the United States, can wield social power that immigrants from the Caribbean may lack. One of the ways in

which this power is expressed is through exclusionary community building by Black Southern migrants and their adult children.

Gina, fifty-four, is a social worker who has lived in Cascades for most of
her life.

> Before, it was mixed. Before when we first moved on this block, it was all
> majority White. We were the first Blacks. They started moving out; some
> of them died; some of them started moving. I guess I was going into my
> high school around that time in the seventies. This neighborhood has
> changed tremendously. Uh, before, 'cause now you have a lot of Indians
> on the block. I think on this block, there are three families that are, origi-
> nally are here. And the rest you know, Spanish, and Jamaican, then the
> Indians been moving in. First it was all White, then the Whites started
> moving out, and then it was all Black, and now the Blacks are moving
> out too.

Like other Black American interviewees, the home Gina currently lives in
was passed down to her from her parents. Gina defined Blacks as Black
Americans. She did not refer to anyone who was not born in the United
States as Black; in her mind, their nationality preempted their belonging
in the Black racial category.

This gatekeeping was apparent in the subtle ways in which Black
Americans described Americans as normative Black people and immigrants as outside the norms of Blackness. They used culture and region to
define this nationality narrative. Black Americans saw themselves as the
arbiters of Blackness. This stance both produced and reflected a rupture
in their ties to the Black diaspora and represented a refashioning of ethnoracial identity. Black Americans explain why they are not below, but
above other nationalities, whom they see as not "Black like us."

Haitian Immigrants = Lower Status

Black Americans believed that the Caribbeanization, particularly the
Haitianization, of Cascades has led to the decline in the status of the middle-
class suburb. While Black Americans construct this belief based on events
and interactions with Haitian families in their neighborhood, they also draw
on popular ideas that stigmatize Haiti as a poor and politically volatile coun-

try. They see their Haitian neighbors as the harbingers of lower-status lifestyles, religious beliefs, and cultural repertoires.

Tania, an office administrator in her fifties, first encountered Haitian immigrants as neighbors. Tania's family was originally from Virginia. Her mother, Coretta, arrived in New York as a teenager, and worked for wealthy White families as a domestic in Manhattan. Coretta and her mother, who shared an apartment in Brooklyn, pooled their resources and bought a house in Cascades just as the desegregation crisis swept across Queens and Long Island. In the midst of White racial resistance to racial integration, Tania watched another Black family, the Pierres, move into a house across the street. The Pierres were Haitian. White ethnic working-class residents who tried to keep Black families out of the neighborhood saw Black American families like Tania's and Haitian families like the Pierres as equal threats. Behind the veil of White domination over space, however, were important cross-diasporic encounters between Black Americans and Haitians.

Tania recalled that growing up on the same block and attending school with Black people from elsewhere created both confusion and opportunities for cross-cultural learning. As she assessed the Pierre family's lifestyle and practices, however, her observations became testimonies of what she saw as Haitian social inferiority and backwardness. When I asked Tania whether she comes into contact with Haitian immigrants today, she replied:

> I don't know too many. Yes, but I have noticed lately that I don't know when someone is Haitian. I know my son's friend is Haitian. They don't look it. They don't look like the Haitians we grew up with. Like the Pierre family across the street. On the block where we grew up, there were like twenty Haitians in a house. I had no clue, not that it made a difference, but I had no clue. They look so Americanized. The Haitians I grew up with were unkempt, they hair wasn't combed, they were wearing hand-me-downs.

Although Haitians comprise the second largest ethnic community in Cascades, Tania described her interactions with them as limited. Her ideas of what it means to be Haitian were shaped by her initial interactions with Haitian neighbors whom she saw as poor and "unkempt." After hesitating and mentioning several times during our interview that she did not want to sound racist, she asserted that Haitians were different back then, marked by what she saw as the poverty and strangeness of their native country, and that now, at least in the next generation, they have been "Americanized" and are indistinguishable from Black Americans. Tania's description of her American-Haitian interactions reflects the internal diasporic meaning making occurring within suburbia. The nationality narratives that emerge from Black American interviewees are embedded in class boundaries and respectability politics.

JAMAICANS: RESENTED COCONUTS OR ELITES

Jamaican immigrants' encounters with Black Americans were colored by resentment and stereotyping. Jamaicans saw themselves as hardworking and unrelenting in the pursuit of social and economic mobility. They experienced confusion and disappointment when they interacted with Black Americans who degraded their achievements or failed to acknowledge their equal position. In similar fashion, they created nationality narratives of Black Americans as lagging behind them culturally and Haitians as "beneath" them. Their development of a diasporic consciousness in and through their encounters with other migrants and immigrants reflected the clash between how they saw themselves and how they were viewed by others. This consciousness varies across the generations and regions of origin.

How They See Us

DAMIAN: You wan sum'n? I'm sendin' Ralphy to the Jamaican restaurant next door.

OC: No, I'm OK. Thanks.

DAMIAN: Alright. Me wan de oxtail with de rice an peas. Oh, an' a pineapple soda.

As I sat in Damian's busy multiservice office, his officemate, Jimmy, was taking orders for their regular lunchtime restaurant run. Damian said that all the businesses on Cascades Boulevard support one another. "The Jamaican butcher across the street, we can order from him and pay him later." The Jamaican restaurant next door had a B rating from the City

Health Department on its window, but was always busy. Damian's business offered assistance with taxes, travel, money transfers, and real estate. "We support each other. The only people that don't support us but we support them is the Chinee restaurant. They neva' bizness wit us."

As I sat facing Damian across his mahogany desk, we were interrupted by a soft-spoken woman who walked in the door. The combination of her low voice and her Jamaican accent made me lean in so I could hear her more clearly. Damian shuffled through his drawer to help her. Then she said: "I need to call Johnny and my grandmother. Make it a ten dollar re-up." Damian reached his hand out to take the five-dollar bill and singles from the woman. He turned to his laptop, adding minutes to Johnny's digicel phone in Jamaica from his desk in Queens. Johnny would now be able to call the family in New York without paying anything. "Al right, ya set," he said. She thanked him, turned around, opened up her flip phone, and walked out the door.

Damian then returned to what he was discussing before the woman entered his office. "What was I sayin? [sucks teeth]. Ya know, de Black American here, they also resent us. They don't like us at all. I think there is something wrong with these Americans here, the ones that are born, not from Caribbean background. I think that they do resent us." He brought up a recent instance in which the host of a popular radio talk show used a slur against a Caribbean immigrant. "You got like, what's this girl on Hot 97 calling the guy from ... she was talking about the Trinidadian bus guy from the MTA. She was saying that 'look at this coconut head coming from his country.' You know, Black Americans, they do resent us." On New York's major hip-hop and R&B radio station, the prominent host, Miss Jones, made comments that enraged many New Yorkers of Caribbean descent. Damian was referring to her discussion of the missteps of the Transport Workers Union director Roger Toussaint amid the controversial transit workers' strike in 2006. Miss Jones had described Toussaint as a "dumb coconut who probably doesn't have a green card." *Coconut* is a derogatory term used to refer to immigrants from island nations in the Caribbean where coconuts are a staple food product. Toussaint is of Trinidadian descent, with an identifiable accent. Miss Jones's inflammatory comment was repudiated by city council member Yvette Clarke, a vocal advocate for New York's Caribbean community and advisor to the major pan-Caribbean organization, who called for a boycott of Hot 97.[6]

This slur caused controversy and intensified existing tensions between New York's Black groups. Hot 97 promotes Black and Latinx music hosts reggae and soca shows to cater to fans of Caribbean musical sounds, making the host's comments particularly inflammatory. Damian pointed to the media scandal as an example of the resentments and stereotypes between Black Americans and Jamaicans that fuel nationality narratives.

Reinventing "Coconuts"

The adult children of Jamaican immigrants traversed different, yet overlapping Jamaican and Black American life worlds every day. Most told me that they had developed both a Jamaican consciousness and a Black American consciousness. Ayana, an accomplished business manager, Great Park resident, and divorced mother of two, understands her coming of age experience as deeply entrenched in these two worlds simultaneously. She grew up during the 1970s in a two-family house in the Bronx that her Jamaican immigrant parents purchased after working in New York for over a decade. Over time, the family blended into the Black working- and middle-class neighborhood. Their next-door neighbors, the Smiths, were also a Jamaican family, and Ayana and her sister spent many weekday afternoons in their home. Her mother worked the afternoon shift at the hospital and would pick them up long after school was out. She recalled growing up in a "very Jamaican household" in a Black American residential area. Adjacent to her neighborhood were housing projects that had a concentration of Black American, Jewish, and Puerto Rican families. She now lives in an elite section of Great Park in a ranch-style home she purchased to establish a multigenerational home her aging parents would feel comfortable living in.

Ayana sees herself as more Jamaican than American at home, but more American than Jamaican in public spaces. As a result, she is misrecognized in public as being a Black American woman until she reveals her Jamaican background. She declared, "I am Jamaican but not a flag waver. I'm both, from both worlds. But my background, I would say I'm

Jamaican. Most people you know, because I can cook, and I'll talk a lot about food, and they're like "Are you a Jamaican? I didn't know you were *coconut*, because your accent doesn't sound like it." And I'm like, "Yes, I'm coconut. And when my mother was here, or if somebody called the house, and she might pick up right away. You hear her accent and that's when you knew."

In Ayana's interactions with Black Americans, they are stunned to learn that she is of Jamaican descent and uses the term *coconut* to describe her cultural background and practices. She reclaims this derogatory word by agreeing that she is "a coconut." For Damian, the term *coconut* precipitated conflict. Ayana, in contrast, embraced the label and redefined it in her own terms. Her culinary habits reveal her bicultural orientation. Ayana was especially good at making jerk pork, and her favorite breakfast was ackee, saltfish, and plantains. Members of the second generation, who do not have the marker of an accent, signal their cultural affiliations through their culinary and related cultural consumption patterns.

Ayana's social network is more heterogeneous than Damian's. She operates in diasporic, multiracial political, religious, and occupational networks on Long Island, while Damian's social world primarily involves interactions with other Jamaicans in Queens. The only exception is Damian's "right han' man," Orin who is his Trinidadian coworker. This difference has implications for how Damian and Ayana are perceived and treated by Black Americans. Ayana is able to operate on both sides of the ethnic boundary in Black Long Island, while Damian's primary identification is Jamaican, and his business links Jamaicans in Queens with their family and friends on the island. The local ethnic hierarchy is more salient to Damian, who is less able than Ayana to blend into the Black American world and feels more deeply the insults launched at Jamaicans.

They Are Beneath Us: Drawing Lines on Top

Camille, a forty-six-year-old nurse practitioner from Jamaica, emits a "cool mom" vibe. She and her family of five live in Great Park. She wore a Black velour jumpsuit with matching Black Nike Air Max sneakers.

Glancing down at her sneakers, I noticed that she crossed her legs and shook her feet when she was excited about a topic we discussed. She was especially animated about the cultural power Jamaicans held in the world, and she was proud to be from a "small island with a lot to offer." She had just finished cooking a large pot of curry crab with a side of rice for dinner that night. Behind the pot, green and red Scotch bonnet peppers were spread out on a wooden cutting board. A separate bowl next to the large iron pot was half filled with the portion of curry crab she was going to send to her sister and mother, who live in a house nearby.

Camille was agitated by the state of race relations in New York and especially her Great Park neighborhood. She also harbored strong feelings about relationships between different Black nationality groups. Camille's first encounters with Black people from other cultures occurred when she arrived in New York in her early twenties. "I never knew of a Haitian or Guyanese or American when I was growing up in Jamaica. You come here and you hear all the accents and languages." The differences among Black groups were more than distinctions between pronunciation and the cadence of their speech, or the types of food served for dinner or the holidays. Residents of Black diasporic New York incorporated these differences into cultural and moral boundaries that defined the superiority or inferiority of nationality groups. Camille explained: "In the West Indian community, Jamaican doesn't like Haitians and Haitians don't like Jamaicans. Like from Haiti. They don't get along because we have a concept that they are beneath us. There is a culture issue, like, we usually relate Haitian people with voodoo. That is prevalent in their country and we identify them with that. It was like a stigma that they were going to put voodoo on you or that's the lifestyle, everybody from Haiti practice voodoo. So that, and we didn't see them as being equal."

Haitians have historically been associated with voodoo and stigmatized as a result. Jamaican interviewees use this stereotype as a feature of the nationality narratives they create about Haitians. This cultural boundary is solidified by middle-class Jamaicans' active disassociation from *obeah* (the term used in Jamaica and Nigeria to refer to voodoo religious practices), which prevalent in Jamaica. Camille's disdainful attitude toward Haitian culture was formulated in the absence of any direct contact with Haitian people. Her notions of Haitianess were transnational and resulted from relationships between the two islands, which were separated by three hundred miles of sea and had strikingly divergent histories in relation to French and British colonialisms. The migration of people and the trade in goods and ideas between Haiti and Jamaica circulated ideas about Haiti and Haitians that Jamaicans brought with them to New York.

Although voodoo is practiced across the Black Atlantic, Haitians are most often constructed as the primary, and sometimes the sole, practitioners of voodoo. Its mysteriousness makes it seem both powerful and threatening. Negative associations with Haitian voodoo, such as the worship of multiple gods, the use of spells for revenge, and the supposed existence of zombies, permeate public discourses about the people and the religion. The stigmatization of voodoo is rooted in colonial condemnation of the spiritual practices and faith traditions of African slaves in Haiti. The promotion of European Christianity at the expense of African religious customs is perpetuated by global narratives about Haitians' cultural "backwardness." The Haitian diaspora's reputation in the White and Black communities in which they live, work, and learn is mired in this anti-African ideology. The nationality narrative suggesting that it is dangerous to befriend or share intimate ties with Haitians shapes relationships in diasporic middle-class suburbia. Jessie, a Black American woman in her late forties, told me: "I don't eat Haitian food. I can't even bear the smell of it." This comment expresses a deep unease with the most fundamental and pervasive form of human interaction, the sharing of food. Food, therefore, becomes an important site of disaccord and rejection among overlapping Black diasporas.

From the vantage point of Jamaicans, the perceived "backwardness" of Haitians helps them to assert that they are at the top of the local diasporic hierarchy. Haitians are not considered equals, but are ranked below Jamaicans. By emphasizing Haitian voodoo and denying Jamaicans' own African-derived religious practices, members of the Jamaican diaspora affirm their civility and respectability. In terms that are strikingly similar to those used by Europeans to categorize African peoples as inferior and to justify their subjugation, they construct Haitians as primitive devil worshippers. Jamaicans create physical and social distance between themselves and Haitians to cement the idea that they are "better." At the same time, their belief that crossing paths with Haitians risks making them targets of imagined sorcery legitimates their fears of the "Haitian other" and helps them deny their own people's history of resistance to European culture and retention of African forms of worship. These reputations and avoidance tactics allow Jamaicans to assert that although they are Black, they are culturally and morally superior to other Black nationality groups. This boundary work animates the social relations between Haitians and Jamaicans in diasporic suburbs.

Jamaicans' fraught relationship to Haitians parallels their constructions of Black Americans. Jamaicans' perceptions of Black Americans are characterized by classic tropes of economic superiority. Camille remarked that Jamaicans arrived in the United States at an economic disadvantage, but because of their work ethic, they have surpassed Black Americans. Camille recounted:

> Now here, you have the African American community that doesn't like the Haitian or West Indian community because they say that we came here and took their jobs. You hear that all the time. They'll say, when I used to work two jobs, I am going to school and working, I had people, Black American coworkers, would tell me that they would never do that. Why are you going back to school, what are you doing all these things for? Yet when I leave that society and move into a better neighborhood, better car or whatever, they would start, oh, she came here and took our job. But the opportunities are there for them to excel but they wouldn't put the work in. It's easier for them to blame and say that Jamaicans came and took their jobs. "You have two and I don't have any." But so many Black Americans would not do what I did, they wouldn't put in the work.

Among the majority of the people I interviewed, upward mobility from working-class to middle-class was the result of acquiring additional education or technical training. For most, it meant earning an associate's or bachelor's degree in nursing, accounting, or education. Camille remarked that in the entry-level jobs where she worked alongside Black Americans, they discouraged her from doing what it took to be upwardly mobile. On the basis of her conversations with Black Americans in the workplace, Camille has created a nationality narrative about Black Americans that reinforces her sense of economic and cultural superiority to them, as well as to Haitians. She posited that Jamaicans are upright Christians, even though she, herself, is not a practicing Christian and does not belong to a church. She also asserted that Jamaicans all work hard and value success, despite her acknowledgment that some Jamaican members of her own family expressed jealousy about her rapid ascent into the middle class. Nationality narratives are constructed from subjective conceptions of self in relation to others. Although these notions often contradict people's lived experiences, they are used as models for interaction and hierarchy building. Jamaicans' definitions of the Haitian and American diasporas, however mythical,[7] shape their social interactions, or lack thereof, in suburbia.

HAITIANS: REJECTS VERSUS RESPECTABLES

In Cascades and Great Park, the Haitian community includes people who come from class and status locations that range from the urban bourgeoisie to the rural proletariat. In diasporic suburbs, Haitians who would never have been neighbors in their class-segregated hometowns lived alongside one another in racially segregated New York suburbs. In addition to navigating the status heterogeneity of other Haitians in diasporic suburbs, members of the Haitian diaspora were actively confronted with their group's lower position in the eyes of Black Americans and Jamaicans, as well as Whites. In the local ethnic stratification system, Black Americans and Jamaicans competed for position as the top Black ethnic group, but did not see Haitians as viable competitors for either moral or cultural superiority. Their Kreyol and French language, complicated citizenship status, and their being perceived as low-income, insular, and backward because they come from "the poorest country in the Western Hemisphere"—all made them seem strange and inferior in the eyes of the other Black ethnic groups they encountered. These perceptions of them collided with how they viewed Jamaicans, Black Americans, and themselves. They used cultural values such as child rearing and family involvement as markers of their social and moral superiority to other Black ethnic groups. Overall, they presented themselves as a quiet, respectful, and therefore culturally superior group in the face of their marginalized position in their Black diasporic community.

How They See Us: Strangers in the House

Haitians I interviewed said that in their encounters with others in the Black world, they were constantly treated as outsiders. They had what Erving Goffman (1963) called a spoiled identity—that is, they had to manage being stigmatized by people whom they encountered. Haitian writer Edwidge Danticat reports that, although the public image of Haitians in New York City and Miami has shifted since musicians such as Wyclef Jean made it "cool" or at least "respectable" to be Haitian in the 1990s, boundaries within the Black community continue to marginalize them.[8] These cultural scripts continue to be significant in middle-class suburban life. Researchers who study Black Caribbeans or West Indians have excluded Haitians from their analyses because they are regarded as a different category of Black people whose culture is impenetrable due to their Haitian Kreyol language and insular community character.[9] The organizational structures of Cascades and Great Park reflect the apartness of the Haitian community. Churches have separate Haitian Kreyol services, Bible study, and youth groups. Haitians have established their own organizations, since Anglophone community organizations serve Black Americans and Jamaicans. Restaurants that serve Caribbean cuisine rarely offer Haitian foods; likewise, Haitian restaurants sparingly serve non-Haitian cuisines.

Haitians are ostracized in the Black communities where they reside (Stepick 1982; Stepick and Swartz 1998; Zephir 1996, 2001). Their consistent exclusion underlines the notion that they are not part of the Caribbean diaspora or the Black American community in the cities they have lived in since the 1960s. This marginalization has persisted even for those who have entered the middle class and moved to the suburbs. Aristide, an engineer in his forties and a Great Park resident, has lived in the United States since he was a young teenager. His memories of encounters with Black Americans, Jamaicans, and Trinidadians are marked by insults and social injuries against Haitian youth. Aristide recalled, "That was back in the days. I remember when I first came there. They used to call Haitians in school—'booty scratchers, Haitian booty scratchers.' You are Haitian, you would be, like, they used to actually pick on you because you were Haitian. They used to actually separate you, like just because you are Haitian, it's like you are not even part of the Caribbean, like it's like you were an alien or something else, and I don't know why. It was so strange, you know?"

The epithet "booty scratcher" emerged from White popular culture's representation of "African booty scratchers" or African bushman who were forced to encounter European social norms through colonization. The term "booty scratchers" refers to first-generation immigrants who are tied to the cultural beliefs and practices of the folk worlds they have left behind. These immigrants are newly immersed in modern, cosmopolitan ways of city life in the United States. The term is an insult targeted to newly arrived Black immigrants. More recently, it has been reclaimed in digital media spaces by millennial African youth who use subversive comedic art to describe their unique coming-of-age experiences as second-generation immigrants.[10] Black Americans' extension of this slur from Africans to Haitians points to the image of Haiti as the place whose culture has remained closest to its African roots in the wake of European colonization. While pro-Black people laud the maintenance of African traditions in Haitian culture, as they do in the radical strands of Jamaican and Black American culture, other Blacks reproduce European colonial logics and disparage Haiti's ties to its African ancestral past. Although Black Americans have historically imagined themselves as descendants of Africa and having pan-African political allegiances (Guridy 2010, Nelson 2016), their initial encounters with Haitian people elucidate cultural tensions and hostilities that require personal and political negotiations between Black ethnic distinction and collective African diasporic identity.

Aristide and several other interviewees observed that anti-Haitian taunts and violence meted out by Black Americans and other Black groups from the Caribbean were tools for segregating Haitians. Although he thought that these nationality narratives about Haiti and aggression toward Haitian youth were more prevalent among New York high school students in the 1980s and 1990s, other interviewees remarked that these tensions have persisted as the Haitian community has become more diverse in its class and spatial location.

As cohorts of Haitian immigrants have come of age and entered white-collar professions and suburban neighborhoods over time, anti-Haitian sentiment has pervaded spaces where Black migrant and immigrant groups work and learn together. In these settings, Haitian professionals I spoke to reported that they were outsiders among their coworkers. Magalie described her encounters in nursing:

> I don't know what it is, but I feel like, like as in my workplace, like if you are Haitian, it's like you're not part of the workplace. Like, can't be in a position, like can't be, you know, like even in a meeting; I could see that. Like if everybody is talking, once a Haitian person get up to say something, they don't really give you time; they don't really. Like, say, they, let's say they would give somebody else two minutes to talk; once the Haitian person start talking, they would cut you off. You know, and that's, we're not now talking about White people, I am talking about Black Caribbean people.

From the perspectives of Haitians and Black Americans, being present in a social space did not mean that you were treated as a respected member of that grouping or as an equal by your peers. This situation was acute for Haitians, who reported constant mistreatment from multiple groups.

The normal human reaction to repeated public embarrassment and social exclusion is physical and emotional stress. Magalie recounted:

> They try to rule. I've been working there for four, over five years. I suffered from anxiety attacks from being attacked by coworkers. Right now, I'm talking to you, I feel the stress. I've been working there for almost six years. I could be home for a couple of days and I feel good. But as soon as I start walking in the workplace, I start panicking. That's how bad it is. I don't know, I really don't know. Sometimes, I'm asking myself why. Is it because we Haitians are more quiet? More classy? I don't know. You don't have to say it, but we have a lot of respect for ourselves at work. I think, I don't wanna say I'm better than anybody else, but I try to do the right thing.

After reflecting on the psychological and physical effects of being a target of discrimination in the workplace, Magalie compared her treatment by other Black people with the way Whites treated her:

> I am not so lucky with Black people. I applied through VNS, Visiting Nurse Service, of New York. They called me for an interview. I was interviewed by four West Indian lady nurses. They put me in a room. Let me tell you something. At some point, I feel like I had to change my clothes because I was wet all over. I don't know. They ask me questions that were irrelevant to the nursing position. I actually, I took a test before the interview and I passed the test, but they still ask me the same questions again, and at some point, they're asking me, "Why do you want to work here? What makes you feel you

should be the one to get this position?" I feel like this is irrelevant; you understand? I am a nurse. And I felt like they treated me such because I was Haitian. Because they're West Indian. And I could tell you this: I've been through probably five to six interviews in Beth Israel, where I was interviewed by White people, [and] not after a single interview [was I] turned down. I always got the job.

Magalie's physical response to work-related stress was anxiety. I noticed during several of our interactions that she expressed signs of this social anxiety. She was suspicious of anyone she did not know and wary about her children's friends. In fact, I was only able to connect with her through a close acquaintance who invited both of us to her home and vouched for me as a trustworthy graduate student trying to complete a thesis project. After this meeting, Magalie opened up to me, and we were able to establish a relationship. She hoped that I would be a positive influence on her teenage and preteen children, whom she struggled to discipline.

Feagin and Sikes's *Living with Racism* (1994) uncovers the enormous amount of cultural work that members of the Black middle class do in White environments where they work, learn, and live. The experiences of Magalie reveal that one's accents and origins are used to target and ostracize others within African diasporic relations. In addition to the weight of White racism, conflicts resulting from Black diasporic encounters in the workplace carry significant social costs for Haitians, Jamaicans, and Black Americans, who report deep social rejection from other Black ethnic groups and one another. In socializing neighborhood and work spaces where Blacks hail from different states, countries, and continents, migrants and immigrants come to grasp how they are viewed by other Black people.

How We See Them and Ourselves: Dignified and Respectable

Members of the Haitian middle class made penetrating observations about their Black neighbors in Cascades and Great Park. They viewed Black Americans as having the same origins in Africa and experiencing the transatlantic slave trade but believed that their family, childrearing, and cultural practices differed significantly.

A reputation for respect and propriety are the building blocks of an acceptable person according to Haitian interviewees. They construct

Black Americans, Jamaicans, and Trinidadians as lacking these traits. Jocelyne, a registered nurse in her late forties and a Great Park resident, believes that there are strict divides between Haitians and non-Haitians. When I asked her about the differences and similarities between Haitians and Jamaicans, she shared:

JOCELYNE: They're rude.

OC: Who's rude? Jamaicans or African Americans?

JOCELYNE: Jamaican, Trinidadian, Black American.

OC: OK.

JOCELYNE: They're rude. They have no respect for others. They say whatever they want in the workplace. They don't treat others the same, you know. I mean that's the reason why I said I don't want to be associated with them.

Jocelyne's encounters with Blacks of other nationalities have been fraught with tension and social exclusion. This experience has led her to question her belonging in the broader Black community. She perceives Jamaicans, Trinidadians, and Black Americans as quite unlike her. Her social isolation from these groups was echoed by Black Americans who experienced repeated disapproval from Jamaican women they interacted with. Jocelyne's views show that encounters between Haitians and other ethnic groups tend to lead to the creation of moral and cultural boundaries between them based on sociability and respectability.

Romantic relationships added another dimension to the conflicted interactions between Haitians and other Black groups. The most intimate of encounters could engender aggrieved battles over cultural differences. People observing these relationships assessed the practices and behaviors of an entire group based on the actions of one person. Consider the views expressed by Chantal, a Haitian woman banker in her fifties, toward Jamaicans. From Chantal's perspective, Jamaicans were not as family oriented as Haitians. She shared the story of a close Haitian male friend of hers who was in the process of getting a divorce from his Jamaican wife to illustrate this point. She learned that the major source of tension in their marriage was that his wife was not open to interacting with his parents, siblings, and extended family. She had decided that she was married to him and that his family was of secondary importance. The husband found this stance unacceptable, and it caused friction in his relationship with his family. This conflict eventually led to the dissolution of their marriage. Saying that "Jamaicans are just different from us," Chantal recounted:

> But Haitians still have a little something against Jamaicans. . . . Haitians, they feel that Jamaican girls when they get married, they only want a guy. They are not married to the guy's family; they only want him. Like the Haitian girl would try to get along with, try to get involved. All they [Jamaican girls] want is the men; that's it. And it's over. That's something that I've seen. They are not involved. . . . If the guy is too much into his family, they're not going to be happy.

In-law relationships are often socially sensitive terrains of interaction. When cultural differences are also involved, people draw on existing narratives that one group has about another. Chantal's assessment of Haitian women as being "involved" with their husband's extended family and Jamaican women as being strategically disengaged is layered with conflict and judgment. This nationality narrative reinforces a sense of Haitian superiority and fortifies cultural boundaries.

Shortly after our interview, Chantal invited me to stay for dinner. It was Friday night. She planned to make fritay, a Haitian fried entrée that includes pork, sausages, plantains, batatas (sweet potatoes) and malanga for her husband and children, who would be home after a long week of commuting to the city for work and college classes. It was a family treat compared to the regular regimen of chicken and rice. Chantal said that she preferred her children to come home with a "tian," not a "can." Confused about what she was referring to, I asked her to explain. She replied with a grin that belied her seriousness that she wanted her children to bring home partners whose nationalities ended with the syllable "tian," meaning Haitian. She would disapprove of those whose nationality ended with "can": American and Jamaican. She laughed. I was stunned that this was such a well-thought-out boundary that she had a saying to accompany it. As I processed this, Chantal's laughter abruptly ended. She said, "No, but seriously, that's my wish."

In White society, Black people are denied the right to have nuanced identities outside of race. When Whites do recognize Black nationality or regionality, they use it to create paradigms of Black immigrants as "better Blacks" or to stigmatize them. These tropes reinforce anti-Black American cultural racism and allow White domination to persisit (Pierre 2004). In this chapter, we have explored Black ethno-national identities through a different lens: from the perspective of the post-Break Black middle class in all their diversity. They engage in constructing and contesting a local ethnic hierarchy that shapes and is shaped by encounters among various groups in the Black diaspora. Prevailing ideas about interactions among different groups of Black people with different origins oversimplify these delicate and sometimes contradictory social interactions. Nationality narratives are created in diasporic suburban spaces as roadmaps for cross-ethnic interaction and for individual and collective identity building. This chapter moves us beyond the argument that members of the West Indian middle-class distance themselves from lower-class Black Americans. It has elucidated the layered cultural hierarchies embedded in each group's racial, color, class, and national politics. Nationality narratives emerge from social interactions that are shaped by preconceived ideas of the other. In the process, they are often negotiating solidarities with their kinfolk and distinctions from their skinfolk.

The cultural rituals of nationality and regionality are important features of Black diasporas. Ethnicity, however, is best understood as a set of identities and practices that group members use to define and police the boundaries of their nationality group. The local ethnic hierarchy among Black Americans, Haitians, and Jamaicans gives shape to a theory of the micro-level power of ethnic categories under the Black racial umbrella. Building on the work of Frederick Barth and Richard Jenkins, I have shown that in Black diasporic suburbs ethnicity is interpreted as "social liability or stigma" (Jenkins 1994, 201) in social interactions, and it leads to the development of ethnic boundaries that define "us" and "them" within a local and transnational Black social field. By deconstructing the pan-ethnic category of West Indians and including the experience of Black Americans, we are able to see the meaning making involved in Black cross-diasporic relationships. Taken together, ethnonational identity is an important fault line in the Black middle class.

What do these nationality narratives mean for the reproduction of social inequalities? Some of the most important Black social movements of the twentieth century have been pan-Africanist. The Atlantic Ocean was a vehicle, not a boundary, for Black political resistance (Kelley 2000).

Cultural differences inevitably colored these social movements. The Break period (1970–present), however, marked a turning point in the social relations across the Black diaspora. The mass movement of Black people from the US South and the Global South brought them together in unprecedented numbers in the cities of the Global North. The distance between them changed from oceans and state lines to boulevards and backyard fences. People from different diasporas lived alongside one another in urban tenements and apartment buildings and now share neighborhoods with spacious homes. As a result of suburbanization, we have entered a new chapter of African diasporic identities, practices and relations.

The meetings of these overlapping diasporas are sometimes cooperative, sometimes conflicted, other times, neutral. Black political mobilization across nationality and class lines is also apparent in diasporic suburbs. On issues of police brutality, organizing to keep senior centers open, discouraging the development of a casino, and protesting the redrawing of district lines, the post-Break Black middle class builds political solidarities across cultural boundaries. They have fought against social inequality in their neighborhoods and defended the soul of the diaspora in the shadows of an oppressive neoliberal city. But this solidarity does not preclude suspicion and misunderstanding, steep cultural learning curves, and questions around loyalty between them. Although these cultural divides do not re-create the racial and class problems that Black peoples wrestle with every day, they do have the effect of creating inequality. This division within the Black middle class undercuts solidarity and mobilization against White supremacy. History has proven that collective political resistance from below has the power to transform the status quo. It remains to be seen, however, whether the urgency of racial and economic justice in the twenty-first-century Obama, Black Lives Matter moment will create solidarities among Black skinfolk whose class, ethnonational, spatial, gender, sexuality and generational differences are now more pronounced than they have ever been before.

Conclusion

MUSTARD SEEDS

On a quiet day in late August, I went to Village Market to gather groceries for the week. As I was choosing d'Anjou pears, I looked up and saw an old friend, Cheyenne, whom I had met in a program for students of color back in college. She was picking out okra in the next aisle. Cheyenne shook her head and chuckled when we recognized each other. Surprised at this reunion in a busy produce aisle of a bustling market in a less-traveled corner of New York, we walked up and down the aisles together and checked out at the same cashier to catch up on the years since we had seen each other. She came to the market to pick up items for her Jamaican uncle, who owned a house nearby. Cheyenne was living with him while completing graduate school.

I have watched as old classmates from Jamaica, childhood friends from the South, and former coworkers from Haiti unexpectedly ran into each other in Cascades and Great Park's public spaces. In the marketplace, I have overheard people ask one another for advice on what meats were best to purchase or debate whose hometown had the best mangoes or cultivated the most vitamin-rich rice. My meeting Cheyenne at Village Market is an example of how local institutions in Black diasporic suburbs connect people in spontaneous yet predictable ways.

Cheyenne and I, the adult children of Black immigrants, were following paths traced by the generation before us. We were daughters of hybrid and overlapping Black diasporas, sorted into schools and neighborhoods by personal choices and structures of segregation outside of our control. As Isabel Wilkerson located herself in her study of the Great Migration, we too were Black southerners, Haitians, Jamaicans, Bajans, Nigerians, and Ghanaians *once removed*. We were transient actors, however, temporarily stopping in Cascades to fulfill our needs in the moment. But our generation writ large stands to inherit suburbs like it. Will Black millennials be attracted to suburban life or pulled into gentrifying cities? Will suburbs be receptive to us socioculturally and economically?

Cheyenne and I stood in the Village Market parking lot and exchanged phone numbers and social media pages. She later sent a text message inviting me to a welcome-back party her grad school friend was hosting in their Brooklyn apartment. I was happy to attend, especially since the party was in Flatbush, my old stomping grounds. It was a typical house party, with a rainbow gathering of students from Turkey, India, Maine, Oregon, and California, all eager to hear and talk about their summer travels and anxieties about their programs. Cheyenne and I were the only Black people there. A circle of others lamented their housing problems; they followed ads for "new Brooklyn" housing options, but the listings disappeared overnight. It was odd to be in the apartment with gentrifiers when my family had been part of the "old Brooklyn." Cities are always undergoing change; dynamism is fundamental to the very existence of a metropolis. But conditions of life for the "old Brooklyn" were not being improved. Instead, it was being radically erased, displaced and dispossessed by local and international real estate developers as well as White and international renters and homebuyers who purchased one-bedroom, one-bath condos for close to a million dollars. South Brooklyn had become a playground for White bankers, lawyers, artists, entrepreneurs, and hustlers. Some were what Loretta Lees (2003) calls super-gentrifiers, affluent financiers for whom places like Brooklyn Heights and Carroll Gardens had become desirable real estate because of their proximity to Wall Street. Many others were tech executives and engineers, social media entrepreneurs, lawyers, doctors, and artists. The wave of Black dispossession in

Bed-Stuy, and Crown Heights was aggressive and had reached the villages of Flatbush.

When I was growing up there, Whites did not consider living on the southeast side of Prospect Park. They never rode on dollar vans, and they did not shop in local Chinese or Korean groceries. Ocean Avenue and Prospect Park separated our racialized zones. The only persons with White skin we saw regularly were cops. There was also our Hasidic Jewish land-lord who came to collect his rent each month. It was said that he made sexual advances toward a mother in my building. Many Black families like my own, left Brooklyn for better housing in the suburbs or the South. In the 1980s and 1990s, Flatbush was inhabited by folks from places like the US South, Puerto Rico, Haiti, Jamaica, Trinidad, Guyana, and Panama. It was rich with life and struggle, love and aspirations. Yet, by the millennium, this community was being aggressively eroded by the "creative class," multinational corporations, and their state sponsors. Cops were harassing corner boys, while White women carrying drug stashes walked by freely. White women brought TJ Maxx and Container Store bags into buildings on Ditmas Ave. with known trap houses. White and Asian couples pushed baby strollers around Albermarle Avenue on street corners my parents had told me to avoid as a teenager. This was the new Brooklyn.

Cheyenne gave me a ride back to Queens in her sandy-colored four-door Corolla. Since it was late August, Brooklyn was preparing for the West Indian Day Parade. When Cheyenne exited the Belt Parkway into Queens, we left the bustling streets of Flatbush behind and turned onto deserted suburban streets. When we entered Cascades, the main signs of life were the brightly lit front porch lights and the glare from flat screen televisions reflected in the windows of English Tudor homes. The sole pedestrians were a group of teenagers who seemed to be returning from a house party; someone had made them a take-home plate, as they were holding plastic containers. A handful of people were waiting at the bus stop, scrolling through their smartphones or pacing back and forth. The detached houses were originally uniform in design, but some residents had added a second story or finished their basement to accommodate growing families. These changes varied in size and style, representing individual tastes and the budgets of residents. The trees arched over the road. The front yards were adorned with colorful flowers that seemed to glow a bit under the street and porch lights. These well-kept properties gave passersby the impression that the neighborhood was a private place where homeowners took pride in their properties. It was a distant world from the busy sidewalks, fire escapes, and front stoops of Brooklyn and Harlem.

"If someone who was not from here drove through this neighborhood right now, they would think that White people lived here," Cheyenne joked. We burst into laughter. On previous occasions, Cheyenne had celebrated living in Cascades. "I love it here. I can find the foods I like to eat, and live with my people." She appreciated the grocery store that stocked fresh foods she liked and offered a taste of her parents' Jamaican heritage. She enjoyed living in a predominately Black neighborhood where people were middle class. She had grown up in a White suburb, and did not know the fullness of Black suburbs like Cascades and Great Park until she moved to New York. As a child, she had belonged to Jack and Jill and other bourgeoisie Black social circles, since her parents wanted her to have some contact with a Black world. She was from the 'burbs, I from working class Brooklyn, but these divergent class upbringings did not seem to matter in that moment. Our knowledge that the neighborhood is predominately Black made the notion that it might appear White to outsiders seem absurd to us.

For outsiders to Cascades and Great Park, however, the old trope of the Whiteness of suburbia was the most likely assumption. The nature of entrenched racial residential segregation in New York gave little hope that this perspective would change. Almost fifty years after the Kerner Commission and twenty years after *American Apartheid*, racial segregation in New York was being refashioned and rationalized by White residents. In the American imaginary, cities in general and ghettoized areas in particular are where Black people belong (Anderson, 2015). Our media and political discourse reinforce this belief, even if it's being challenged by the settler colonial logics of gentrification. While on the campaign trail 2016, presidential candidate Donald Trump equated the African American community with the inner-city ghetto, where he conjectured that rampant violence, joblessness, and poor schools abound. Although New York is lauded as a diverse city, most non-Black New Yorkers never visit Black urban areas, let alone segregated areas on the margins of the boroughs and suburbs. Their rich diversity and entrenched disparities are unknown and deemed unremarkable, its residents shunned and distorted. This book has unveiled the sociological layers of Black life on the margins of the metro and its cultural and economic interconnectedness with the so-called global city and the American South and Global South.

While the Blackness of Cascades and Great Park is hidden from outsiders, the multinational and transregional character of its residents is even less visible. Visitors would be surprised that the Black people who live here come from many places, speak many languages and dialects, and belong to diverse spiritual communities. This surprise is rooted in American cultures denial of Black complexity. The cultural plurality of this Black world is revealed when you walk down the main commercial streets. On any given day, the banners of Mae's Soul Food Restaurant, the Rastafarian Natural Juice & Herbs Shop, and the Nollywood Movie & Music store reveal the cultural variety of this suburb within city limits and suburban towns like Great Park. The community boards, civic associations, block associations, religious groups, rotary clubs, Kiwanis clubs, senior citizen centers, and alumni association meetings are animated by the sounds of Southern, Caribbean, and African accents, and catered with jambalaya, collards, sorrel, white pudding, fried plantains, pork and grits.

The vibrant colors of suburban cultural life illuminate a new chapter in Black spatial history. Its residents are the descendants of Africans who were scattered across the Americas by the transatlantic slave trade. They have come to New York from these locales, striking back at this empire city in their own ways. By seizing the city's opportunities for mobility, or creating their own mobility pathways, they are challenging generations of racial oppression by boldly striving for the ordinary comforts of middle-class suburban life they have historically been denied. Government subsidized home loans, federal loans to support small businesses, and tuition coverage to complete college degrees were a form of affirmative action for Whites only, and the suburbs were their exclusive American dream. Black families took more circuitous paths to middle-class suburbia, having to rely on a mixture of controversial governmental policies and community resources to move up the economic ladder. The people I interviewed reported many sacrifices they and their parents made and the losses incurred in their pursuit of upward mobility. They worked their way through the city's educational and training systems, while clocking in to arduous work environments in factories, White offices, homes, and hospitals. They endured racism and xenophobia on the job from coworkers, clients, and managers, some became their own bosses in order not to have to answer to racist supervisors. In their private lives, they wrestled with family separations, petty jealousies, and feelings of loneliness as they aspired to a better life for themselves and their children. Often, they could not take all their kin along with them, but instead became pillars of economic support. They rose out of the dust and chaos of New York's competitive landscapes to become middle-class suburbanites. In their encounters with one another across differences of color, class, language, and religion, they have made Cascades and Great Park into *places of their own* (Wiese, 2005).

On the night Cheyenne and I drove back to Queens, Brooklyn residents were preparing for the Labor Day Parade. It was a little over a week away, and although the parade has been a Brooklyn institution for decades, the festivities leading up to it are celebrated throughout Black New York. The smell of jerk smoke and the sounds of Jay Z, Beenie Man, Bobby Shmurda, Sanchez, and Wyclef playing from car radios and restaurants in the main boulevard signaled that the area was preparing for its own smaller, satellite Labor Day festivities. Since Phil Kasinitz's (1992) depiction of Brooklyn's West Indian Day Parade as an important site of the development of pan–West Indian consciousness and political solidarity, many Black immigrants have left central Brooklyn, Harlem, and the Bronx and joined Black Americans settled in the suburbs of Queens, Long Island, Westchester County, and New Jersey.[1] The majority of my interviewees were living in their second, third or fourth address in New York. On the morning of Labor Day, many walk to the subway or the Long Island Railroad sporting their national flags and wearing comfortable shoes, prepared to descend into Brooklyn for the day's festivities. Others sleep over at family or friends' houses not too far from Eastern Parkway to limit their commutes and stretch their leisure time playing dominoes with old friends or reuniting with former classmates from the old country.

Some of those who moved out of Brooklyn have brought their festivals, cultural institutions, and religious organizations with them to their new neighborhoods. West Indian Day activities are echoed across the metropolis, and now include BBQs and dance club parties, as well as rehearsals and preparations for the parade, in suburban neighborhoods. Labor Day weekend is one of the times when suburban communities reproduce the cultural celebrations taking place in the central Brooklyn neighborhoods where diasporic Black residents first settled after arriving in New York. Red Stripe and Prestige beers sell out; chickpeas and bara are on kitchen islands for Trinidadian doubles. Bodegas and grocery stores stock American and Caribbean flags, soca and reggae CDs are sold from the trunks of cars, and jerk pits pop up in various locations off major streets and highways.

Over the past thirty years, as Jamaicans and Haitians emerged as the largest immigrant groups from the Caribbean, they have become more visible participants in carnivals. Black Americans, particularly those of mixed US and Caribbean ancestry or friendships, have forged hybrid cultural identities there. At the same time, White gentrification has led to rapid increases in housing prices around the Eastern Parkway. Once dominated by Black Americans and Caribbean immigrants, areas such as Crown Heights and Flatbush have seen large out-migrations of Blacks to outer boroughs and suburbs[2]. In contrast to what was once seen as the ghettoization of the West Indian Parade, which mainly Black New Yorkers knew about and joined, the Labor Day Parade in Brooklyn has become a part of the city's ethnic tourism, and stories about it are carried by magazines and websites with a large White audience, such as *Time Out New York*. In recent years the parade has been accompanied by controversy over the eruption of violence and the number of deaths that have occurred during the multiday festivities. The Labor Day Parade is still well attended, but efforts by organizers and the city are focused on turning around its image as a site where violence interrupts the goals of community enjoyment. The event is now hyper-policed, with armed officers screening participants and spectators for weapons at checkpoints, practices that have intensified already problematic relations between the NYPD and the Black community.

Carnival, with its anticolonial and anti-enslavement politics and diasporic cultural roots, celebrates self-expression and communal resistance through performance, song, dance, and theater. Once observed mainly in Rio, the Caribbean, New Orleans, and Harlem, the festival also takes place in distant cities such as Hartford, Montreal, and London's Notting Hill, which rock to its cultural traditions from May until September every year. Steel pan bands and whistle calls to "report to the dance floor" are heard in Queens and on Long Island, suburban nodes of a global Black diasporic traditions. Carnival echoes in these middle-class neighborhoods represent the continuity of this tradition across space, time, and class for a diaspora on the move, a people in constant motion trying to define who they are in relation to Black America, the Caribbean, and the African Diaspora (Dodson and Diouf 2004).

BLACK DIASPORIC SUBURBS

This ethnography has explored the cultural identities, interactions, and micro-practices of Black diasporic groups to generate new sociological insights into the politics of belonging and boundary work in suburbia. Middle-class Black Americans, Haitians, and Jamaicans have constructed dynamic cultural codes around race, class, and nationality. This cultural system is rooted in their trans-geographical identities and practices and shapes their relationships with one another and to the New York metropolitan area. The local cultural space reveals the complex intersections of Blackness, middle-classness, diasporic identity, and suburban place making. The analysis presented in this book challenges us to think more inclusively about cities, migration, mobility, and citizenship.

The New Noir move us beyond traditional and current understandings of suburbia. Although suburbs are defined as located on the periphery of cities, Cascades is a suburb within city limits, offering suburban amenities without burdensome suburban taxes. In contrast to the prevailing image of suburbs as White preserves, Cascades and Great Park residents are majority Black and Latinx. Moreover, unlike the Black American suburbs portrayed in recent books, they are home to people from across the African diaspora. The regions and nations from which residents come, are core to the identities that they negotiate in their interactions with neighbors, church members, coworkers, friends, and relatives. Their belonging, and boundary work animates the spaces in which they live and the politics of mobility amid social exclusion (Silver, 1994) give shape to how they understand their place in their local social stratification system and the global political economy. This dynamic can be seen in the herbs they grow in their backyards, the foods they prepare in their suburban kitchens, the freedom celebrations that bring the US South and the Global South into their homes (i.e., Juneteenth and Jamaican Independence Day), the flags hanging from their rearview mirrors, the national and regional diversity of the organizations and businesses they create, the affinity organizations they participate in at work, and the religious communities in which they worship.

Black diasporic suburbs are glocal places, whose culture, economy and politics are deeply tied both to New York and to trans-geographical home places. Yet the chapters in this book have demonstrated that Black diasporic suburbs differ in crucial respects from often cited ethnoburbs. Studying Asian suburbanization in California's San Gabriel Valley, Wei Li (1998) defines ethnoburbs as global economic outposts for upwardly mobile Chinese, Korean, and Japanese immigrants who have created homes and suburban communities reflective of their transnational identities. The formation of these ethnic suburbs has been facilitated by the passage of the Immigration Act of 1965 and the targeted recruitment of highly skilled immigrants in information technology and medicine. Although Asian immigrants and their descendants have encountered White supremacist policies designed to exclude them, the social-historical racialized conditions of the Asian and Black diasporas in the United States are fundamentally different. Asians were brought to the Americas primarily as exploited wage laborers to expand the economy, often to dilute Black rebellion from chattel slavery and colonialism (Lowe 2015). Therefore, the relationship of Black diasporas to migration, land, property, and capital is fundamentally different from that of Asians because of this living history.

The sagas of Asian and African migrations, mobilities, and suburban geographies reflect the different racial strata into which they are sorted by White society. The Black diasporic suburb reflects an internal as well as external colonial dynamic between the African diaspora and the cities where they have come to improve their life chances. The term *diaspora* reflects the unique social condition of Africans in the Americas. The Black diasporas are constantly in conversation with their real or imagined ties to their common African roots, their hybrid identities as a people constantly in motion and intermixing (Gilroy, 1993; Hall, 1990). Tiffany Patterson and Robin Kelley (2000) remark that the Black diaspora is not only a condition of dispersion, but also a process of being made and remade through migrations. The soils upon which real estate developers and the US government collaborated to create suburbs as technologies of White supremacy and capital accumulation through the housing market are sullied by the history of colonialism, racial slavery, and racial segregation that Black residents are the descendants of and inherit. Black Americans have a longer history of this as the descendants of slavery in the United States. However, as discussed in chapter 2, migrations across the Black Atlantic, and European and American colonialisms complicate any clear definition of nationality and ethnicity for Black peoples. These actions were met with radical pan-African Black thought, organized political resistance and cultural creativity. The relationship of Black Americans, Haitians, and Jamaicans to slavery in the US South, the Global South, and New York embodies the strange journey from being the property and labor of European empires to occupying the position of a *class moyenne* in urban capitalism. Therefore, I use the term *Black diasporic suburbs*, as opposed to ethnoburbs, to reflect the particular racialized condition of Black middle-classness and subordination.

A GENERATION IN MOTION

The extraordinary people whose lives fill this book were part of the post-Break generation whose possibilities and trajectories were transformed by the global challenges to White supremacy between World War II and deindustrialization (Winant 2000). Widespread antiracist and anticolonial insurrections denounced Whites' control over the resources, bodies, and destinies of the *darker races* (Du Bois 1900, 1903). Migration was a primary tool of political protest, and millions of Black people from the US and Global South came to cities to make new futures for themselves. The Haitian, Jamaican, and Black Americans who are now in the middle class are the result of this process of racial, demographic, political, and cultural change. The opportunities available to them are the outcomes of large and small acts of freedom fighters who came before them, Black people who used their feet, the ballot, and voices to protest racial caste systems in their rural and urban villages.

Prior to his in depth analysis of "The Dawn of Freedom," the watershed period between 1861 and 1872 of the emancipation of enslaved Africans, Du Bois presciently declared that the "the problem of the twentieth century is the problem of the color-line,—the relation of the lighter and darker races of men in Asia and Africa, in America and the islands of the sea"[3] Although the Great Migration from the US South, the mass migration of Black people from postcolonial Jamaica, and the flight from the repressive dictatorship in Haiti are usually seen as separate movements, they had similar world-historical causes; each exodus flowed through and enlarged small tears in the fabric of global White domination over the "darker races." This crisis was the result of the weakening of European and American colonial legitimacy by two world wars and multiple, yet simultaneous, political mobilizations from below to overturn centuries of racial and economic oppression. Together, these Black migrants have followed the footprints of generations before them and forged diasporic communities in cities never created with them in mind, and hostile to their progress. Congregating in the largest numbers in New York, Black migrants have moved through the boroughs to the suburbs, and their cultural encounters and exchanges with one another mandate that we remake how we theorize mobility and displacement in America.

Although in becoming a middle-class suburban homeowner my interviewees achieved what represents the epitome of the "American Dream," their sense of belonging and citizenship remained elusive and contested. One resident described Cascades and Great Park as "fish bowls," where one's actions are scrutinized and status is questioned by local elites. To others, they were places where people from varying classes and ethnic or national origins could make a claim to "*movin' on up*," like the television sitcom family in *The Jeffersons*. They simultaneously blended together and drew lines among themselves. Some had grown up in poverty in Jamaica and made their way to New York suburbs when there seemed to be limited possibilities. Others cast their nets wide in order to recapture the middle-class status they lost when they left Haiti. Still others saw their current status as middle-class suburbanites as beneath them; some raised in Harlem's small Black bourgeoisie had been unable to retain that privileged position in adulthood. The salience of class origins and status journeys in the consciousness of my interviewees compels us to recognize that beyond education, occupation, income, and homeownership, the pathway to the middle class is not linear or unidirectional, and this goal is never attained once and for all. Not only are positions in the middle class precarious, but also the subjective sense of class identity is changeable as people encounter social and economic boundaries and possibilities over their life course. Because the people I interviewed came from various places and took different paths to these diasporic suburbs, they made sense of their class status and that of others through the prism of class hierarchies both here and in their place of origin[4] in other parts of New York, the US South, Haiti, and Jamaica.

Racial consciousness is shaped not only by the problems of the color line, but also by the myriad of cultural meanings that take shape behind racial lines. My interviewees migrated from places with unique yet interconnected racial stratification systems. When sociologists treat Black identity as a fixed category, they miss the varied ways in which Black people themselves define Blackness. Black diasporic groups continuously shape and reshape the parameters and content of Blackness through their self-identifications and practices. For example, their immersion in White spaces at work, in their neighborhoods, and in school leads the Black middle class to seek and nurture connections with the Black world, particularly for their children (Lacy 2007). Recognizing the multiple diasporic worlds that exist within the Black middle class further complicates the cultural meanings of Blackness.

The racial consciousness spectrum frames the multinational Black middle class through a lens that corresponds more closely to how they see themselves and each other. Phenomenological methods of listening and observing culture help us center how folks racialized as Black define the contents of Blackness and practice these contexts in everyday life. From this perspective, the dynamic spectrum of racial identities emerges. We find a continuum of cultural positions from pro-Blackness to post-Blackness that shows the breadth and depth of Black cultural production. The post-Break Black middle class is a self-directed cultural group whose members' attitudes toward Blackness not only vary widely but often depend on the contexts in which they find themselves.

This spectrum is an entrée into the expansiveness of Black cultural politics. The cultural spaces on the spectrum are not fixed; rather, individuals move to and through them depending on the racialized political landscapes in which they came of age, their experiences and exposures, and their stage of life at decisive historical political moments. Researchers are invited to expand the racial consciousness spectrum so that it includes the intersectional identities articulated by the Black diaspora across physical and digital spaces. The framework can be extended in various directions. For example, Black feminists have identified Black men who espouse pro-Blackness yet condone the oppression of Black women as "hoteps"; they are invested in racial liberation yet articulate sexist, homophobic, and transphobic beliefs. For example, one cannot be pro-Black, yet oppress the Black transgender community. Calls for inclusion into "the culture"—Black culture, that is—are being made by LGBTQIA communities, who have historically been excluded from discussions of Blackness but have always been central to its cultural creativity and liberation struggles. I open up this sociological exercise to scholars of race and identity for future research. Identity and consciousness can reflect strategies of resistance, but they also constitute spaces for expression, creativity, and solidarity outside of White supremacy. As the poet Sonia Sanchez said, "Black people are interested in two thousand and one things, and White oppression is only one of them."[5] The members of the post-Break Black middle class are constantly engaged in making sense of their relationship with one another along and across lines of region or nation of origin. It is imperative that we explore how identity and culture are articulated from the ground up.

The racial consciousness spectrum elucidates how nationality shapes people's cultural pathways to pro-Blackness, selective Blackness, and post-racial Blackness. History is at the core of this process. For example, Jamaicans in the pro-Blackness space espoused pan-African repertoires inspired by Rastafarianism. Black Americans articulated pro-Blackness from the perspective of the Black Power movement and Black is Beautiful iconography. Haitians evoked their historical status as the harbingers of global Black liberation, being descendants of the Haitian Revolution.

Mary Waters (1999b) argues that middle-class Black Caribbean immigrants distance themselves from Black identities and bolster their ethnic identities instead to separate themselves from the stigma of being Black Americans (or at least they do so more than their working-class counterparts). Middle-class Haitians and Jamaicans in New York suburbs, however, vary in the meanings they give to Blackness, and sometimes have more contentious relations with one another than with Black Americans. Black Americans have sets of beliefs and attitudes about compatibility between Blacks from the US South and Black immigrants. They interpret the social rejection they experience from other Black ethnic groups and define boundaries around Blackness that exclude immigrants. The cultural scripts these ethnic groups write about one another are what I call *nationality narratives*, and they give shape to local diasporic hierarchies. These narratives are animated with racial, color, and class boundaries and are created in the ongoing encounters of Black diasporic groups inside and outside of their suburban settings. Like a pepper sauce, this view livens a menu of encounters. But nationality narratives also potentially distract and overpower community building and critical pan-African solidarities needed in order to challenge the destructive agendas of White supremacy. The interactional nature of this hierarchy makes it dynamic, demonstrating the ongoing cultural work occurring among Black diasporas continuously reinterpreting their sense of their belonging and solidarity with one another. The hope is that in revealing the complex cultural boundaries negotiated within Black suburbia, this body of work makes plain the urgent need for a unified, radical Black political agenda. If it cannot be created by the post-Break generation, then the hope lies in their children.

HANGIN' IN THE CHOW LINE

I immersed myself in the research for this book during the Great Recession in 2008. The gutting of the economic advancements that the Black middle class had made since the civil rights movement set up a strange but important landscape for sociocultural inquiry into a group whose housing, jobs, and neighborhoods were under a great deal of economic and political precarity. Cascades and Great Park were being transformed in real time. Queens's foreclosure crisis ravaged the dream of owning a home for many families, and new waves of renters were ushered in to keep other families whose mortgages were underwater afloat. Residents were profoundly affected by this new normal. I sat in the living room of a Jamaican woman in Cascades who started crying ten minutes into our interview because her home loan payments were in arrears and her children had just discovered a foreclosure notice on the front door. She had come home from work one day and found them crying, asking if they were going to lose their home.

The economic collapse triggered by the crisis in the finance and real estate sectors inspired the rise of the grassroots Occupy Wall Street movement. Discussions of class status among the diasporic Black middle class were grounded in the tensions between the 99 percent and the 1 percent. The "Wall Street vs. Main Street" dichotomy became an important site of class consciousness discourse. Neckerman, Carter, and Lee (1999) argued that the Black middle class has unique social experiences based on a host of racial and class problems they face in their encounters with the White middle class and the Black lower class. The Great Recession had bought heightened attention to wealthy Whites living in the Upper East Side and Long Islands Northshore estates. As the Black middle class was being undermined by the foreclosure crisis, mass layoffs, and salary freezes, their class identities were in conversation with the White economic elites who prospered while the masses suffered right in their own city. Although middle-class Blacks have been found to build moral boundaries between themselves and the lower class (Neckerman, Carter, and Lee 1999; Pattillo-McCoy 1999; Haynes 2001 Lacy 2007) the economic crises made it difficult for them to justify any moral claims to status in terms of hard work and achievement. Instead, they believed that the economic distinctions between themselves and lower-income Blacks were blurring. They increasingly saw themselves as being "in the same pot" with lower-income Blacks. "Scratching and surviving, like in *Good Times*. Make a little chow line" is how Ayana, a Black American accountant who lives in Great Park, characterized the economic atmosphere. With humor and seriousness, she described to me in detail how she and her husband constantly strategize to keep their eldest child in college, launch their teenager on the same trajectory, and pay off their debts.

SPOILED MILK, ROTTEN HONEY

During my time in the field, Great Park was undergoing a set of changes that Cascades and other postwar suburbs to which Whites had fled during desegregation had already experienced. The anxieties produced by plummeting home values were exacerbated by racial tensions within the multiracial community. Pockets of White residents tried to redraw lines within the town to make sure that new Black children on the block did not have access to "their" schools. White neighbors used community organizations to tell Black residents how they should keep their yards. Others engaged in racial avoidance so they would not have to socialize with their Black neighbors. Some called the police when Black children played basketball on the street where they both lived. These tactics of racial control over suburban space were responses to increases in the numbers of Black and Latinx families in the area over the past fifteen years.

A local Black American librarian shared that she has watched the public schools hemorrhage White students since the 1980s. When the Great Recession occurred, White families were largely unable to sell their homes, but well before that they were sending their children to private schools in order to keep them away from the Black children in the neighborhood. Since the "recovery," White families have more opportunities to leave the area. It remains to be seen how significant White population decline in Great Park will be by the 2020 census. This pattern of suburban racial change is comparable to that in other inner-ring suburbs throughout the United States. The majority Black and Latinx composition of Great Park and similar suburbs of color reflects past patterns of Black and Latinx urbanization, as well as the future of America's racial geography. Interviewees were not only wrestling with racial problems with Whites but also negotiating complicated relations with lower-income and middle-class Latinx residents. The atmosphere of Great Park in particular was affected by the growing number of interracial families in the area. They selected Great Park because they believed it would be a more elite residence than places like Cascades but also a more welcoming place for biracial Black-White or Black-Asian families than Long Island's exclusively White towns. These dynamics of conflict and harmony reflect the complex landscape of racism and solidarity in suburbia. The cultural and political implications of these multiracial, diasporic suburban places for the politics of citizenship and democracy are far reaching.

Since the 1970s, new freedoms from racial discrimination in education, employment, and housing have helped to form a much larger and more diverse Black middle class. For some, the green and open spaces of suburban landscapes remind them of the rural places they left behind in the American and Global Souths. For others, suburbs are alien and alienating environments. How Black people—monied, working class, and poor—will fare in these spaces remains in question. As younger Whites reject returning to the suburbs of their parents' and grandparents' generation and seek urban centers designed according to their comforts and interests, America's racial geography is looking more like *vanilla cities and chocolate suburbs*. In the interim, although Black suburbanites sometimes earn more than Whites, the inequality in their accumulated wealth compromises Black families' hopes of attaining economic parity through suburban homeownership. The most expensive housing markets are now in central urban areas. In "inner-city" Brooklyn, multimillion-dollar new-construction apartment buildings have waiting lists; renovated homes are on the market only briefly as insider digital sites notify gentrifiers of properties that will be on the market long before they are advertised on StreetEasy and Zillow. As the Black pioneers of suburbs like Cascades and Great Park age and transition, their children will inherit properties that are lower in value than those of Whites in the same generation. This squeeze affects Black Americans and Caribbean immigrants alike. As the rise of restrictive immigration. The rise of anti-immigration practices in post-9/11 New York and America, in the form of mass deportations during the Obama Presidency and White supremacist rhetoric and executive orders during the Trump administration, has slowed immigrant flows. Millennial youth's opportunities for mobility in a bifurcated economy have been compromised; their economic futures remain uncertain.

A TAKE-HOME PLATE

I have devoted my research for this book to the experiences of middle-class Black Americans, Haitians, and Jamaicans in New York. However, there

are a myriad of group experiences of migration, mobility, and suburbanization that are just as sociologically important. Immigrants from other Black
Caribbean countries such as, but not limited to, Barbados, Trinidad,
Panama, Guyana, Puerto Rico, and the Dominican Republic are making
significant contributions to the cultural geography of suburbs. African
immigrants, from Nigeria, Ethiopia, and Ghana, for example, are one of the
fastest growing immigrant populations in the United States. The majority
of African immigrants reside in New York, but they are less concentrated in
major gateways like New York than Caribbean immigrants (Kent 2007).

From Harlem to Long Island, the micro-practices of heterogeneous
African immigrant groups stir the pot of Black diasporic identities in different directions. Unlike Black Americans and Caribbean immigrants,
contemporary African immigrants were free, voluntary migrants to the
West, but their societies have long and deep histories with European colonialism and US imperialism. African nationality groups are the fastest
growing group of immigrants. They enter the United States largely
through family reunification pathways. However, a higher proportion of
immigrants from Africa enter the U.S as refugees or through the diversity
visa program (Capps et al. 2012). A significant number of sub-Saharan
African immigrants are college educated; they are more likely to hold a
college degree than other immigrant and native-born groups in the United
States (Capps et al., 2012; Kent, 2007) and work in middle-class health
care and education occupations. Cascades and Great Park have an important presence of Nigerian and Ghanaian immigrants who have established
churches, organizations, and clothing and media shops. Future research
on the suburbanization of African immigrants and how they negotiate
race, racism, and class mobility are critical to our understandings of how
Black Diasporic culture is being remixed in twenty-first century cities.

Migration, urbanization, and suburbanization are phenomena that are
also reshaping state societies in African, European, and Asian societies.
The local, regional, and international Black migrations that created Black
diasporic suburbs are one part of a larger reality of global population
movements in response to rising economic inequality, middle-class formation, state policy, and social exclusion in the neoliberal era. The Black
Atlantic is on the move, and their encounters in state societies that continue to hyper-segregate them call on ethnographers and demographers

to document a new era of Black spatial history. For examples, France's structural racism is articulated through its urban inequalities (Wacquant 2008, 1992); Paris is perceived as a beacon of Black American "inclusion," yet the pervasive marginalization of Black and Arab immigrants in the city and its *banlieues* demonstrate the racial limits that limit access to full French citizenship (Beaman 2017, Keaton 2009).

Many sub-Saharan African cities are being configured by rapid population growth, inequalities, and (im)migration (Mberu and Pongou 2016, White, Mberu, and Collinson 2008). From Nigeria to Kenya to South Africa, these dynamics require urgent state policies to meet the increasing need for economic growth; however, cultural studies are also imperative for understanding how poor, working-class and middle-class migrants understand, challenge, and reproduce their ethnoracial exclusions. Similar to the US, Black migration patterns in South Africa were historically intertwined with resistance politics from below to state-sanctioned racial segregation (Reed 2013). Other postcolonial societies are also seeing unprecedented patterns of geographical and cultural change. In major Indian cities, the caste system persists as a major fault line and shapes residential patterns more so than social class (Vithayathil and Singh 2012). In Korea, urban residential space is used as a site of nurturing the norms of a state-developed new middle class (Yang 2012). Therefore, the cultural and political geography of Black diasporic suburbs is one strand in an international fabric of peoples from below trying to make a way for themselves in a postcolonial and postindustrial globalized world never designed to truly include them.

MUSTARD SEEDS

A century ago, Harlem was the hotbed of an emerging urban, cosmopolitan Black identity. 125th Street was a central site of new Black cultural formations. Migrants from the US South and the Caribbean were both leaving their rural folk cultures and remaking themselves anew in a city that offered them the freedom of urban anonymity as well as new opportunities to earn money, support family, interact with strangers, and explore their self-determination. The intellectuals, writers, artists, and activists who created the Harlem Renaissance were ambivalent about how to represent this changing Black experience. Some thought it best for migrants to leave rural folk cultures behind and embrace their new cosmopolitan selves. Their Southern accents and ways of being seemed tied to slavery, too traditional, and unchanging. If this culture were perpetuated in the city, they feared, it would hinder the progress of a people already thwarted by White supremacy. A new cosmopolitan Negro was preferable to these urban elites. Others sought to represent rural folk culture in the domains of high culture in order to commodify and mystify it. Some rushed to capture and preserve the authenticity of a rural Black culture that was rapidly vanishing. These tensions about the meanings and articulations of Black life among a myriad of diverse social groups have taken a new form a century later. As Black people leave cities for the suburbs, they are forging new cultural geographies that merge their rural and urban sensibilities, evoking diasporic micro-practices and undermining any neat notions about suburban places, Black identity, migration, and mobility. In their journeys from Harlem to Long Island, Brooklyn to Queens, and the South Bronx to Westchester, they are stirring up a new cultural era of Black life.

Central to the extraordinariness of Black middle-class suburbanization is the ordinariness of their human desires—a nice home, a guaranteed parking space, a large kitchen, a garden in the backyard, a place to give their children a better life. Whether it's Haitian parents seeking a school that teaches French, Black American parents helping their child study for the entrance exam to Brooklyn Tech, or Jamaican parents worrying about sending their child to an all-White Catholic high school on Long Island, these parents are unified in their commitment to launching their children. How Black youth coming of age in these diasporic homes understand their relationship to the suburbs, race, class, and nationality is an important piece of the story of Black diasporic suburbia.

Over half of Black millennials live in suburbs (Rogowski and Cohen 2015). In the next phase of this project, I will explore the situation of the children of the post-Break generation, the multinational Black millennials growing up in the suburbs. The adults in this book saw much of themselves through the lens of being parents to a generation that has great technological opportunities but faces extraordinary social and economic challenges. Black millennials were the seeds that the post-Break Black middle class planted in their home gardens, hoping that with watering, love, care, affection, and attention they will grow and achieve more than their parents could imagine. They hoped that with the help of their villages both in the suburbs and in their original homes, they would see the fruits of their own labor and those of the generations before them manifest in their children. Their teenagers and young adults not only inherit these scripts, but form their own views about how the past and present come together to shape their aspirations for the future.

Initial explorations of their narratives highlight that the children of the post-Break generation found great hope in seeing a Black family in the White House. President Barack and Michelle Obama symbolized possibilities and left an indelible imprint on their consciousness and aspirations. Yet their hope was often eclipsed by fear and frustration. In New York and across the country, diasporic Black families received regular news reports of the murders of unarmed Black youth by police. Residents of the suburbs were not exempt from this danger. The anti-Black atmosphere that had formed the suburbs was waiting for Black families seeking to escape the problems they faced in the cities. The police killing of Michael Brown in Ferguson, a suburb of St. Louis, Missouri; the murder of Trayvon Martin by a Latinx member of the neighborhood watch in suburban Sanford, Florida; the fatal shooting murder of Renisha McBride in suburban Dearborn Heights, Michigan, by a White homeowner who answered the door when she came to ask for help after an accident; and too many other cases have awakened a generation of Black youth to the unrealized promises of the civil rights movement, racial integration, middle-class attainment, and suburbanization.

The vulnerability of their children in the outside world led parents to tighten their hold on their children and home. Their concept of "their children" was broadly inclusive, and with an ethic of caring they extended their hand to me, as a researcher, on countless occasions. "If you were my daughter, I would want someone to look after you, make sure you get home alright," Anna told me as she backed her luxury SUV out of her driveway to take me to the bus station after dark. They knew the dangers a young Black woman could encounter in their suburb walking alone at night. Suburbanization, therefore, did not always equate safety and freedom.

Black Lives Matter (BLM) has emerged as a primary social movement to resist the murders of unarmed Black youth across cities and suburbs.

BLM has inserted Black liberation politics into an American political arena that has been largely satisfied with the racial status quo. For young antiracist activists, second-class integration is not enough. They have organized a multiracial social movement across the United States to fight police brutality and systemic racial inequality. Close sociological attention to the contributions of both urban and suburban youth to this movement will elucidate how a generation of Black teenagers and young adults growing up in spatial worlds that are racially hostile to them despite being middle class or integrated are shaping the future of Black political thought, identity, and resistance.

Lastly, the formation of BLM demonstrates the intersectionality of Black social protest. This is reflected in the seeds of Black Lives Matter, which was founded by Black immigrant, queer women. Any movement led by today's Black youth will inevitably be animated by the nationality narratives and cultural hierarchies of the diaspora. Millennials are the most ethnoracially diverse generation America has yet seen, and the children of immigrants comprise a significant segment of the population. The increased ethnic heterogeneity of Black students at selective colleges, for example, is accompanied by questions of who deserves access to affirmative action policies designed to address the historical racial subjugation of the descendants of African slaves in the United States (Massey, Mooney, Torres, and Charles 2006). College campuses, too, have been hotbeds of collective Black student political organizing. Their antiracist efforts have been accompanied by tensions between Caribbean, Black American, and African students, which are overlaid with questions involving loyalty and solidarity by class origins; urban, suburban, or rural background; gender politics; and sexuality. Black millennials are a diverse group who, like their parents, wrestle with their class journeys, diasporic cultures, and Black consciousness as they build their adult lives. The future of middle-class Black youth requires close attention, and my hope is that this book's focus on the suburban backyards, lakous, and communities where they have come of age has provided a roadmap of their contemporary sociocultural foundations.

Appendix

DIGESTIF

The data analyzed in this book is a part of a larger, National Science Foundation–funded research project called the Black Ethnic Middle Class–New York (BEMP–NY) Study. Started in the summer of 2008, its first phase was a study of community and identity among middle-class Haitian families. This research was originally designed in an immigrant parent-child interview format, modeled after the Children of Immigrants Longitudinal Study.[1] In 2010, the project entered its second phase, expanding to include Black American as well as Jamaican families in Queens. By 2011, the comparative cultural analysis of three Black diasporic groups was extended to include families on Long Island. This research was designed to study cross-cultural interactions in middle-class Black diasporic spaces among adults and youth. Most of the sociological work that dealt with these groups described the experiences of Black people living in low-income areas in the urban core. What Black middle-class out-migration from cities (Wilson 1987) looked like for families of multiple nationalities and regional identities was yet to be written. It would have been easier to focus on just one nationality group and its cultural politics, but that would have limited the breadth of the project's insights. The project's multigroup, comparative design enabled me to examine how Black people who come from different vantage points but share the same residential space experience identity and belonging. The community explorations were inspired by the ethnographic legacies of Zora Neale Hurston, W. E. B. Du Bois, and the generations of scholars whose research have extended their traditions (Anderson, 1978; Charles, 2006; Drake & Cayton, 1945; Duck, 2015; Eason,

251

2017; Frazier, 1957; Hunter, 2013; N. Jones, 2009; Lamothe, 2008; Lewis-McCoy, 2014; Nelson, 2011; Z. F. Robinson, 2014; Wright & Calhoun, 2006).

I entered the field intending to find a balance between using theory to drive my inquiries and allowing the organic identities and interactions of Cascades and Great Park residents to shape the development of my theoretical findings. I borrow from Michael Burawoy's extended case method "to identify the general from the unique, to move from the "micro" to the "macro," and to connect the present to the past in anticipation of the future, all by building on preexisting theory" (Burawoy 1998, 5). I engage with theories of segmented assimilation (Portes and Zhou 1993), the minority culture of mobility (Neckerman et al. 1999), and the Black middle-class toolkit (Lacy 2007, Pattillo-McCoy 1999). However, the patterns of everyday life in Black diasporic suburbs and the narratives of my interviewees required me to add more ingredients to the theoretical pot. Cross-disciplinary perspectives from history, Black studies, cultural studies, and anthropology were essential to the development of the project's theoretical standpoint. Only an interdisciplinary recipe of texts could help capture the complex identities of this extraordinary generation of strivers; with the help of these broader intellectual frameworks, I was able to generate sociological insights from the quotidian interactions of Black diasporic life.

After moving to Cascades, I used several strategies to insert myself into the neighborhood. I wanted to know the rhythm of cultural life as residents did. I worked in ethnic and pan-ethnic organizations that were located on busy commercial streets. I volunteered in nonprofit organizations and afterschool programs. Spending time in these spaces helped me to understand their internal workings, and their relationships to the larger New York community. Once I became a regular face and built trust with their staff, I requested interviews with their professional and volunteer workers. My affiliation with these organizations was a key tool for recruiting interviewees. Families that frequented an organization's programs were more open to being interviewed because they knew that I was a part of a community institution they trusted. My volunteer work gave me legitimacy in the eyes of residents, who would otherwise be skeptical of a young woman with a clipboard asking a battery of questions about their lives. Religious leaders were also key interlocuters; they gave their "blessings" to the project. Pastors and priests disseminated information about my research activities and encouraged families in the congregation to welcome me and take part in a study of their neighborhood. The rapport I gained with these organizations and families became the springboard for recruiting other families in their neighborhood networks (Biernacki, 1981, Axinn and Pearce, 2006).

In order to recruit from a broad cross section of residents, I approached businesses and organizations that catered to nationality-specific as well as multinational groups. Business owners and organizational directors were important interlocuters. A Jamaican-owned barbershop became a key site for recruiting Jamaican men, for example. Nationality faultlines emerged during this process. If I wanted to recruit Haitian families, the established Catholic churches or newer storefront Baptist churches were more fertile ground than African Methodist Episcopal churches. Afterschool programs in their neighborhood for arts and culture were frequented mostly by Black American families. For a more multinational mixture of parents from across the Black diaspora, Parent Teacher Organizations, community boards and afterschool program leaders were invaluable resources.

Once I established a routine and rapport in Cascades, I replicated elements of this recruitment approach in Great Park. The Nassau County suburban area was less densely populated and more racially diverse than Queens, which mandated that I use more targeted recruitment strategies. There were fewer Black organizations in Great Park to volunteer for; therefore, I relied on my initial contacts with adults at school-, church-, and neighborhood-related events to identify families to be a part of my project. I also turned back to some Cascades residents who mentioned that they had members of their social network who lived on Long Island to help me find eligible interviewees.

Fieldwork requires a commitment to ongoing flexibility. A researcher has to learn the pace of life and social order of the places they study. My time was organized around the schedules of the local community. I volunteered as a tutor and grant writer for afterschool programs. I spent the earlier parts of the day canvassing busy commercial areas and approaching business owners and the latter part of the day attending church Bible study groups and youth meetings. Late evenings were devoted to attending the convenings of community boards, parent-teacher associations, civic associations, and church services. The weekends were dedicated to observing business patterns and attending social events such as birthday parties, fundraisers, first communions, Black History Months shows, church services, or hanging out in the neighborhoods.

To get from one place to the next, through the seasons, I walked on commercial and residential streets but also used dolla vans (which cost $2), rode MTA and Nassau County buses, took the subway, and rarely the Long Island Railroad. Understanding how residents got from point A to point B revealed their relationship to the spatial configuration of the suburbs in relation to the city. Using public transportation in Queens was a more democratic, accessible experience. Relative to Nassau County, Queens's buses ran more frequently in order to accommodate the large number of residents who needed to move in and out of the area. However, Nassau's bus lines did not accommodate the needs of suburban residents or the city residents who were traveling to the suburbs for work, school, or leisure. Nassau's bus lines were used mostly by the suburban poor or working class who could not afford a car. The morning and evening commutes were the exceptions, when professionals and service workers alike crammed into buses heading to the subway, eager to report to work on time. On my walks and subway and train rides, I talked to strangers; some became transportation friends I would see regularly. I also witnessed driver-rider interactions where the politics of race, class, nationality, and gender were palpable.

I used the services of local businesses and entered them with a watchful ethnographic eye for interactions between workers, owners, and clientele. I become a regular at local restaurants and bakeries, shopped in grocery stores and bodegas, went to beauty supply stores for my hair products, and frequented music stores for my media. Like my neighbors, I shoveled snow during blizzards, cleaned the front yard of debris in the mornings, and went to religious services weekly, especially during the holidays. I attended public fund-raisers for the organizations where I worked and private parties held by people who took a liking to me and invited me into their homes.

Newbies in the field have a steep learning curve and make many mistakes. I was no exception. The social world is complex, and when you have spent most of your adult life in classrooms and the past several years fretting over theory and methods, basic rules of nature are easy to miss. For instance, it is not wise to start fieldwork in the dead of winter, when people are less likely to go outside. It is important to recruit students at the beginning of the school year, not toward the end of it. The spatial dimensions of fieldwork are as crucial as the temporal ones. Moving in new spaces among the unfamiliar and unpredictable entails unanticipated challenges as well as opportunities for growth.

When I reflect on how the people I met might have seen me when I entered the field ten years ago, I recognize that the fact that I was a young Black woman of working-class background and Haitian descent shaped my motivations and experiences in the field. I am a native New Yorker, and much of my sense of self has been shaped by growing up as a city kid. I do not believe that objectivity is possible for any line of research, be it qualitative or quantitative. We all arrive at the research process with backgrounds, identities, and beliefs that shape the questions we ask, the theories we use or reject, and the methods we employ. The best that we can do is engage in reflexivity and make room for social nuance. For example, my Black identity was not a passport in every space I frequented. At times I was a fish out of water in diasporic Black middle-class suburban settings, unfamiliar with certain cultural codes and discovering things I could learn only by listening to an older generation of Black diasporic people tell their stories. Nevertheless, my Black identity and the culture and history it carried allowed me access to Black public and private spaces that my White, Asian, Latinx, or Indigenous peers would not have had. When the people I met learned that I was a graduate student at Brown University, their eyes would often light up, and a sense of pride set in. Some saw their hopes and aspirations for their children in me. Others asked me to help their kids with homework, SATs, and college applications. These parents were not only working to pass on their class status to their children, but they also activated the "it takes a village to raise a child" repertoire by helping someone else's child complete what they would often refer to as "homework." This attitude opened many doors for me.

Being Black in the field also closed other doors. In Great Park, Whites had a strong hold over public institutions. Their declining numbers in the area likely heightened their exclusionary practices toward people they deemed as racial outsiders. When I approached school officials, Black administrators were more open to setting up meetings with me and facilitating connections with the parents of their students than White administrators. White school officials required more documentation in order to legitimize my status and my research. After multiple meetings and phone calls, two institutions decided that they would not participate in this study and would not allow me to recruit affiliated families. Long Island's reputation for being racially segregated and exclusive, even in quasi-integrated settings, was reflected in these refusals.

During the participant observation phases of this research, I worked in gender-diverse environments; however, the interview settings were anchored by gendered politics. I gathered more narratives from women than from men. I was a young woman in a world of middle-class men and woman, many of whom were in heterosexual marital relationships. When a young woman "hangs out" in a setting with middle-aged men or requests an interview with them, taboos about cross-gender relations emerge. For example, after explaining who I was and why I wanted to speak with them, Black men were reluctant to set up one-on-one meetings with me. Instead, they often told me that their wife had to be a part of the meeting. At other times, I was instructed to get in touch with their wife and schedule a time to talk to her and their teenaged child. "Take my wife's number," they often said. Doing research on relations of family and kin, class, and race necessarily involves many sensitive subjects, and interactions proceed through unspoken rules that become clear only through encounters in the process of fieldwork. Although both women and men were busy juggling their jobs and family responsibilities, women more often made themselves available to me for interviews. Food and cooking became a central theme in the book because I spent significant amounts of time with women as they juggled participating in the study and preparing family meals. Their husbands sometimes joined us at kitchen tables. The unspoken rules of heterosexual relations among non-kin were observed between husbands and wives.

"Where are you from?" is a fraught question for an ethnographer attempting to understand social interactions and ethnoracial attitudes among Black diasporic groups. I entered the field intent on concealing my family's nationality so it would not affect how people interacted with me or answered research questions. Eventually I adopted a situation-specific answer to the question. Black New Yorkers will ask "where are you from" for many reasons; they are seeking to locate one another in the mosaic of American, Caribbean, and African diasporas. At first, I would reply that I would be happy to share my background after the interview was completed to avoid influencing their interview answers. Most were satisfied, yet some saw this evasion as an invitation to do detective work. One Black American woman said, "Your last name sounds French; you must be Haitian." Some Haitians recognized my last name, noting that they knew a Clerge family back on the island. In other encounters, it was important to disclose my background to Haitians I wanted to take part in the study, but who were reticent to speak to people whom they felt were outsiders. Another person called over some of her friends to play the game "Let's try to guess where Orly is from? She has locs, maybe she's Jamaican?" I went along in these situations, mortified on the inside that bias would make an interview that had taken weeks to schedule unusable. Nevertheless, these interactions were also common in everyday social life and provided a window into the sociocultural nature of Black diasporic encounters. Methodologically, these dynamics add to the body of research on the complex negotiations of research positionality and the researcher as interview instrument in the qualitative research process (Cassell 2005; Ganga and Scott 2006; Pezalla, Pettigrew, and Miller-Day 2012).

The tradition of fieldwork and ethnography is a White patriarchal practice of writing culture about the racial and economic "other." This study departs from this tradition by employing the Black ethnographic tradition of Zora Neale Hurston and W. E. B. Du Bois. Both of these Black scholars developed an understanding of how to study and write about Black cultures in a profession and academic setting that has often acted as an arm of White scientific and cultural racism. Hurston provided tools for writing ethnography in race- and gender-conscious ways, especially as an *insider outsider* in the social field (Du Bois 1899, Zuberi 2004). Black feminism has given students of sociology the tools to navigate systems of oppression within the academy, with an eye for how to translate research effectively when you are an *outsider within* the profession (Collins 2002).

The conception and analysis of fieldwork was also shaped by preeminent anthropologist Zora Neale Hurston's ethnography of spiritual and religious life in Haiti and Jamaica in the early 1900s. Although Hurston is now lauded mainly as a literary giant for her world-renowned work *Their Eyes Were Watching God*, her fiction writing was secondary to her training as an anthropologist. Literary critics have both praised her for celebrating southern Black folk culture and criticized her for exploiting vulnerable Black populations. Her ethnographic genius lies in her ability to use her insider status as a Black woman in racially divided and unequal Eatonville, Florida, to know and share the experiences of Black people from across the diaspora and, at the same time, use her outsider position as a trained ethnographer to analyze the Black cultures she observed. I have harnessed a similar insider/outsider status as ethnographer. Although I grew up in a working-class urban setting rather than a middle-class suburb, and had to learn the cues of middle-class lifestyles, my lifelong immersion in Black diasporic worlds in the U.S. and abroad facilitated my ability to interact with the people I studied and interviewed, blending in and becoming a part of their social world. Hurston's folk ethnography of Florida, Haiti, and Jamaica presented in *Tell My Horse: Voodoo and Life in Haiti and Jamaica* (1990) was an important model for how I should engage the cultural translation required when studying various Black nationality groups. I conducted this research intent on both respecting their common experiences with slavery and colonialism and honoring the integrity of their unique cultural fabrics and inter- and intra-group differences.

Hurston traveled abroad to write back into existence Black cultures that had been forgotten and maligned. A century later, the stories of migrations from the US South, the Caribbean, and Africa to suburban neighborhoods in the United States remain largely unwritten. A combination of White domination and Black desire has segregated these diasporas. In these bounded neighborhoods, Du Bois became a compass for how to write narratives about Black life in a specific spatial location with an eye to internal diversity, the distinct histories of the people, and the place they now live, as well as the importance of using multiple methods to shed light on their lives. From 1896 through 1899, Du Bois collected extensive archival information, conducted a survey, interviewed residents, and participated in the everyday life of Philadelphia's Seventh Ward in the Black ghetto for *The Philadelphia Negro* (Du Bois [1899] 1996). Isabel Eaton, a Black settlement house worker, conducted a detailed study of women's employment in domestic service for the project. The writings we have inherited, together with the passion, wit, spirit, and foresight of Hurston, Du Bois, have provided unparalleled guidance to me in this project from concept to completion.

Notes

PREFACE

1. A. Wiese, *Places of Their Own: African American Suburbanization in the Twentieth Century* (Chicago: University of Chicago Press, 2005).

CHAPTER 1. VILLAGE MARKET: ENCOUNTERS IN
BLACK DIASPORIC SUBURBS

1. Village Market and the names of the majority of people and places in this text are pseudonyms used to protect the identities of interviewees.

2. "Edwidge Danticat on Immigrant Experience" Jean Appolon Expressions, https://www.youtube.com/watch?v=ZHD0ik9JReM/

3. For more on the literature on the foodways of the African diaspora, see: Bower (2008), Williams-Forson and Sharpless (2015), Henderson (2007), Terry (2014), Twitty (2017).

4. Pew Research Center, "Black Immigrant Population in the U.S. Rose to 4.2 Million in 2016." January 24, 2018, www.pewresearch.org/fact-tank/2018/01/24 /key-facts-about-black-immigrants-in-the-u-s/ft_18-01-24_blackimmigrants _us_pop/. The Black category includes those of Hispanic origin.

5. See discussion of asset-deficit model in (Hunter and Robinson 2016).

6. Yaba Blay, "Diaspora is a verb. . . . We must physically see and feel what Blackness means in the world." As quoted by Dr. Lauren Powell on Twitter April 8, 2017.

7. The term Black American refers to people who are racialized as black and were born in the United States of America. In this book, they are seldom referred to as African American or native-born Blacks with no recent foreign born ancestry.

8. "New York Metropolitan Data in Diversity and Disparities, Trends in Racial and Ethnic Diversity," (Providence, RI: Spatial Structures in the Social Sciences, Brown University), https://s4.ad.brown.edu/projects/diversity/DiversityPages2/Default.aspx#menu

9. Amanda Fung, "Southeast Queens Is Foreclosure Central," *Crain's New York Business*, October 3, 2010, https://www.crainsnewyork.com/article/20101003/REAL_ESTATE/310039983/southeast-queens-is-foreclosure-central.

10. Christopher Dunn, *Stop and Frisk during the Bloomberg Administration—2002-2013* (New York: NYCLU, 2014). Data analysis by Sara LaPlante.

11. "Income, Poverty, and Health Coverage in the United States: 2008. US Census Bureau, https://www.census.gov/prod/2009pubs/p60-236.pdf

12. American Community Survey, 5 year estimates, 2008–2012. https://factfinder.census.gov/faces/tableservices/jsf/pages/productview.xhtml?src=bkmk

13. New York City Department of Planning, *The Newest New Yorkers—2013 Edition*, (New York: NYCDOP, 2013), https://www1.nyc.gov/site/planning/data-maps/nyc-population/newest-new-yorkers-2013.page.

14. John Logan and John Mollenkopf, *People and Politics in America's Big Cities* (New York: New York City Labor Market Information Service), 52.

15. The American Community Survey for 2008–2010 shows that some parts of Great Park are more affluent than others. In 2010 there were sections of Great Park with median household incomes of approximately $99,800 and $95,700, while that of another section was $69,000. To preserve the anonymity of interviewees I provide only generalized data here.

16. American Community Survey, five-year estimates, 2008–2012.

CHAPTER 2. CHILDREN OF THE YAM: ENSLAVED
AFRICAN TO THE BLACK MIDDLE CLASS IN THE
UNITED STATES, HAITI, AND JAMAICA

1. See Lori White, "7 Mouthwatering Dishes That Show the African Origins of Southern Soul Food," Upworthy, February 19, 2016, https://www.upworthy.com/7-mouthwatering-dishes-that-show-the-african-origins-of-southern-soul-food.

2. Nathaniel Bacon was a wealthy Englishmen who sought to eradicate the Indigenous population of Virginia and seize their land for settler colonists. The rebellion he led was supported by a multiracial coalition of Europeans and Africans. Here we see an early instance of the manipulation of "race" in order to sup-

port the planter class's drive for dominion over land and labor. Racial categories were shaped by enslaved men and women as well. (Brown 2012)

3. I use the term *mulatto* aware of its controversial status, historical evolution, and varied and changing meanings. In this section, it refers to a historical class of people with mixed European and African ancestry which emerged as a result of racialized gendered violence of White men against enslaved Black women. The social experiences of this class of mixed-race people are distinct from those whom I refer to as "Black" or "White." Most important, the use of the term *mulatto* illuminates the specific racial classification and stratification structures of the U.S., Jamaica, and Haiti. I recognize that in the U.S. many people who were identified and self-identified as Black also had European ancestry. Indeed, I aim to decenter the popular but historically inaccurate assumptions that proliferate about race in the United States. The one-drop rule that has defined any persons with visible African features as solely Black does not reflect the actual hybridity of the so-called Black population. Instead, it allowed White Americans to deny the paternity of the children whom White slave owners fathered but continued to enslave, sold away, or freed. A less rigid racial classification system that designed a continuum of Whiteness existed in both the South and the North before the Civil War and Emancipation in the United States.

4. In his autobiography, W. E. B. Du Bois wrote of his grandfather, Alexander:

> My grandfather was apprenticed to a shoemaker. Just what happened to [his brother] John, I do not know. Probably he continued as White, and his descendants, if any, know nothing of their colored ancestry. Alexander was of stern character. His movements between 1820 and 1840 are not clear. As the son of a "gentleman," with the beginnings of a gentleman's education, he refused to become a shoemaker and went to Haiti at the age of perhaps 18. . . . Of grandfather's life in Haiti from about 1821 to 1830, I know few details. From his 18th to his 27th year he formed acquaintanceships, earned a living, married and had a son, my father, Alfred, born in 1825. I do not know what work grandfather did, but probably he ran a plantation and engaged in the growing shipping trade to the United States. Who he married I do not know, nor her relatives. He may have married into the family of Elie Du Bois, the great Haitian educator. Also why he left Haiti in 1830 is not clear. It may have been because of the threat of war with France during the Revolution of 1830. . . . England soon recognized the independence of Haiti; but the United States while recognizing South American republics which Haiti had helped to free, refused to recognize a Negro nation. Because of this turmoil, grandfather may have lost faith in the possibility of real independence for Haiti.

5. See Blain (2018) for the role of Black women in transnational liberation movements.

CHAPTER 3. BLOOD PUDDING: FORBIDDEN
NEIGHBORS ON JIM CROW LONG ISLAND

1. Rieder legitimates the racist viewpoints of Canarsie residents by providing a sympathetic view of their racial hysteria about having poor Black neighbors.

Rather than consistently critiquing the racial extremism of Canarsie residents, their racial fears are verified as rationale responses to being forced to adopt liberal ideals and welcome racial integration.

2. George Vecsey, "Rosedale Service Evokes Rights Era," *New York Times*, January 13, 1975, https://timesmachine.nytimes.com/timesmachine/1975 /01/13/76323282.html?action=click&contentCollection=Archives&module=Led eAsset&region=ArchiveBody&pgtype=article&pageNumber=33.

3. See Peter Ross, "Slavery on Long Island," in *A History of Long Island from Its Earliest Settlement to the Present Time* (New York: Lewis, 1902) at https:// babel.hathitrust.org/cgi/pt?id=mdp.39015003945162;view=1up;seq=155.

4. See New Netherland Institute, "Slavery in New Netherland," https://www.new netherlandinstitute.org/history-and-heritage/digital-exhibitions/slavery-exhibit /half-freedom/.

5. Ross, "Slavery on Long Island," https://babel.hathitrust.org/cgi/pt?id=mdp .39015003945162;view=1up;seq=165.

6. WPA Writers, Hick's Neck: The Story of Baldwin, Long Island (Baldwin, NY: Baldwin National Bank and Trust, 1939) https://babel.hathitrust.org/cgi /pt?id=uc1.$b728188;view=1up;seq=57

7. Douglas Harper, "Emancipation in New York" Slavery in the North, http:// slavenorth.com/nyemancip.htm.

8. Deborah Sontag, "Canonizing a Slave: Saint or Uncle Tom?" *New York Times*, February 22, 1992, https://www.nytimes.com/1992/02/23/nyregion/canonizing -a-slave-saint-or-uncle-tom.html

9. Flushing Town Hall, http://www.flushingtownhall.org/

10. See Michael Henry Adams, "Protecting the House Where Lena Lived!" *Huffington Post*, December 6, 2017, http://www.huffingtonpost.com/michael -henry-adams/protecting-the-house-wher_b_574420.html.

11. See Nicholas Hirshon, "House Where Civil-Rights Leader W. E. B. Du Bois Lived Not Landmarked," *New York Daily News*, March 24, 2008, http://www .nydailynews.com/new-york/queens/house-civil-rights-leader-w-e-b-du-bois -lived-not-landmarked-article-1.287235.

12. "Fred C. Trump, Postwar Master Builder of Housing for Middle Class, Dies at 93," *New York Times*, June 26, 1999, http://www.nytimes.com/1999/06/26 /nyregion/fred-c-trump-postwar-master-builder-of-housing-for-middle-class -dies-at-93.html?mcubz=3.

13. Crystal Galyean, "Levittown: The Imperfect Rise of the American Suburbs," U.S. History Scene, http://ushistoryscene.com/article/levittown/

14. Joanne Jacobson, "Jew vs Jew in Levittown," *Forward*, April 13, 2009, http://forward.com/culture/104767/jew-vs-jew-in-levittown/.

15. Margery Sly, "From the Philadelphia Archive: 'The Levittown Problem,'" *History News* (blog), Temple University Libraries, October 24, 2016, https://sites .temple.edu/historynews/2016/10/24/from-the-philadelphia-jewish-archives-the -levittown-problem/.

16. See CORE NYC, http://www.corenyc.org/omeka/items/show/248, for a 1965 photo of Dr. Martin Luther King with a group of Long Island CORE members. He is addressing a rally in the Lakeview area of Long Island.

17. "LI's Non-White Population Jumps 113% in 7 Years," *Long Island Daily Press*, November 19, 1957; "218,240 Negroes Live on Long Island," *The Long Island Daily Press*, February 18, 1962.

CHAPTER 4. CALLALOO: CULTURAL ECONOMIES OF OUR BACKYARDS

1. Rich Schapiro and Ginger Adams Otis, "Crown Heights Erupts in Three Days of Race Riots after Jewish Driver Hits and Kills Gavin Cato, 7, in 1991," *New York Daily News*, August 13, 2016. http://www.nydailynews.com/new-york /brooklyn/crown-heights-erupts-days-race-riots-1991-article-1.2750050.

2. Methodologically, it was more feasible to ask prospective respondents about their overall household income. Asking about their individual earnings would have unnecessarily deterred participation in the study.

3. "Income, Poverty and Health Insurance Coverage in the United States: 2010. " https://www.census.gov/prod/2011pubs/p60-239.pdf

4. The international recruitment of Caribbean teachers is colored by racial discrimination. Teachers recruited from the Caribbean campaigned against the New York City Department of Education since they learned that they were given lower wages and less secure visa permissions than recruits from European countries brought to New York to solve the teacher shortage. A report by the Black Institute demonstrates that teachers recruited to fill the needs of low-income, low-performing schools in the city do not have a clear pathway to citizenship for themselves and their families. Some have been forced to return to their home countries after being enticed to move to New York by promises of support in gaining housing, further education, and permanent residency. http://nationbuilder.s3.ama zonaws.com/the-Blackinstitute/pages/66/attachments/original/brokenpromises.pdf?1308529431.

5. Note that the US-born children of Black immigrants are listed among the native-born, alongside those whose parents and grandparents were born in the United States.

6. The Moynihan Report, published in 1965 by Daniel Patrick Moynihan, contended that the absence of fathers and the rise of single mother households kept Black people in a cycle of urban poverty. Opponents of desegregation used this poorly researched and prejudiced report to blame poverty on Black culture rather than acknowledging historical structural racism. "Black matriarchs" were erroneously held responsible for economic disadvantage, and the report played into the hands of conservatives. Social science research was used to undercut social welfare policy and exacerbate racial economic inequality (see Greenbaum 2015).

7. Sociologist Kris Marsh and colleagues (2007) argue that declining rates of marriage and childbearing have created a larger number of Black middle-class

households that consist of single persons living alone (SALA). In addition to income, homeownership, education, and occupation as parameters for defining who is middle class, Marsh and her colleagues believe that it is important to see "households as the unit of analysis" (p. 743). The authors demonstrate that two-parent households with children are not always the norm. In 2000, 11 percent of Black middle-class households were twenty-five- to fifty-four-year-old SALA, nearly double the proportion in 1980. I argue that this redefinition of middle-class households should include both single-parent *and* multigenerational families.

8. Richard V. Reeves and Katherine Guyot, "Black Women Are Earning More College Degrees, but That Alone Won't Close Race Gaps." The Brookings Institute. https://www.brookings.edu/blog/social-mobility-memos/2017/12/04/Black-women-are-earning-more-college-degrees-but-that-alone-wont-close-race-gaps/.

9. Mark Ellis and Richard Wright, "Assimilation and Differences between the Settlement Patterns of Individual Immigrants and Immigrant Households." *Proceedings of the National Academy of Science* 102 (43): 15325–30, http://www.pnas.org/content/102/43/15325.full.pdf.

10. In Cascades and Green Park, young adults who went away to reputable colleges and universities found lucrative jobs in the city or out of state. Others struggled to find jobs while in school or after graduation that would enable them to pay rent for their own apartments. Many remained at home with their parents in order to manage the high cost of living in New York while getting started in their careers. This pattern is in sharp contrast with the middle-class American ideal of the transition to adulthood and intergenerational mobility. For Black as well as White families, this middle-class norm became increasingly impossible to achieve as the Great Recession and the student loan debt epidemic kept millions of high school and college educated young people from launching into adult economic independence. This reality resonated with parents, who sought to prolong their child's transition to independence and adulthood and frowned upon the White American idea that a child should leave home at eighteen. Some parents encouraged their adult children to remain in the household until they married. Parents used their homes to protect their children from the economic hardship involved in renting single or shared apartments in New York's expensive housing market.

11. Richard Fry, "For the First Time in Modern Era, Living with Parents Edges Out Other Living Arrangement for 18- to 34-Year-Olds." Pew Researcher Center, May 24, 2016. http://www.pewsocialtrends.org/2016/05/24/for-first-time-in-modern-era-living-with-parents-edges-out-other-living-arrangements-for-18-to-34-year-olds/.

12. For example, Baruch College, Hunter College, the College at New Paltz, the College of Staten Island, Brooklyn College and Stony Brook University have helped people of color to acquire the skill sets, credentials, and networks to become medical professionals, legal secretaries, employees of nonprofit organi-

zations, and retail managers. CCNY graduates are largely comprised of people who grew up in poor and working-class families of color in New York. Tuition and room and board costs at private out-of-state colleges were prohibitively high. These schools and occupations, although not regarded as elite or part of the "creative class" (National Center for Education Statistics, 2016), are opportunities for escaping low-wage service work and entering the middle class.

CHAPTER 5. FISH SOUP: CLASS JOURNEY ACROSS TIME AND PLACE

1. In Cascades and Great Park, those who were bourgeois in Haiti had neighbors whose families were rural farmers or urban domestic servants. The most widely known story of how migration to the United States can lead to liberation from a rigid class structure is that of Jean Robert Cadet. Cadet belonged to the lowest stratum of Haitian society: a child slave. Cadet's *Restavec: From Haitian Slave Child to Middle-Class American* (1998) testifies to how a migrant escaped the colonial legacy of child slavery in Haiti through emigration.

2. Haitian militiaman Emanuel "Toto" Constant fled Haiti with funding from the CIA and used this money to purchase property and start businesses in Queens. Once his compatriots in the diaspora discovered that a man who had commissioned death squads under the Front for the Advancement and Progress of Haiti (FRAPH), committing widespread political crimes against humanity to suppress support for then-president Jean Bertrand Aristide in Haiti, was trying to make himself into someone else in New York, they exposed him through social protests and media campaigns. He was arrested and sentenced in 2008 for his participation in grand larceny and mortgage fraud at a New York brokerage company. The crimes he committed in Haiti remain unpunished.

3. Gillian B. White, "How Black Middle-Class Kids Become Poor Adults," *Atlantic*, January 19, 2015, https://www.theatlantic.com/business/archive /2015/01/how-Black-middle-class-kids-become-Black-lower-class-adults/384613/.

CHAPTER 7. GREEN JUICE FAST: SKINFOLK DISTINCTION MAKING

1. The Daniel Fast is a twenty-one-day fast where Christians restrict their food intake for spiritual growth. During the fast, one emulates the sacrificial eating regimen upheld by the Prophet Daniel, who survived being thrown into a lion's den in the Old Testament of the Bible. During this fast, one enters into a period of extended prayer while restricting the consumption of sugar, meat products, dairy, bread, processed foods, fried foods, and alcoholic beverages.

2. *Caribbeans* can also include the children of immigrants from Caribbean islands. The term is also used by Black immigrants from the Caribbean to describe themselves and at times is used interchangeably with *West Indian*. *Caribbeans* encompasses people from the myriad of islands in the Caribbean Sea occupied by various European and American empires, while *West Indian* more often refers to Black immigrants from postcolonial nations of the Anglophone British Empire.

3. Wilson's sense of alienation was compounded by the fact that his father, a German immigrant from the Sudetenland (then part of Czechoslovakia), had deserted his mother, a migrant from North Carolina. The family lived in a poor neighborhood of Blacks and Jews near downtown Pittsburgh until his mother remarried a Black man and they moved to a predominantly White neighborhood in the city, where they were met with racist violence and forced to move again.

4. Aida Amoako writes, "The only victor of diaspora wars is white supremacy." *The Badger,* April 2017, thebadgeronline.com/2017/04/victor-diaspora-wars-white-supremacy/.

5. Cultural racism, the contemporary manifestation of socially constructed differences between Whites and racialized groups, has substituted cultural beliefs and practices for biology in order to justify why racialized groups are concentrated in lower socioeconomic positions. For more on the manipulation of culture in the name of racism, see Bonilla Silva (2003), Kelley (2001), and Pierre (2004).

6. In 2006 Yvette D. Clarke (D) was elected to the US House of Representatives by the Ninth Congressional District of New York. She now serves as cochair of the Caribbean Caucus, chair of the Multicultural Media Caucus, and cochair of the Black Women and Girls Caucus. A Brooklyn native of Jamaican heritage, she is the daughter of former City Council member Dr. Una S. T. Clarke.

7. This conception of nationality narratives and its relationship to the local ethnic hierarchy is shaped by W. I. Thomas's theory that if people believe a situation to be real, it will have real consequences. (Merton 1995)

8. Garry Pierre-Pierre, "Hip-Hop Idol Is the Pride of a People: Young Haitian Americans Get Help against Stigma," New York Times, March 28, 1998, https://www.nytimes.com/1998/03/28/nyregion/hip-hop-idol-pride-people-young-haitian-americans-get-help-against-stigma.html

9. Haitian Kreyol (also referred to as Haitian Creole) is the language of the people of Haiti. It is stereotyped as a secondary, inferior language compared to French, which is the official language of Haiti. Recent anticolonial, liberatory movements to alphabetize Haitian Kreyol aim to expand educational and linguistic access for the majority of the Haitian people; only an educated minority speaks French in Haiti.

10. There are multiple interpretations of how "booty scratcher" was first applied by Black Americans to African immigrants and then extended to Haitians. It appears to be derived from the saying that Black slaves had to scratch their masters' derrieres because Whites were too lazy to do it themselves. It was

directed not against Whites, but against Black people by other Black people who thought they were subservient and accommodating to Whites. It was, thus, analogous to Malcolm's critique of "house niggers." The idea (repeated on Wikimedia) that it had to do with African bushmen who sat passively and scratched as they were bitten by flies seems apocryphal. The phrase has recently been taken up by a projected TV sitcom of that name whose Nigerian creator, Damilare Sonoiki, who has a degree in economics from Harvard and worked on Wall Street before becoming a writer on the sitcom *Black-ish*. Sonoiki explains: "It is how people with an African accent in USA are called by the African Americans. I used to be called this way in school. . . . I just like the idea of taking something negative and poking fun at it. We are going to turn around and actually take away the power from it." See http://inspireafrika.com/en/are.

CONCLUSION: MUSTARD SEEDS

1. New York's Black suburban population increased by 30 percent between 1990 and 2000. The rate of increase varied by nationality: African Americans increased by 16.8 percent, Afro-Caribbean immigrants by 87.6 percent, and African immigrants by 74.9 percent. Source: http://www.s4.brown.edu/cen2000 /BlackWhite/DiversityBWDataPages/5600ccBWCt.htm.

2. For Black immigrant population change: The Newest New Yorkers: Characteristics of the City's Foreign Born Population. 2013. Department of City Planning, New York City. https://www1.nyc.gov/assets/planning/download/pdf /data-maps/nyc-population/nny2013/nny_2013.pdf. For general multinational Black population change: William H. Frey's "Melting Pot Cities and Suburbs: Racial and Ethnic Change in Metro America in the 2000s." Brookings Institute Metropolitan Policy Program. https://www.brookings.edu/wp-content/uploads /2016/06/0504_census_ethnicity_frey.pdf

3. From "The Dawn of Freedom" (Du Bois 1903, 9).

4. See Joseph (2015) for her discussion of how Brazilian migrants navigate global racial hierarchies.

5. Sonia Sanchez. Featured Guest Speaker. Association for Black Sociologist Meeting, Sonesta Hotel, Philadelphia, 2018.

APPENDIX: DIGESTIF

1. Alejandro Portes and Rubén G. Rumbaut, *Children of Immigrants Longitudinal Study (CILS), 1991–2006*. Ann Arbor, MI: Inter-university Consortium for Political and Social Research, January 23, 2012. https://doi.org/10.3886 /ICPSR20520.v2.

References

Adams R. L. Jr. 2005. "Black Gotham: African Americans in New York City, 1900–2000." *Identities: Global Studies in Culture and Power* 12 (3): 363–84.

Addo, F. R., J. N. Houle, and D. Simon. 2016. "Young, Black, and (Still) in the Red: Parental Wealth, Race, and Student Loan Debt." *Race and Social Problems* 8 (1): 64–76.

Alba, R., P. Kasinitz, and M. C. Waters. 2011. The Kids Are (Mostly) Alright: Second-Generation Assimilation—Comments on Haller, Portes and Lynch. *Social Forces* 89 (3): 763–73.

Anderson, E. 1978. *A Place on the Corner: A Study of Black Street Corner Men*. Chicago: University of Chicago Press.

———. 1999. *Code of the Street*. New York: W. W. Norton.

———. 2011. *The Cosmopolitan Canopy: Race and Civility in Everyday Life*: W. W. Norton.

———. 2015. "The White Space." *Sociology of Race and Ethnicity* 1 (1): 10–21.

Axinn, W. G. and L. D. Pearce. 2006. *Mixed Method Data Collection Strategies*. Cambridge: Cambridge University Press.

Bailey, E. K. 2013. "From Cultural Dissonance to Diasporic Affinity: The Experience of Jamaican Teachers in New York City Schools." *Urban Review* 45 (2): 232–49.

Bald, V. 2006. "Overlapping Diasporas, Multiracial Lives: South Asian Muslims in US Communities of Color, 1880–1950." *Souls* 8 (4), 3–18.

———. 2013. *Bengali Harlem and the Lost Histories of South Asian America*. Cambridge, MA: Harvard University Press.

Beaman, J. 2017. *Citizen Outsider: Children of North African Immigrants in France*. Oakland: University of California Press.

Berlin, I., and Harris, L. M. 2005. *Slavery in New York*: New York: The New Press.

Biernacki, P., and D. Waldorf. 1981. Snowball Sampling: Problems and Techniques of Chain Referral Sampling. *Sociological Methods & Research* 10 (2): 141–63.

Blain, K. N. 2018. *Set the World on Fire: Black Nationalist Women and the Global Struggle for Freedom*. Philadelphia: University of Pennsylvania Press.

Bonilla-Silva, E. 2003. *Racism without Racists: Color-Blind Racism and the Persistence of Racial Inequality in the United States*. Lanham, MD: Rowman & Littlefield.

———. 2004. From Bi-racial to Tri-racial: Towards a New System of Racial Stratification in the USA. *Ethnic and Racial Studies* 27 (6): 931–50.

Bonilla-Silva, E., C. Goar, and D. G. Embrick. 2006. "When Whites Flock Together: The Social Psychology of White Habitus." *Critical Sociology* 32 (2–3): 229–53.

Bower, A. L., ed. 2008. *African American Foodways: Explorations of History and Culture*. Urbana: University of Illinois Press.

Bowls, J., Joel Katkin, and David Giles. 2009. *Reviving the City of Aspiration: A Study of the Challenges Facing New York City's Middle Class*. Retrieved from Center for an Urban Future. https://nycfuture.org/research/reviving-the-middle-class-dream-in-nyc.

Brown, A. 1979. *Color, Class, and Politics in Jamaica*. New Brunswick, NJ: Transaction Publishers.

Brown, K. L. 2018. *Gone Home: Race and Roots through Appalachia*. Chapel Hill: University of North Carolina Press.

Brown, K. M. 2012. *Good Wives, Nasty Wenches, and Anxious Patriarchs: Gender, Race, and Power in Colonial Virginia*: Chapel Hill: University of North Carolina Press.

Brown-Glaude, W. 2011. *Higglers in Kingston: Women's Informal Work in Jamaica*. Nashville, TN: Vanderbilt University Press.

Browne, I. 1997. "Explaining the Black-White Gap in Labor Force Participation among Women Heading Households." *American Sociological Review* 62 (2): 236–52.

Brutus, E. 1948. *Instruction publique en Haïti, 1492–1945*. Vol. 1. Port-au-Prince, Haiti: Éditions Panorama.

Burawoy, M. 1998. "The Extended Case Method." *Sociological Theory* 16 (1): 4–33.

Buffonge, A. E. Gordon. 2001. "Culture and Political Opportunity: Rastafarian Links to the Jamaican Poor." In *Political Opportunities Social Movements, and Democratization*, edited by Patrick G. Coy, 3–35. Bingley, UK: Emerald Group Publishing.

Cadet, J.-R. 1998. *Restavec: From Haitian Slave Child to Middle-Class American*: Austin: University of Texas Press.

Campbell, M. C. 1988. *The Maroons of Jamaica, 1655–1796: A History of Resistance, Collaboration and Betrayal*. Granby, MA: Bergin & Garvey.

Capps, Randy, Kristen McCabe, and Michael Fix. 2012. Diverse Streams: Black African Migration to the United States. Washington, DC: Migration Policy Institute.

Cassell, C. 2005. "Creating the Interviewer: Identity Work in the Management Research Process." *Qualitative Research* 5 (2): 167–79.

Cassiman, S. A. 2007. "Of Witches, Welfare Queens, and the Disaster Named Poverty: The Search for a Counter-Narrative." *Journal of Poverty* 10 (4): 51–66.

———. 2008. "Resisting the Neo-liberal Poverty Discourse: On Constructing Deadbeat Dads and Welfare Queens." *Sociology Compass* 2 (5): 1690–1700.

Chamberlain, M. 2003. "Rethinking Caribbean Families: Extending the Links." *Community, Work & Family* 6 (1): 63–76.

———. 2017. *Family Love in the Diaspora: Migration and the Anglo-Caribbean Experience*. New York: Routledge.

Charles, C. Z. 2006. *Won't You Be My Neighbor: Race, Class, and Residence in Los Angeles*. New York: Russell Sage Foundation.

Chatelain, M. 2015. *South Side Girls: Growing up in the Great Migration*. Durham, NC: Duke University Press.

Chiteji, N. S., and D. Hamilton, D. 2002. "Family Connections and the Black-White Wealth Gap among Middle-Class Families." *Review of Black Political Economy* 30 (1): 9–28.

Clerge, O., G. Sanchez-Soto, J. Song, and N. Luke. 2017. "'I Would Really Like to Go Where You Go': Rethinking Migration Decision-Making among Educated Tied Movers." *Population, Space and Place* 23 (2): e1990.

Collins, P. H. 1986. Learning from the Outsider Within: The Sociological Significance of Black Feminist Thought. *Social problems* 33 (6): s14–s32.

Collins, P. H. 1998. "Intersections of Race, Class, Gender, and Nation: Some Implications for Black Family Studies." *Journal of Comparative Family Studies* 29 (1): 27–36.

———. 2002. *Black Feminist Thought: Knowledge, Consciousness, and the Politics of Empowerment*. New York: Routledge.

Conley, D. 2010. *Being Black, Living in the Red: Race, Wealth, and Social Policy in America*. Berkeley: University of California Press.

Cook, M. 1948. *Education in Haiti*: Washington, DC: Federal Security Agency.

Coupeau, S. 2008. *The History of Haiti*: Westport, CT: Greenwood Publishing Group.

Cox, L. C. F., and J. H. Cox. 1973. *Reconstruction: The Negro, and the New South*. Columbus: University of South Carolina Press.

Crenshaw, K. 1990. Mapping the Margins: Intersectionality, Identity Politics, and Violence against Women of Color. *Stanford Law Review* 43: 1241.

Cromartie, J., and C. B. Stack. 1989. "Reinterpretation of Black Return and Nonreturn Migration to the South 1975–1980." *Geographical Review* 79 (3): 297–310.

Darity, W. Jr., and M. J. Nicholson. 2005. "Racial Wealth Inequality and the Black Family." *African American Family Life: Ecological and Cultural Diversity*, edited by Vonnie C. McLoyd, Nancy E. Hill, and Kenneth A. Dodge, 78–85. New York: Guilford.

Dawson, M. C. 1995. *Behind the Mule: Race and Class in African-American Politics*. Princeton, NJ: Princeton University Press.

Day, Lynda R. 1997. *Making a Way to Freedom: A History of African Americans on Long Island*. New York: Empire State Books.

Dodson, H., and Diouf, S. A. 2004. *In Motion: The African-American Migration Experience*. Washington, DC: National Geographic Society.

Drake, S. C., and H. Cayton. 1945. *Black Metropolis*. 2 vols. New York: Harper and Row.

Dubois, L. 2005. *Avengers of the New World*. Cambridge, MA: Harvard University Press.

Du Bois, W. E. B. (1899) 1996. *The Philadelphia Negro*. Philadelphia: University of Pennsylvania Press.

———. 1900. The Present Outlook for the Dark Races of Mankind. *AME Church Review* 17 (2): 95–110.

———. 1901. *The Black North in 1901: A Social Study*. New York: Arno Press. New York Times.

———. 1903. *The Souls of Black Folk*. Chicago: A. C. McClurg.

———. 1935. *Black Reconstruction: An Essay toward a History of the Part Which Black Folk Played in the Attempt to Reconstruct Democracy in America, 1860–1880*. New York: Harcourt, Brace and Company.

———. 2014. *The Autobiography of W. E. B. Du Bois: A Soliloquy on Viewing My Life from the Last Decade of Its First Century*. Edited by H. L. Gates Jr. Oxford: Oxford University Press.

Duck, W. 2015. *No Way Out: Precarious Living in the Shadow of Poverty and Drug Dealing*. Chicago: University of Chicago Press.

Dunn, R. S. 2012. *Sugar and Slaves: The Rise of the Planter Class in the English West Indies, 1624–1713*. Chapel Hill: University of North Carolina Press.

Dupuy, A. 2004. "Class, Race, and Nation: Unresolved Contradictions of the Saint-Domingue Revolution." *Journal of Haitian Studies* 10 (1): 6–21.

Eason, J. M. 2017. *Big House on the Prairie: Rise of the Rural Ghetto and Prison Proliferation*. Chicago: University of Chicago Press.

Feagin, J. R., and M. P. Sikes. 1994. *Living with Racism: The Black Middle-Class Experience*. Boston: Beacon Press.

Feimster, C. N. 2009. *Southern Horrors: Women and the Politics of Rape and Lynching*. Cambridge, MA: Harvard University Press.

Field, K. T. 2018. *Growing Up with the Country: Family, Race, and Nation after the Civil War*. New Haven, CT: Yale University Press.

Florida, R. 2002. *The Rise of the Creative Class: And How It's Transforming Work, Leisure and Everyday Life*. New York: Basic Books.

Foner, N. ed., 2001. *Islands in the City: West Indian Migration to New York*. Berkeley: University of California Press.

Fordham, S. 1993. "'Those Loud Black Girls': (Black) Women, Silence, and Gender 'Passing' in the Academy." *Anthropology & Education Quarterly* 24 (1): 3–32.

Frazier, F. 1957. *Black Bourgeoisie*. New York: Simon & Schuster.

Ganga, D., and S. Scott. 2006. "Cultural 'Insiders' and the Issue of Positionality in Qualitative Migration Research: Moving 'across' and Moving 'along' Researcher-Participant Divides." *Forum: Qualitative Social Research* 7 (3): Art. 7. http://www.qualitative-research.net/index.php/fqs/article/view/134/289.

Gay, C. 2006. Seeing Difference: The Effect of Economic Disparity on Black Attitudes toward Latinos. *American Journal of Political Science* 50 (4): 982–97.

Geggus, D. P. 2001. *The Impact of the Haitian Revolution in the Atlantic World*. Columbus: University of South Carolina Press.

Gellman, D. N. 2006. *Emancipating New York: The Politics of Slavery and Freedom, 1777–1827*. Baton Rouge: Louisiana State University Press.

Gilroy, P. 1993. *The Black Atlantic: Modernity and Double Consciousness*. Cambridge, MA: Harvard University Press.

Glenn, C. L. 2011. "Jim Crow North." In *African-American/Afro-Canadian Schooling: From the Colonial Period to the Present*, 109–25. New York: Palgrave Macmillan.

Go, J. 2013. "For a Postcolonial Sociology." *Theory and Society* 42(1): 25–55.

Goffman, E. 1963. *Stigma: Notes on the Management of Spoiled Identity*. New York Simon & Schuster.

Goldin, C. 1977. "Female Labor Force Participation: The Origin of Black and White Differences, 1870 and 1880." *Journal of Economic History* 37 (1): 87–108.

Gottesdiener, L. 2013. *A Dream Foreclosed: Black America and the Fight for a Place to Call Home*. Westfield, NJ: Zuccotti Park Press.

Graham, L. O. 2000. *Our Kind of People: Inside America's Black Upper Class*. New York: HarperCollins,

Greenbaum, S. D. 2015. *Blaming the Poor: The Long Shadow of the Moynihan Report on Cruel Images about Poverty.* New Brunswick, NJ: Rutgers University Press.

Greer, C. M. 2013. *Black Ethnics: Race, Immigration, and the Pursuit of the American Dream.* Oxford: Oxford University Press.

Gregory, S. 1998. *Black Corona: Race and the Politics of Place in an Urban Community.* Princeton, NJ: Princeton University Press.

Griffin, F. J. 1996. *"Who Set You Flowin'?": The African-American Migration Narrative.* New York: Oxford University Press.

Guridy, F. A. 2010. *Forging Diaspora: Afro-Cubans and African Americans in a World of Empire and Jim Crow.* Chapel Hill: University of North Carolina Press.

Hall, S. 1990. *Cultural Identity and Diaspora.* London: Lawrence and Wishart.

Hamilton, D., W. Darity Jr., A. E. Price, V. Sridharan, and R. Tippett. 2015. *Umbrellas Don't Make It Rain: Why Studying and Working Hard Isn't Enough for Black Americans.* New York: The New School.

Harris, M., Carlson, B. and Poata-Smith, E. S. (2013). "Indigenous identities and the politics of authenticity." In *The Politics of Identity: Emerging Indigeneity,* edited by M. Harris and M. Nakataand B. Carlson, 1–9. Sydney: University of Technology Sydney E-Press.

Harris-Perry, M. V. 2011. *Sister Citizen: Shame, Stereotypes, and Black Women in America.* New Haven, CT: Yale University Press.

Haynes, B. D. 2001. *Red Lines, Black Spaces: The Politics of Race and Space in a Black Middle-Class Suburb.* New Haven, CT: Yale University Press.

Haynes, G. E. 1913. "Conditions among Negroes in the Cities." *The Annals of the American Academy of Political and Social Science* 49 (1): 105–19.

———. 1918. "Negroes Move North." *The Survey,* no. 40, 115–22.

Henderson, L. 2007. "'Ebony Jr!' and 'Soul Food': The Construction of Middle-Class African American Identity through the Use of Traditional Southern Foodways." *Melus* 32 (4): 81–97.

Horton, J. O., and L. E. Horton. 1998. *In Hope of Liberty: Culture, Community and Protest among Northern Free Blacks, 1700–1860.* Oxford: Oxford University Press.

Hunter, M. A. 2013. *Black Citymakers: How the Philadelphia Negro Changed Urban America.* New York: Oxford University Press.

Hunter, M. A., and Z. F. Robinson. 2016. "The Sociology of Urban Black America." *Annual Review of Sociology* 42: 385–405.

———. 2018. *Chocolate Cities: The Black Map of American Life*: Oakland: University of California Press.

Hurston, Z. N. 1990. *Tell My Horse: Voodoo and Life in Haiti and Jamaica.* New York: Harper Collins.

Ignatiev, N. 2009. *How the Irish Became White.* NewYork: Routledge.

Itzigsohn, J. 2009. *Encountering American Faultlines: Race, Class, and the Dominican Experience in Providence.* New York: Russell Sage Foundation.

Itzigsohn, J., and K. Brown. 2015. "Sociology and the Theory of Double Consciousness: WEB Du Bois's Phenomenology of Racialized Subjectivity." *Du Bois Review: Social Science Research on Race* 12 (2): 231–48.

Jackson, J. L. 2001. *Harlem World: Doing Race and Class in Contemporary Black America.* Chicago: University of Chicago Press.

Jackson, S. N. 2007. "What Is This Thing Called Callaloo? An Introduction." *Callaloo* 30 (1): 14–22.

Jefferson, M. 2016. *Negroland: A Memoir.* New York: Vintage.

Jenkins, R. 1994. "Rethinking Ethnicity: Identity, Categorization and Power." *Ethnic and Racial Studies* 17 (2): 197–223.

Johnson, R. 2016. *Slavery's Metropolis: Unfree Labor in New Orleans during the Age of Revolutions.* Cambridge: Cambridge University Press.

Jones, J. 2009. *Labor of Love, Labor of Sorrow: Black Women, Work, and the Family, from Slavery to the Present.* New York: Basic Books.

Jones, N. 2009. *Between Good and Ghetto: African American Girls and Inner-City Violence.* New Brunswick, NJ: Rutgers University Press.

Joseph, T. D. 2015. *Race on the Move: Brazilian Migrants and the Global Reconstruction of Race.* Stanford, CA: Stanford University Press.

Jung, M.-H. 2006. *Coolies and Cane: Race, Labor, and Sugar in the Age of Emancipation.* Baltimore: Johns Hopkins University Press.

Kasinitz, P. 1992. *Caribbean New York: Black Immigrants and the Politics of Race.* Ithaca, NY: Cornell University Press.

Kasinitz, P., and M. Vickerman. 2001. "Ethnic Niches and Racial Traps: Jamaicans in the New York Regional Economy." In *Migration, Transnationalization, and Race in a Changing New York*, edited by Hector Cordero-Guzman, Rovert C. Smith, and Ramon Grosfoguel, 191–211. Philadelphia: Temple University Press.

Katznelson, I. 2005. *When Affirmative Action Was White: An Untold History of Racial Inequality in Twentieth-Century America.* WW Norton.

Keaton, T. 2009. "'Black (American) Paris' and the French Outer-Cities: The Race Question and Questioning Solidarity." In *Black Europe and the African Diaspora*, edited by D. C. Hine, T. D. Keaton, and S. Small, 95–118. Urbana: University of Illinois Press.

Kelley, R. D. 2000. How the West Was One: On the Uses and Limitations of Diaspora. *The Black Scholar* 30 (3–4): 31–35.

———. 2001. *Yo' Mama's Disfunktional! Fighting the Culture Wars in Urban America.* Boston: Beacon Press.

Kent, M. M. 2007. "Immigration and America's Black Population." *Population Bulletin* 62 (4).

Lacy, K. 2007. *Blue-Chip Black: Race, Class, and Status in the New Black Middle Class.* Berkeley: University of California Press.

———. 2012. All's Fair? The Foreclosure Crisis and Middle-Class Black (in) Stability. *American Behavioral Scientist* 56 (11): 1565–80.

Laguerre, M. S. 1984. *American Odyssey: Haitians in New York City.* Vol. 1. Ithaca, NY: Cornell University Press.

———. 1998. *Diasporic Citizenship: Haitians in Transnational America.* New York: St: Martin's Press.

Lamont, M. 2009. *The Dignity of Working Men: Morality and the Boundaries of Race, Class, and Immigration.* Cambridge, MA: Harvard University Press.

Lamothe, D. 2008. *Inventing the New Negro: Narrative, Culture, and Ethnography.* Philadelphia: University of Pennsylvania Press.

Lavergne, M., and S. Mullainathan, S. 2004. "Are Emily and Greg More Employable Than Lakisha and Jamal? A Field Experiment on Labor Market Discrimination. *American Economic Review* 94 (4): 991–1013.

Lees, L. 2003. "Super-Gentrification: The Case of Brooklyn Heights, New York City." *Urban studies* 40 (12): 2487–509.

Lemann, N. 2011. *The Promised Land: The Great Black Migration and How It Changed America.* New York: Vintage.

Levitt, P. 2001. *The Transnational Villagers.* Berkeley: University of California Press.

Lewis, E. 1995. "To Turn as on a Pivot: Writing African Americans into a History of Overlapping Diasporas." *American Historical Review* 100 (3): 765–87.

Lewis-McCoy, R. H. 2014. *Inequality in the Promised Land: Race, Resources, and Suburban Schooling.* Stanford, CA: Stanford University Press.

Li, W. 1998. "Anatomy of a New Ethnic Settlement: The Chinese Ethnoburb in Los Angeles." *Urban Studies* 35 (3): 479–501.

Lichter, D. T., D. Parisi, and M. C. Taquino. 2012. "The Geography of Exclusion: Race, Segregation, and Concentrated Poverty." *Social Problems* 59 (3): 364–88.

Lowe, L. 2015. *The Intimacies of Four Continents.* Durham, NC: Duke University Press.

Lung-Amam, W. 2017. *Trespassers? Asian Americans and the Battle for Suburbia.* Oakland: University of California Press.

Marable, M. 1983. *How Capitalism Underdeveloped Black America.* Boston: South End Press.

Marrow, H. 2011. *New Destination Dreaming: Immigration, Race, and Legal Status in the Rural American South.* Stanford, CA: Stanford University Press.

Marsh, K., W. A. Darity Jr, P. N., Cohen, L. M. Casper, and D. Salters. 2007. "The Emerging Black Middle Class: Single and Living Alone" *Social Forces* 86 (2): 735–62.

Massey, D. S. 2007. *Categorically Unequal: The American Stratification System*. New York: Russell Sage Foundation.

Massey, D. S., and N. A. Denton. 1993. *American Apartheid: Segregation and the Making of the Underclass*. Cambridge, MA: Harvard University Press.

Massey, D. S., M. Mooney, K. C. Torres, and C. Z. Charles. 2006. "Black Immigrants and Black Natives Attending Selective Colleges and Universities in the United States." *American Journal of Education* 113 (2): 243–71.

Mberu, B. U., and R. Pongou. 2016. "Crossing Boundaries: Internal, Regional and International Migration in Cameroon." *International Migration* 54 (1): 100–118.

McKay, C. 1928. *Home to Harlem*. Lebanon, NH: University Press of New England.

Merton, R. K. 1995. "The Thomas Theorem and the Matthews Effect." *Social Forces* 74 (2): 379–422.

Mirabal, N. R., and E. Danticat. 2007. "Dyasporic Appetites and Longings: An Interview with Edwidge Danticat." *Callaloo* 30 (1): 26–39.

Model, S. 1991. Caribbean Immigrants: A Black Success Story? *International Migration Review* 25 (2): 248–76.

———. 2008. *West Indian Immigrants: A Black Success Story?* New York: Russell Sage Foundation.

National Center for Education Statistics. 2016. *Status and Trends in the Education of Racial and Ethnic Groups 2016*. Washington, DC: US Department of Education. Retrieved from https://nces.ed.gov/pubs2016/2016007.pdf.

Neckerman, K. M., P. Carter, and J. Lee. 1999. "Segmented Assimilation and Minority Cultures of Mobility." *Ethnic and Racial Studies* 22 (6): 945–65.

Nelson, A. 2011. *Body and Soul: The Black Panther Party and the Fight against Medical Discrimination*. Minneapolis: University of Minnesota Press.

———. 2016. *The Social Life of DNA: Race, Reparations, and Reconciliation after the Genome*. Boston: Beacon Press.

Nicholls, D. 1996. *From Dessalines to Duvalier: Race, Colour, and National Independence in Haiti*. New Brunswick, NJ: Rutgers University Press.

Niedt, C., and I. W. Martin. 2013. "Who Are the Foreclosed? A Statistical Portrait of America in Crisis." *Housing Policy Debate* 23 (1): 159–76.

Ogbar, J. O. 2010. *The Harlem Renaissance Revisited: Politics, Arts, and Letters*: Baltimore: Johns Hopkins University Press.

Oliver, M., and T. Shapiro. 2013. *Black Wealth/White Wealth: A New Perspective on Racial Inequality*. New York: Routledge.

Omi, M., and H. Winant. 1994. "Racial Formations." In *Racial Formation in the United States: From the 1960s to the 1990s*, 53–76. New York: Routledge.

Ostine, Regine. 2007. "Beyond Social Distancing: Intermarriage and Ethnic Boundaries among Black Americans in Boston." In *The Other African Americans: Contemporary African and Caribbean Immigrants in the*

United States, edited by Y. Shaw-Taylor and S.A. Tuch, 217–254 Lanham, MD: Rowman & Littlefield.

Pager, D. 2003. "The Mark of a Criminal Record." *American Journal of Sociology* 108 (5): 937–75.

Patterson, T. R., and R. D. Kelley. 2000. "Unfinished Migrations: Reflections on the African Diaspora and the Making of the Modern World. *African Studies Review* 43 (1): 11–45.

Pattillo-McCoy, M. 1999. *Black Picket Fences: Privilege and Peril among the Black Middle Class*. Chicago: University of Chicago Press.

Pendergrass, S. 2013. "Perceptions of Race and Region in the Black Reverse Migration to the South." *Du Bois Review: Social Science Research on Race*, 10 (1): 155–78.

Pezalla, A. E., J. Pettigrew, and M. Miller-Day. 2012. Researching the Researcher-as-Instrument: An Exercise in Interviewer Self-Reflexivity. *Qualitative Research* 12 (2): 165–85.

Pierre, J. 2004. "Black Immigrants in the United States and the 'Cultural Narratives' of Ethnicity." *Identities: Global Studies in Culture and Power* 11 (2): 141–70.

Portes, A., and R. G. Rumbaut. 2001. *Legacies: The Story of the Immigrant Second Generation*. Berkeley: University of California Press; New York: Russell Sage Foundation.

Portes, A., and M. Zhou. 1993. The New Second Generation: Segmented Assimilation and Its Variants. *Annals of the American Academy of Political and Social Science* 530 (November): 74–96. doi: 10.1177/0002716293530001006.

Putnam, L. 2013. *Radical Moves: Caribbean Migrants and the Politics of Race in the Jazz Age*. Chapel Hill: University of the North Carolina Press.

Rabaka, R. 2015. *The Negritude Movement: W. E. B. Du Bois, Leon Damas, Aimé Césaire, Léopold Senghor, Frantz Fanon, and the Evolution of an Insurgent Idea*: Lanham, MD: Lexington Books.

Reed, H. E. 2013. "Moving across Boundaries: Migration in South Africa, 1950–2000." *Demography* 50 (1): 71–95.

Rieder, J. 1985. *Canarsie*. Cambridge, MA: Harvard University Press.

Robinson, C. J. 1983. *Black Marxism: The Making of the Black Radical Tradition*. Chapel Hill: University of North Carolina Press.

Robinson, Z. F. 2014. *This Ain't Chicago: Race, Class, and Regional Identity in the Post-Soul South*. Chapel Hill: University of North Carolina Press.

Rodney, W. 1972. *How Europe Underdeveloped Africa*. London: Bogle L'Ouverture.

Rogers, B. F. 1955. "William E. B. DuBois, Marcus Garvey, and Pan-Africa." *Journal of Negro History* 40 (2): 154–65.

Rogers, R. R. 2006. *Afro-Caribbean Immigrants and the Politics of Incorporation: Ethnicity, Exception, or Exit*. Cambridge: Cambridge University Press.

Rogowski, J.C., and C.J. Cohen. 2015. *Black Millennials in America*. Chicago: Black Youth Project. https://blackyouthproject.com/wp-content/uploads /2015/11/BYP-millenials-report-10-27-15-FINAL.pdf.

Rothstein, R. 2017. *The Color of Law*. New York: Liveright.

Rudwick, E.M. 1959. DuBois versus Garvey: Race Propagandists at War. *Journal of Negro Education* 28 (4): 421–29.

Sanjek, R. 2000. *The Future of Us All: Race and Neighborhood Politics in New York City*. Ithaca, NY: Cornell University Press.

Sellers, R.M., N. Copeland-Linder, P.P. Martin, and R.H. Lewis. 2006. "Racial Identity Matters: The Relationship between Racial Discrimination and Psychological Functioning in African American Adolescents." *Journal of Research on Adolescence* 16 (2): 187–216.

Shannon, S.G. 1997. A Transplant That Did Not Take: August Wilson's Views on the Great Migration. *African American Review* 31 (4): 659–66.

Sharfstein, D.J. 2006. "Crossing the Color Line: Racial Migration and the One-Drop Rule, 1600–1860." *Minnesota Law Review* 91, 592–656.

Shimkin, E.M., and D.A. Frate. 1978. *Extended Family in Black Societies*. New York: Walter de Gruyter.

Silver, H. 1994. "Social Exclusion and Social Solidarity: Three Paradigms." *International Labour Review* 133 (5): 531–78.

Stack, C. 1996. *Call to Home: African Americans Reclaim the Rural South*. New York: Basic Books

Stepick, A. 1982. "Haitian Boat People: A Study in the Conflicting Forces Shaping US Immigration Policy." *Law and Contemporary Problems* 45 (2): 163–96.

Stepick, A., and D.F. Swartz. 1998. *Pride against Prejudice: Haitians in the United States*. Boston: Allyn and Bacon.

Tchen, J.K.W. 2001. *New York before Chinatown: Orientalism and the Shaping of American Culture, 1776–1882*. Baltimore: Johns Hopkins University Press.

Terry, B. 2014. *Afro-vegan: Farm-Fresh African, Caribbean and Southern Flavors Remixed*. Berkeley, CA: Ten Speed Press

Thomas, D.A. 2004. *Modern Blackness: Nationalism, Globalization, and the Politics of Culture in Jamaica*. Durham, NC: Duke University Press.

———. 2007. "Blackness across Borders: Jamaican Diasporas and New Politics of Citizenship." *Identities: Global Studies in Culture and Power* 14 (1–2): 111–33.

Tienda, M., and J. Glass. 1985. "Household Structure and Labor Force Participation of Black, Hispanic, and White Mothers." *Demography* 22 (3): 381–94.

Treitler, V.B. 2013. *The Ethnic Project: Transforming Racial Fiction into Ethnic Factions*. Stanford, CA: Stanford University Press.

———. 2015. "Social Agency and White Supremacy in Immigration Studies." *Sociology of Race and Ethnicity* 1 (1): 153–65.

Trotter, J. W. 2004. "The Great Migration, African Americans, and Immigrants in the Industrial City." In *Not Just Black and White: Historical and Contemporary Perspectives on Immigration, Race, and Ethnicity in the United States*, edited by Nancy Foner and George M. Fredrickson, 82–99. New York: Russell Sage Foundation.

Trouillot, M.-R. 1990. *Haiti: State against Nation*. New York: New York University Press.

Twitty, M. 2017. *The Cooking Gene: A Journey through African American Culinary History in the Old South*. New York: Amistad.

Vallejo, J. 2012. *Barrios to Burbs: The Making of the Mexican American Middle Class*. Stanford, CA: Stanford University Press.

Vargas, S. R. L. 2000. "History, Legal Scholarship, and LatCrit Theory: The Case of Racial Transformations Circa the Spanish American War, 1896–1900." *Denver University Law Review* 78 (4): 921–63.

Velsor, Kathleen. 2013. *The Underground Railroad on Long Island: Friends in Freedom*. Charleston, SC: The History Press.

Verga, Christopher Claude. 2016. *Civil Rights on Long Island*. New York: Arcadia Publishing.

Vickerman, M. 1999. *Crosscurrents: West Indian Immigrants and Race*. Oxford: Oxford University Press.

Vithayathil, T., and G. Singh. 2012. "Spaces of Discrimination: Residential Segregation in Indian Cities."*Economic and Political Weekly* 47 (37): 60–66.

Wacquant, L. 1992. "Banlieues françaises et ghetto noir américain: De l'amalgame à la comparaison." *French Politics and Society* 10 (4): 81–103.

———. 2008. *Urban Outcasts: A Comparative Sociology of Advanced Marginality*. Malden, MA: Polity.

Walters, R. W. 1997. *Pan Africanism in the African Diaspora: An Analysis of Modern Afrocentric Political Movements*: Detroit: Wayne State University Press.

Waters, M. C. 1990. *Ethnic Options: Choosing Identities in America*. Berkeley: University of California Press.

———. 1999. *Black Identities: West Indian Immigrant Dreams and American Realities*. New York: Russel Sage; Cambridge, MA: Harvard University Press.

Watkins-Owens, I. 1996. *Blood Relations: Caribbean Immigrants and the Harlem Community, 1900-1930*. Bloomington: Indiana University Press.

Weil, F. 2004. *A History of New York*. New York: Columbia University Press.

Wen, M., D. S. Lauderdale, and N. R. Kandula. 2009. Ethnic Neighborhoods in Multi-ethnic America, 1990-2000: Resurgent Ethnicity in the Ethnoburbs? *Social Forces* 88 (1): 425–60.

Wesley, C. H. 1917. "The Struggle for the Recognition of Haiti and Liberia as Independent Republics." *Journal of Negro History* 2 (4): 369–83.

White, M.J., B.U. Mberu, and M.A. Collinson. 2008. African Urbanization: Recent Trends and Implications. In *The New Global Frontier: Urbanization, Poverty and Environment in the 21st Century*, edited by George Martine, 301–16. New York: Earthscan.

Wiese, A. 2005. *Places of Their Own: African American Suburbanization in the Twentieth Century*. Chicago: University of Chicago Press.

Wilder, C.S. 2000. *A Covenant with Color: Race and Social Power in Brooklyn 1636–1990*. New York: Columbia University Press.

Wilkerson, I. 2011. *The Warmth of Other Suns: The Epic Story of America's Great Migration*. New York: Vintage.

Williams-Forson, P., and R. Sharpless. 2015. *Dethroning the Deceitful Pork Chop: Rethinking African American Foodways from Slavery to Obama*. Fayetteville: University of Arkansas Press

Wilson, W.J. 1987. *The Truly Disadvantaged: The Inner City, the Underclass, and Public Policy*. Chicago: University of Chicago Press.

Winant, H. 2001. *The World Is a Ghetto: Race and Democracy since World War II*. New York: Basic Books.

Wingfield, A.H. 2007. "The Modern Mammy and the Angry Black Man: African American Professionals' Experiences with Gendered Racism in the Workplace." *Race, Gender and Class* 14 (1–2): 196–212.

Wingfield, A.H., and R.S. Alston. 2014. Maintaining iHerarchies in Predominantly White Organizations: A Theory of Racial Tasks. *American Behavioral Scientist* 58 (2): 274–87.

Wright, E., and T.C. Calhoun. 2006. "Jim Crow Sociology: Toward an Understanding of the Origin and Principles of Black Sociology via the Atlanta Sociological Laboratory. *Sociological Focus* 39 (1): 1–18.

Yang, M. 2012. "The Making of the Urban Middle Class in South Korea (1961–1979): Nation-Building, Discipline, and the Birth of the Ideal National Subjects." *Sociological Inquiry* 82 (3): 424–45.

Zephir, F. 1996. *Haitian Immigrants in Black America: A Sociological and Sociolinguistic Portrait*: Westport, CT: Greenwood Publishing Group.

———. 2001. *Trends in Ethnic Identification among Second-Generation Haitian Immigrants in New York City*. Westport, CT: Bergin and Garvey.

Zips, W. 1999. *Black Rebels: African-Caribbean Freedom Fighters in Jamaica*. Princeton, NJ: Markus Wiener Publishers.

Zuberi, T. 2004. "WEB Du Bois's Sociology: The Philadelphia Negro and Social Science." *Annals of the American Academy of Political and Social Science* 595 (1): 146–56.

Zunz, O. 2000. *The Changing Face of Inequality: Urbanization, Industrial Development, and Immigrants in Detroit, 1880–1920*. Chicago: University of Chicago Press.

Index

NOTE: The italicized abbreviations *fig.*, *map* and *tab.* following a page number indicate a figure, map, or table, respectively.

Founded in 1893,
UNIVERSITY OF CALIFORNIA PRESS
publishes bold, progressive books and journals
on topics in the arts, humanities, social sciences,
and natural sciences—with a focus on social
justice issues—that inspire thought and action
among readers worldwide.

The UC PRESS FOUNDATION
raises funds to uphold the press's vital role
as an independent, nonprofit publisher, and
receives philanthropic support from a wide
range of individuals and institutions—and from
committed readers like you. To learn more, visit
ucpress.edu/supportus.